I0124466

Surviving the Prison Place

Suicide in prison is a growing problem across the developed world. Originally published in 2001, this book sets out to enlarge understanding of the complexities of suicidal feelings and of the part played by some inalienable features of prison life. It does this by presenting and analysing prisoners' accounts of their most intimate responses to the deprivations of prison, in particular the stringent control and management of their personal time and space. These accounts show, in more graphic form than previous literature, the depth of suffering as well as the range of creative responses produced in prisoners through interaction with the prison environment. Prisoners themselves have enormous need for more humane and interactive management of the problem, and their accounts show clearly how prisoner expertise could be utilised in profoundly significant ways. This book will be of interest to all who research, live or work in prison, as well as to students and practitioners in criminology, penology, criminal justice, sociology, psychology, psychiatry and health.

Surviving the Prison Place

Narratives of Suicidal Prisoners

Diana Medlicott

Routledge
Taylor & Francis Group

First published in 2001
by Ashgate Publishing Limited

This edition first published in 2024 by Routledge
4 Park Square, Milton Park, Abingdon, Oxon, OX14 4RN

and by Routledge
605 Third Avenue, New York, NY 10017

Routledge is an imprint of the Taylor & Francis Group, an informa business

Publisher's Note
The publisher has gone to great lengths to ensure the quality of this reprint but points out that some imperfections in the original copies may be apparent.

Disclaimer
The publisher has made every effort to trace copyright holders and welcomes correspondence from those they have been unable to contact.

A Library of Congress record exists under ISBN: 0754617076

ISBN: 978-1-032-80303-6 (hbk)
ISBN: 978-1-003-49636-6 (ebk)
ISBN: 978-1-032-80309-8 (pbk)

Book DOI 10.4324/9781003496366

SURVIVING THE PRISON PLACE

SURVIVING THE PRISON PLACE

For Oliver, Charlotte, Annabel and Flora

In memory of Dr. Rod Fallaw

Surviving the Prison Place

Narratives of suicidal prisoners

DIANA MEDLICOTT
Buckinghamshire Chilterns University College

Ashgate

Aldershot • Burlington USA • Singapore • Sydney

Published by
Ashgate Publishing Limited
Gower House
Croft Road
Aldershot
Hants GU11 3HR
England

Ashgate Publishing Company
131 Main Street
Burlington, VT 05401-5600 USA

Ashgate website: http://www.ashgate.com

British Library Cataloguing in Publication Data
Medlicott, Diana
  Surviving the prison place : narratives of suicidal
  prisoners
  1.Prisoners - Suicidal behavior - Great Britain
  I.Title
  365.6

Library of Congress Control Number: 2001089071

ISBN 0 7546 1707 6

Printed and bound by Athenaeum Press, Ltd.,
Gateshead, Tyne & Wear.

Contents

List of Tables

Acknowledgements

I should like to thank all the prisoners who took part in this research. Without their bravery, openness and willingness to share their thoughts, there would be no book. I should also like to thank the Governor and staff at the prison where I did my research for their support and co-operation. The Suicide Awareness Support Unit (Prison Service Headquarters) were a constant source of encouragement and support, and thanks are particularly due to Martin McHugh. John Lea and Mick Ryan read the manuscript at an early stage and provided valuable help. Buckinghamshire Chilterns University College have provided lots of assistance in a variety of ways. My family and friends have been patient with my absent-mindedness whilst my head was filled with turbulent narratives. Oliver has provided valuable argument and technical help. Joe, thank you for your patience. And, finally, grateful thanks to Pete Archard who opened the door just a chink to let a mature student into an academic career. To all of you, thank you. The faults, however, are mine alone.

Introduction

This book has a very particular rationale. It aims to present prisoners' own experiences as central to the debate over self-inflicted death and suicidal feelings in prison. It does so by analysing a set of prisoner accounts gathered in a large local male prison, chosen because it is representative of the type of establishment which has experienced a disproportionate amount of self-inflicted death.

Self-inflicted death is a formidable challenge to HM Prison Service, and one that has attracted considerable attention in the policies of recent years without appearing to make inroads into the size and scale of the problem. So Chapter One begins with a brief overview of this attention, and tries to capture the broad thrust of both research and policy initiatives over the last few years.

The problem of self-inflicted death in prison suffers from a lack of visibility, and, moreover, a failure of legitimacy in the eyes of those who should be most concerned about it. Almost lost in a welter of other problems surrounding the management of a rapidly increasing prison population, it is sometimes easy to gain the impression from policy makers that they are more concerned to have a demonstrable policy in place than to actually reduce the numbers of self-inflicted deaths. Implementation of the policy is problematic and uneven. Amongst the general public, a researcher in this area regrettably meets all too often an attitude that doubts whether this is a problem worth investigating at all. Relatively well-educated people have pointed out to me that prisoners bring their own fate upon themselves, and if this fate is death in custody, society should feel relieved of a problem. This attitude is one indication of the ignorance and irrationality which can underpin public thinking about punishment, and indicates the strength of public attachment to authoritarian penal policy (Garland 1990).

So Chapter Two strenuously asserts that the abstract worth of a prisoner's life is equal to any other life. No one can read this book in the spirit in which it was written if they are not prepared to consider this principle. Once this is accepted, it follows that in terms of policy and practice, prisoners are human subjects and unique spheres of value. The difference between them and the general population is that the state has taken them into its care on our behalf, and therefore has a special responsibility to do all that it reasonably can to ensure that they remain alive and well cared for. This principle, embodied in the Prison Service Mission Statement, is not in dispute in a bureaucratic sense: its implementation, however, on the level of daily practice, is more vulnerable to variation.

The failure to recognise prisoners as fully human subjects can lead to doubts about the veracity of their accounts of prison experience. My methodology is integrally bound up with the principle that prisoners, as human subjects, have a right to be heard. So this, too, is covered in Chapter Two, and I go into some detail in order to redress often unconsciously held views that prisoners' voices are a marginal consideration in policy initiatives. Just as one listens to friends who give *their* account of a painful event, and expect us to recognise the pain from *their* perspective, so those who make and implement suicide awareness and prevention policy must be prepared to listen to prisoners and say in response, 'Yes, I recognise that that is how it seems to be for you'.

In Chapter Three, I introduce the prisoners whose accounts form the heart of this book. I call them Tellers, to indicate something of the magnitude of what they do when they disclose to a stranger their innermost thoughts and pain. I have given them aliases in terms of names and any details that would enable others to recognise them. It is, however, perfectly possible that they will recognise themselves, and they all knew this principle when they agreed to talk to me. The chapter finishes by listing the starter questions about Time, Place and Self which were put to prisoners in interview.

Chapter Four presents an analysis of prisoner accounts in response to the questions about Place. The importance of a prior place identity is established, and the way in which this is harmed by the grief and disruption that accompanies entry into the prison place. Chapter Five uses the same analytic approach to the questions about Time, and Chapter Six synthesises what prisoners say about the effects of time and spatial deprivation upon their sense of self. A typology is presented of different types or stages of telling, and discusses the relationship of these different stages with suicidal behaviour. Chapter Seven presents two prisoners who used to be seriously suicidal but whose narratives show them to have managed important internal changes, which have led to an enlarged sense of self. Prisoners who used to be suicidal but have overcome that crisis have much to contribute to developing policy responses.

The last chapter draws on the issues raised in the prisoner narratives gathered in this research, discusses the special characteristics of the prison place and suggests that a more humane model of Attention, Care and Talk needs to be inculcated into the entire prison culture, in ways consistent with the Healthy Prison advocated by the Chief Inspector (HM Chief Inspector 1999). Perhaps the first step to achieving this positive cultural change is for all staff working in prisons, and all policy makers, to take the leap of recognition which involves accepting that prisoners themselves have a huge part to play in policy responses to the problem of suicidal feelings in prison, and that, moreover, it is of benefit to us all if they are enabled to play that part.

References

Foucault, M. (1979), *Discipline and Punish*, Penguin, Harmondsworth.
Garland, D. (1990), *Punishment and Modern Society*, Oxford University Press, Oxford.

1 Suicide in Prison

The Problem and Its Research Contexts

The problem of prisoners who commit suicide whilst in prison is a complex one with no simple set of solutions. It is a difficult problem to research, and those who could best illuminate causation are dead. Despite increased attention to it on the part of the Prison Service, and the development, since 1991, of a coherent strategy of awareness and prevention, it is not diminishing. Researchers in the United Kingdom up until that time tended toward a psychiatric model, and focused on the problems of establishing rates, conducting retrospective analyses of completed suicides, and seeking for the emergence of significant patterns of one kind or another. In 1992, research was published (Liebling 1992) which departed significantly from that approach.

The first modern empirical study into suicides in prison (Topp 1979) focused on calculating trends in rates, retrospectively examined completed suicides and undertook analyses of available written records. It adopted a largely medical perspective to the problem which was echoed in policy and practice approaches for some time. Phillips (1986) also adopted a retrospective examination, but at a particular institution, defining her sample according to coroners' verdicts and studying 34 suicides at HMP Brixton.

Dooley's (1990) work reviewed the written case records for 295 deaths in prison during the 1972-1987 period, during which time the annual number of suicides in prisons in England and Wales rose by 121%, a much greater increase than might have been predicted from the rise in the prison population. Until 1986, the annual numbers of suicides had remained relatively stable at around 20-25, even in the context of the rising prison population of the early and mid 1980s. But in 1987, the annual number rose sharply to 46. Dooley (1990) tried to draw inferences about motivation from the available but highly variable records in Prison Service files and other sources. This retrospective analysis of written records had some methodological difficulties which may have influenced the findings (Crighton 2000), but a finding which replicated Topp's (1979) work, and which was to be replicated in future research, concerned the significance of the early period of imprisonment. 17.3% of Dooley's sample suffered suicide within the first week of reception into prison, 28.5% within a month, 51.2% with three months, and 76.9% within a year.

Liebling's (1992) research in relation to suicidal behaviour by young prisoners used a rich variety of methodological approaches, including interviews with young offenders with a history of serious self-intentional injury and a control group of random young prisoners. She hypothesised that suicidal behaviour could be shown to exist at one end of a continuum of self-harming behaviours, in contrast to those more medically inclined researchers who viewed suicide and self-harm as two phenomenologically distinct forms of behaviour. Her research showed that a narrowly psychiatric perspective was inappropriate, because it was so often difficulty in coping with custody which was productive of suicidal behaviour rather than psychiatric disorder. Predictors of suicidal behaviour, such as previous psychiatric history, domestic murder, sexual offence charges, social isolation, drug misuse, and a history of self-injury have only a limited usefulness in indicating the risk of suicide in prison, for a large proportion of the inmate population exhibit such predictors and only a small and unpredictable cohort go on to complete suicide (Liebling 1992). In the 60 self inflicted deaths for the period 1st January 1994 to 31st March 1995, for instance, 17 had previous psychiatric history, 27 did not, and for 16 this item was not known (SASU, HM Prison Service 1995).

The basis of suicide prevention has traditionally been viewed as residing in the relationships prevailing on the landings between inmates and staff (HM Prison Service 1992). 1987 saw the introduction of "Fresh Start": in consequence, the nature of relationships between prison officers and prisoners changed in sometimes disturbing ways (McDermott and King 1989). In the same period, the Service introduced new suicide prevention measures, and sought to heighten awareness of the problem within a broad context of medical solutions. The increase in England and Wales that year was matched by similar and unexplained increases in Canada and Australia (HM Prison Service 1992).

Over the next twelve years, the figures for England and Wales showed an overall rise, as the following table shows:

Table 1.1   Self-Inflicted Deaths (S.I.D.) in H.M. Prison Service Establishments in England and Wales 1st January 1988 - 31st December 2000

	Total S.I.D.	Male S.I.D.	Female S.I.D.
1988	37	37	0
1989	48	46	2
1990	50	49	1
1991	42	42	0
1992	41	39	2
1993	47	46	1
1994	62	61	1
1995	59	57	2
1996	64	62	2
1997	70	67	3
1998	82	79	3
1999	91	86	5
2000	82	74	8

Source: Suicide Awareness Support Unit, H. M. Prison Service

From 1982 to 1996, the suicide rate in the general population as a whole has tended to fall, by 9% for men and by 43% for women. But there were significant rises in the younger age groups for both men and women in the same period, including a 30% rise for men in the 25-34 age group (HM Chief Inspector 1999). It is this age group which dominates the male prison population, and the social trends which underpin the rise in suicide in the community also contribute to the heightened levels of vulnerability within the prison system (HM Prison Service 1992). In 1984, the rate in the general population for males between the ages of 15 and 59 was 14 per 100,000; the rate for male prisoners in the same year was 60 per 100,000 population. Fifteen years later, the rate per 100,000 average population was 140 (McHugh and Snow 2000).The prison population, however, is a constantly shifting one, and a satisfactory measure of the suicide rate might acknowledge the number of receptions into custody each year and the time spent in custody by each inmate.

But it is important to stress that the actual numbers of completed suicides in prison, and the rates, however they are calculated, are only markers and, of themselves, are not indicative of the nature and scale of the problem of suicidal disposition. They may be viewed as the tip of a largely invisible iceberg. Many almost successful suicides are prevented, because of the way in which prisoners are invigilated and/or cared for in the prison situation. No-one can measure the depth and extent of suicidal feelings in prison: what is known is that much self-injury and many suicidal attempts are unrecorded (Liebling and Krarup 1993; HM Chief Inspector of Prisons 1990).

Completed suicides in prison are most prevalent in male local prisons, where overcrowding, operational pressures and high numbers of receptions of remand prisoners are daily stresses. In 1878, the then medical inspector for local prisons observed that rates at local prisons were four times greater than at convict prisons, and surmised that remand prisoners underwent specific torture through suspense and anxiety about outcomes (Second Report of the Commissioners of Prisons 1878-9). Local prisons continued to figure persistently and disproportionately as the site of suicides, and still do so today, despite avowed efforts to implement the suicide awareness policy and enrich the regimes in local prisons.

Table 1.2   Suicides in Local Prisons

	Suicides in Local Prisons	Total Prison Suicides
1990	35	50
1991	24	42
1992	22	41
1993	34	47
1994	40	62
1995	35	59
1996	41	64
1997	38	70
1998	60	82

Source: Hansard: column 546 4/2/1997, Richard Tilt (1997) and for 1997-1998, Suicide Awareness Support Unit, H.M. Prison Service

In the local male prison where the research for this particular study was carried out, there was a relatively high level of suicide awareness, in that 75% of all staff had received training in Prison Service procedures for dealing with those considered to be at risk of suicide or self-harm. But however widespread suicide awareness is within an establishment, realistically it can never wholly overcome the operational pressures which stem from overcrowding. In this particular local male prison, the normal operating capacity over the period of my fieldwork was held to be 480, but the average number of held prisoners was 598, and the highest number at any one time reached 621.

There have always been notorious suicides that have contemporaneously touched the public and the policy makers' consciences. These include John Rawlings, a 'lunatic' convicted of murder, who hanged himself in 1812 with a stocking in an underground cell at Lancaster Castle Gaol, after a terrible beating by the turnkey, and a 16 year old called Andrews, sentenced to three months hard labour in Birmingham Gaol in 1853 for stealing a piece of meat, and under restraint as a punishment for being too weak to complete his quota on the crank (Playfair 1971).

It is easy for the contemporary observer to feel righteous indignation when faced with historical cases such as these, because of the displays of overt cruelty involved. However, knowledge of the historical past paradoxically does a disservice to our present understanding of suicide in prison, because it enables the present-day observer to feel reassured that, because the worst barbarities of a physical nature are indeed things of the past, there is no cause for concern. It is difficult to convey to a public, largely ignorant of the true nature of the modern prison and sometimes coached by the media to regard it as a soft and benevolent setting, that prison is still a place where people suffer extremes of desperation and despair. There may indeed have been a historical transition, from punishment of the body in the classical age, to punishment of the soul or psyche in the modern era (Foucault 1979), but punishment through imprisonment is productive of a high level of suffering, all the more subtle because it is largely experienced mentally.

Shortly after the Prisons Act of 1877, which established a single authority to manage all prisons in England and Wales, the then Medical Commissioner, observing the high number of suicides as well as of mentally disturbed prisoners, undertook a research inquiry and concluded that fear was the greatest motive (Second and Third Reports of the Commissioners of Prisons, 1878-9, 1880). Since then, suicides have traditionally been seen primarily as an aspect of mental health, and have formed part of the domain of the Prison Medical Service which, since its inception through the Act of 1779, and in the wake of John Howard's review of prisons in Europe, has retained its autonomy as the oldest civilian medical service in Britain (CIBA

Foundation 1973). It is only recently that this autonomy has become blurred as the medical care of prisoners becomes a community health issue in which the N.H.S. will collaborate in various forms of partnership.

Policy Contexts

Although the statistics are of some importance, they must be approached within the overall context of the impact of the whole Criminal Justice 'System' upon the offender, and consideration of the wider social problems which impact upon the experience of imprisonment (HM Prison Service 1992). The Prison Service has struggled in very difficult circumstances to implement a policy of awareness and prevention over the past few years, and its progress cannot be judged by recourse to crude statistics. It is important to trace in outline the development and type of policy responses which affect present practice, and a useful starting point is the first Circular Instruction in 1973 which laid the foundations for current strategies on suicide prevention (McHugh and Snow 2000). This emphasised the need for general awareness of the problem, and identified the period immediately after reception as significant. It also dealt with risk factors, the need for communication with the inmate as a source of relevant information, and the requirement for support and care.

Circular Instructions (1983) tackled the management of suicide prevention, suggesting the formation of a management group in establishments to oversee and co-ordinate implementation of a prevention policy. It dealt with reception procedures, staff awareness, referral procedures, medical assessments, and appropriate recording documentation.

In 1982, the death of an eighteen year old prisoner on remand in Ashford Remand Centre had received an inquest verdict of 'lack of care' on the part of the Prison Service. This led to a review of suicide prevention procedures by HM Chief Inspector of Prisons, which was published in 1984 (Home Office 1984). Consultation was wide, and a number of limitations in current policy were identified. General improvements in the conditions for all prisoners were recommended. Overall, the report reinforced the view that suicide was a medical problem, and the responsibility for prevention lay with the medical officer. Improvements in screening, referral and treatment were advised.

Circular Instructions (1989) followed up on the issue of managing suicide prevention, and made it mandatory for governors to set up a management group in each establishment, called a Suicide Prevention

Management Group (SPMG). Reception procedures were refined, and all prisoners were required to be screened by a doctor within the first 24 hours of reception into prison. Staff were alerted to the importance of certain risk indicators, such as previous self-harm, a psychiatric history, a history of substance misuse, certain offence categories and apparent social isolation. Prisoners identified as at risk were to be referred for medical assessment. Documentation was to be put in place which would ensure full recording of assessment, together with plans for management. This documentation would accompany the prisoner's medical and personal records. Medical officers were made wholly responsible for assessing risk and defining appropriate management. They would decide the appropriate location, be it shared cell, in a hospital ward or room, or an unfurnished cell in protective clothing. Support and interaction was considered advisable, with staff, family, prison visitors and, where possible, Samaritans.

These developments in successive sets of circular instructions and reports were not a seamless story of willing progress and increasing sensitivity to the phenomenon of prison suicide on the part of the prison service and the Home Office. Progress did not occur without pressure from the many lobby and voluntary groups which take a critical interest in issues of policy and practice in relation to suicide in custody, particularly as the numbers grew in the 1980's in the context of worsening regimes. These organisations include INQUEST, Prison Reform Trust, Howard League for Penal Reform, CRUSE, Samaritans and others. In the late 1980s and the early 1990s there were particular clusters of suicide amongst young prisoners which drew increased attention from the media as well as from pressure groups. The Chiswick Report (1985) was prompted by a spate of suicides in a Scottish institution, and addressed specific comments to the problem of apparent clusters of suicide. The Prison Reform Trust were highly active in this period in a wide variety of penal matters, and in 1997 published its critique of the worsening position in suicide prevention in prison (Prison Reform Trust 1997).

A brief description of the research and lobby effort by just one voluntary organisation gives some idea of the energy and commitment with which suicides in prison in general and in particular establishments were pursued. INQUEST pursued its goals through parliamentary questions, submissions to the Home Office, to the Prisons Inspectorate and to Select Committees. It submitted evidence for the preparation of the 1984 Home Office report on prison suicides, pressing in particular for acknowledgement of the problems caused in this area by overcrowding, isolation and poor quality regimes. INQUEST also stressed that Standing Orders and Circular Instructions on suicide prevention must be more fully implemented, and, where they could not be implemented, governors should be obliged to state the reasons in writing to service headquarters. Following publication of the 1984 report, INQUEST took issue with the detail, as well as the general thrust, of the report, pointing out its failure to properly recognise the overwhelming evidence that suicide in prison was not primarily a medical problem but a social one induced by certain characteristics of the prison place (Ryan 1996).

There is evidence that official concern with the Circular Instruction on Deaths in Custody, which lead to amendment and re-issue, was provoked largely by pressure from lobby groups such as INQUEST (Ryan 1996). In 1986 the Home Office set up a Working Party on Suicide Prevention, and commissioned independent research on deaths in custody (Home Office 1986).

A further general enquiry, Suicide and Self-Harm in Prison Service Establishments in England and Wales, was set up in 1990. As it canvassed for views, the inquiry group largely echoed the almost exclusively psychiatric and procedural focus of the 1984 report, and it was only following extensive submissions from INQUEST and other sources that the resultant report recognised the dangers of medicalising suicide in prison, and the importance of decent environments, constructive regimes and good relationships in preventing suicide (Ryan 1996).

The Review of Suicide and Self Injury in prisons was carried out by Sir Stephen Tumim, the then Chief Inspector of Prisons, in 1990 (HM Chief Inspector of Prisons 1990) at the request of the Home Secretary, in the light of the continuing rise in suicide despite the introduction of the new 1987 policy of prevention. In this review, the Chief Inspector was critical of the Circular Instruction of 1989, because it was overly concerned with formal procedures, rather than with a proper philosophy of care for inmates. He also took issue with the policy of treating suicide in prison as solely a medical problem, and emphasised the social dimensions of self-harm and self-inflicted deaths in custody. He pointed out the significance of the environment, and the importance of constructive activities to help inmates to cope with anxiety and stress. It is clear that this review recognised the importance of supportive relationships in prison, both from the perspective of the prisoner and also from the perspective of staff attitudes, experience and culture.

The Medical Model Approach To Suicides in Prison

Much research in this field carries an explicit or implicit acceptance of the authority of a medical and psychiatric model, and yet there are many definitional difficulties that are associated with this dominant paradigm. Recognising the difficulties is all the more important because, despite the recommendation in 1990 by the then Chief Inspector for the problem to be shared, and despite the thrust of suicide prevention policies over the last few years, this powerful paradigm continues to dominate, sometimes by stealth, both overall policy and day-to-day practice, and therefore feeds directly in to prisoner experience. At the most basic level, in the prevailing approach, the traditional search for a risk profile that will identify the suicide-prone (Liebling 1992) still feeds the tenacious assumption that persons can be identified and diagnosed as suicidal. This, after all, in the difficult, rushed and challenging environment of prison, seems to provide a model whereby staff, overwhelmed by multiple problems, can be comforted by a measure of apparently scientific knowledge about an intractable and deeply distressing aspect of their work.

But over-identification with this model can lead to an approach to specific prisoners which is not conducive to suicide awareness in relation to all prisoners. For instance, certain characteristics of prisoners may be taken, during rushed reception procedures and/or medical assessments, to be definitive of their mental health status, when it would be more appropriate to view them as a set of fluctuating capacities which will wax and wane in relation to time, place and social relations. Such definitions may stimulate responses that are counter-productive to those who are so defined, and may fail to define tomorrow's successful suicide. Additionally, the comfort that this model has afforded staff and prisoners may well prove worse than illusory when a successful suicide occurs in a person whose despair has not even been noticed.

In an attempt to shift the debate about responses to and treatment of the potential suicide, from the sphere of individualised pathology, only understandable from within a psychiatrised domain of knowledge, Sir Stephen Tumim (HM Chief Inspector of Prisons 1990) had declared unequivocally that the majority of suicides were not mentally disordered within the meaning of the Mental Health Act 1983, and that suicide prevention in prison was essentially a social problem rather than exclusively a medical one. Individual pathology as causative of suicidal behaviour must always remain one explanatory option for some prisoners, but it cannot be an exclusively appropriate focus, for only a proportion of successful suicides have a recognised mental health illness:

> This group represent less than a third of all prison suicides, compared with 90% of suicides in the community with a history of mental illness (HM Prison Service 1993:8).

On the other hand, the prison population as a whole has high levels of mental disturbance, much of it undiagnosed. It is suggested that only 10% of the prison population are free of any kind of mental disturbance (HM Chief Inspector 1999). About three quarters of self-inflicted deaths indicate a history of substance abuse, a much higher proportion than in community suicides.

Profound definitional problems surround the wide range of psychological, psychiatric and medical disorders so often associated with suicide. The most common psychological disorder associated with suicidal and self-harming behaviour is depression (Crighton 1997), and, although there are disagreements over its precise definition, a medical model would hold to the fact that it is a discrete illness, with a range of specific symptoms that are latent or manifest in all cases.

As criteria for diagnosing Major Depressive Disorder, the diagnostic manual of the American Psychiatric Association contains a list of symptoms, five or more of which need to have been present for at least a two week period, and are a change from previous functioning (Crighton 1997). Additionally, symptoms 1 or 2 must be present:

- Depressed mood for most of the day nearly every day
- Loss of interest or pleasure in activities
- Significant weight loss when not dieting
- Insomnia or hypersomnia
- Psychomotor agitation or retardation
- Fatigue or loss of energy
- Feelings of worthlessness or guilt
- Loss of concentration or indecisiveness
- Recurrent thoughts of death

Leaving aside the arbitrary nature of these criteria, and the grouping of oppositional states as a single criterion, the problem with using this or a similar disease model of depression in the prison setting is that, to some extent, some of these symptoms are naturally induced by the prison environment (e.g. 2, 4 or 8), and some could be said to be part of the adjustment process to the situation of conviction and/or incarceration (e.g. 1 or 7). It might indeed be difficult to find substantial numbers of prisoners who did not fulfil some of these criteria. This suggests that the place characteristics of prison need close scrutiny, with a view to identifying those that are symptomatically productive in ways that threaten mental 'health'.

Other clinical measures of depression, such as the Beck Depression Inventory, do go some way toward recognising and attempting to measure the individual's positioning in varied contexts, times and places. Beck et al.'s (1979) suggestion of the factors which may predispose individuals toward depression revolve around the themes of loss, lowered self-esteem and sudden change in their social valuation by others. Specific environments, such as the prison or the camp, are powerful enough to entail changes in self-esteem and personal identity. In its natural function, prison causes tangible losses of home, companionship, friends and all the ingredients of the daily round of ordinary life. It inevitably causes a lowering of self-esteem, and it provokes a changed image in the eyes of significant others. So negative automatic thoughts and a conviction that things can get no better are cognitive and emotional responses which may very well be highly appropriate, given the individual's situation.

In short, depending on the way in which it is defined, "depression" may well be an entirely natural response to some or all stages of incarceration. Given its Statement of Purpose, the Prison Service has a responsibility, therefore, to attempt to ameliorate these responses by making the environment as positive as possible within the overall function of deprivation of freedom.

One of the matters which is supposed to be established at reception is whether or not a prisoner has a previous psychiatric history. There are obvious difficulties in gathering this information from incoming prisoners and in ensuring its accuracy and reliability. The term *previous psychiatric history* is itself ambiguous and open to a wide range of interpretations. During my pilot study, I found that this aspect almost never correlated accurately with what the prisoners themselves told me about their past life. In just one of many such instances, a prisoner identified as having no previous psychiatric history told me that he had suffered bi-polar disorder since his teens, and had frequently been prescribed lithium, but that there had been no opportunity to convey this information to staff. The issue of prior mental health is obviously a crucial one, if the Prison Service intends to fully implement a policy of screening with a view to risk assessment. A haphazard conversation about general health can never be an adequate substitute for a properly conducted mental health assessment.

Much energy is currently expended in the Prison Service in discussing and developing risk assessment strategies. It is claimed that although individuals will have differing levels of risk at different times, nevertheless the risk of a prisoner committing suicide can theoretically be expressed as a statement of probability (Crighton and Towl 1997). Risk assessment not only estimates this probability but considers the consequences of such occurrences. It would seem logical to suppose that if risk assessment were implemented as standard policy, then the assessment would take some time and would involve a detailed knowledge of the prisoner's background and history. However, it is difficult to understand how such a policy could be realistically implemented, given that prisoners do not enter prison accompanied by the sort of documentation which could aid the gathering of a full history. The trauma of admission to prison, an ignorance of such history, an unawareness of the purposes to which such a history might be put are only some of the reasons why the prisoners themselves can not provide the relevant information.

But even if such "in-depth" assessment of prisoners were to become routine practice, the taking of prisoners' histories would present severe challenges to risk assessment strategies. For the very factors which have been identified (Diekstra and Hawton 1987) across a wide range of research studies as increasing an individual's risk of suicide are precisely those factors which are associated with crime (Crighton and Towl 1997) and therefore disproportionately present in the histories of those who make up the prison population - a disrupted family background, drug and alcohol addiction, school failure, unemployment, depression and a family background containing suicide. So there are inherent difficulties in adopting an actuarial approach to the assessment of risk, despite the growing tendency to do so in an increasingly managerialised criminal justice system (Feeley and Simon 1994). Such inherent difficulties attend most aspects of managerialism, where it is deployed with a tendency toward an exclusive approach to the problems of the prison system.

Risk assessment strategies logically require a basis of definitions which are sound and consistent. Depression and other psychological disorders claimed to be associated with suicidal behaviour do not currently provide that sound definitional base. Even if there were a sound definitional basis, there are enormous difficulties with implementing the strategy, and prisons with different starting points in terms of suicide awareness will achieve differing levels of implementation. Currently, identifying those prisoners at reception who might be unduly at risk of suicide has not enjoyed much success. The assessment procedures at reception may in practice be implemented in a cursory and hurried manner, and the rate of implementation will vary in different prisons with different cultures and different resource demands and pressures (McHugh and Towl 1997).

The current policy has been developed at a time of enormous strain for the Prison Service: it is moving from a centralised model toward a more devolved one, in the contexts of public expenditure cuts, increased privatisation, efficiency drives, organisational changes at every level, and a prison population which is constantly exceeding budgeted forecasts. Above and around all of this is a complex political, economic and societal backdrop, where political expediency jousts with established public sensibilities and ideological ambition competes against the principle of financial constraint, and the values of austerity, security and welfare pull against each other, with differing professional interests articulating different impulses (Garland 1990). In such a climate, it is regrettable that previous research been too pre-occupied with extending the tools of prediction in relation to prison suicide (Liebling 1996:47).

Thus a broader social scientific approach to causation, prevention, awareness and response has been shown to be legitimate both by inspection reports and by research. It is important to recognise the significance of mental health factors, but life history, current location, current life events, demographic, social and economic factors are also significant variables. Any prior and underpinning generalised commitment to any one point and location of cause predetermines findings, and, in so doing, may foreclose on fruitful avenues of awareness and prevention. Historically, there has not been much recognition of the validity of prisoner contribution to knowledge of the problem, and this study aims to follow Liebling's (1992) research which stressed the importance of that dimension. Additionally, there has been a significant tendency in the research to treat all suicides as the same (Liebling 1996), and to neglect the fact that each one represents a different set of reactions to individually experienced pain. That this pain is in part associated with the place characteristics of prison, and the forced interaction of inmates with each other and with this complex environment seems incontrovertible in the light of the consistently robust finding that the initial period of custody is one of heightened risk.

Responses Post 1991

Problems in Policy Implementation, Language, and Definitions

In response to the force of messages coming from a variety of directions, HM Prison Service set up the Suicide Awareness Support Unit in 1991, dedicated to improving awareness and prevention of suicide and self harm. A guidance pack, *Caring for The Suicidal in Custody*, was developed and implemented in training and practice in a number of prisons. The F2052SH documentation was developed, which could be initiated by any member of staff who is concerned about a prisoner who is judged to be at an unacceptably high risk of suicide (Towl and Hudson 1997). It is completed by staff, and kept in the same location as the prisoner. It serves as an available summary of the prisoner's history since the form was opened, and of the difficulties experienced and expressed by that prisoner. The F2052SH is a policy initiative that aims for effective monitoring, good communications and help for the individual (HM Prison Service 1992). It is just part of a more dynamic, de-medicalised, multi-disciplinary approach to suicide prevention which has been widely welcomed (Council of Europe 1996).

Implementation across the entire prison estate has, however, been difficult and patchy for a wide variety of reasons. The scale and pace of change which has been demanded of the Service over the past few years has been considerable, staff training is notoriously inconsistent across the prison estate, and the phenomenon itself is complex and essentially unpredictable. In addition, whilst there has been commitment to putting this particular problem high on the managerialist and bureaucratic agenda, there has not been the same commitment to the necessary change of culture which would be needed for a real change in atttitudes toward the suicidal (HM Chief Inspector 1999).

Quite apart from the context of a dominant culture which is unsympathetic to prisoner vulnerability, there are pragmatic problems of definition surrounding the labels which get affixed to inmates and their actions (McHugh and Towl 1997). Whenever a prisoner is deemed to be *suicidal*, a judgement has been made about complex aspects of behaviour and intention, despite a widespread awareness that deliberate self-harm is confused, confusing, and has mixed motives. Even if the suicide is successfully completed, the definitional problems do not end, and legal criteria fight with semantics. All deaths in custody result in an inquest in public in front of a jury. But coroners' verdicts adopt narrow legal criteria and, where possible, avoid suicide verdicts in favour of verdicts of "open" or "misadventure" (McHugh and Towl 1997). The last two decades have seen growing public disquiet about the apparent determination of the relevant authorities to minimise investigation into particular deaths in custody and disclosure of the circumstances surrounding them (Ryan 1996).

In order to arrive at a realistic picture of the extent of the problem, the Prison Service now uses the term *self-inflicted death* to describe all deaths classified by coroners' courts as suicide, death by misadventure, open verdicts and accidental deaths. This definition dates from the setting up of the Suicide Awareness Support Unit in 1991 and marks the claim of an enhanced commitment on the part of the Prison Service to learn from such events and use this understanding in risk assessment strategies and the management of those in custody (HM Prison Service 1992).

The definition and classification of the broad range of acts of "self-injury" is just as complex. Approximately 3,000 incidences of self harm/self mutilation are recorded annually by the Prison Service, and many more go unrecorded. The relationship between self-injury and self-inflicted death is a complex one. Most of those who self-injure in prison do not kill themselves and do not appear to have had this intention (HM Prison Service 1992). In a review of 60 self-inflicted deaths in custody between 1st January 1994 and 31st March 1995, it was stated:

In around two thirds of cases (43 in number), there was no indication of suicidal intent or behaviour prior to death, thus demonstrating the difficulty and dangers inherent in predicting individual behaviour (SASU, HM Prison Service 1995).

In eleven of these 43 particular cases, there was a documented history of self harm either prior to or earlier in custody, which may indeed demonstrate the difficulty and dangers inherent in predicting individual behaviour, but also points up the dangers of classifying any acts of self injury as *only* a cry for help. World-wide evidence points to the fact that many successful suicides have a history of self-injury. But:

These factors are poor predictors. There is no sure way of 'diagnosing' suicidal intentions or predicting the degree of risk. Assessments can only be of temporary value because moods and situations change. Self harm can be an impulsive reaction to bad news or a sudden increase in stress (HM Prison Service 1993 (Part I):5).

The Prison Service is well aware that however the factors that precipitate suicide are expressed, such facts - familial and social circumstances, hopelessness and uncertainty about the future, an inability to cope with the prison environment - are not sound predictors and cannot be pursued as if they were.

Nevertheless, it is clear that self-harm is evidence of extreme vulnerability: out of the vast pool of vulnerability in prison, some prisoners go on to commit suicide. Additionally, some suicides particularly amongst young prisoners, are as a result of acts of self-injury which misfire. The ambiguity of self-harming behaviour, which may conceivably at some future point in time prove fatal, baffles mental health practitioners, prison officers and the self-harmers themselves. Clinicians do not agree as to whether it is appropriate to classify the wide range of self-damaging behaviours under a single classification (Livingston 1997) or to classify them according to the strength of the individual's intention to kill himself (Pattison and Kahan 1983).

But to make this latter judgement provokes the tendency, always latent in institutional life, to classify this kind of behaviour as *manipulative* (Livingston 1997). The implication of this judgement is that the inmate is wilfully and self-consciously harming him/herself out of a desire to exploit the system and those within it. I found the use of this classification to be widespread amongst staff. Some of my interviewees were identified by staff as *manipulative* or *attention-seeking*, whilst others were deemed *genuine*. Some were attributed with *threatening suicide* to a member of staff, as if it were a weapon wielded solely with the object of harming that staff member. The overall effect of this labelling is part of the general tendency amongst staff and inmates in prison to deny suicide and suicidal behaviour (Toch 1992). Such cultural ideology promotes the myth that inmates can cope with any situation, and so suicidal actions cannot possibly be real acts of desperation but mere manipulations (Douglas Grant 1985).

Many historical parallels can be found between the usage of the classification of *manipulative* or *genuine* to categorise those who harm themselves, and the usage of the terms *deserving* and *non-deserving* to describe the poor in the wake of the 1834 Poor Law. The dividing practices (Foucault 1979) of language helped to erect complex and self-nourishing ideologies in the nineteenth century, in which the unfortunate were blamed for their own misfortune, and judged according to their ability to help themselves out of their predicament. The *lack of capacity* to help themselves was conflated with an attributed *unwillingness* to help themselves, resulting in a judgement about their moral worth, or *deservedness* status.

This conflation is common in the prison environment, despite widespread awareness that, by definition, prison populations contain disproportionate numbers of people with limited capacities for problem-solving. Some behaviours, such as violence toward others, do not necessarily differ from behaviour on the outside, but suicidal behaviour is a response *which is markedly more common when men are incarcerated than when they are not* (Douglas Grant 1985). The place setting of it is, therefore, a proper focus of enquiry, but the qualitative and experiential aspects of the prison place from the prisoner's perspective have been neglected in pre-1992 research, which largely relied upon statistical information and a medical model of suicide risk (Liebling 1996:45). Such a model depends upon the robustness of detailed descriptions and classification of disorders. But professionals in different disciplines use differing terminology and explanatory models, and the very definitions they use are dependent upon varying social and cultural standards (Towl and Crighton 2000). Liebling's (1992) work was a valuable corrective to the previous over-emphasis of the role of psychiatric illness in prison suicide and self-injury.

Recent research has pointed out that the application of the label *manipulative,* to prisoners who inflict harm upon themselves, serves to legitimate a hostile response from staff (Dexter and Towl 1995). I found in my research, however, that its usage also served more self-protective functions. Staff who were thoughtful and reflective used this term to me, in the context of generally insightful observations. It was obviously considered to be an expert observation which would help me in my fieldwork. I came to see it as a significant dimension of staff coping strategies, for it was not only an attitude that looked out upon the chaos and attempted to classify it in manageable terms, but also an internal and defensive refuge. Labelling an inmate as manipulative could be said to excuse the member of staff from employing anything other than minimal good practice in dealing with that inmate, or even justify overt hostility. But, at a deeper level, since it was a moral judgement about a prisoner's deservedness of real help and attention, it protected the staff member from empathising with the inmate's desperation and hence was a much needed shield against the discomfort and pain that would result from such empathy. The prison is a working environment with more than its share of stress, much of which comes from working with the explicit distress of so many people At the same time, it is not an environment where all staff feel well supported in relation to this stress. Defences against such stress are naturally grasped and become amplified in a culture where constant personal change is demanded to keep up with policy changes and frequent overcrowding. Suicides of prison officers rose from one in 1997 to seven in 1999, and since 1990, 51 prison staff have killed themselves (Howard League 2000).

Such defences, however, have the capacity to be treacherous. Completed suicides have damaging effects upon staff morale, producing feelings of failure in those involved, a factor which has influenced the development of recent strategic responses (McHugh and Towl 1997). How much greater this feeling of failure must be within an individual or a team, if the label of *manipulative* was one that had persistently been applied to an inmate who subsequently completes suicide. The consequences of its usage, and of similar semantic dividing practices, are deeply injurious to both staff and prisoners' well-being: research in this area is much needed, with a view to changing awareness and practice. Such change, however, in requiring staff to relinquish this defence, would necessitate deeper and more sustained support for staff.

There is a deeper irony behind the usage of the term *manipulative*. Prisons can only be run by consent, and in order to achieve consent, those who manage custody must *manipulate* both colleagues and inmates, as well as regimes, in order to achieve desired ends. In that sense, it is a necessary virtue in staff in such a challenging arena. But the capacity to manipulate is a virtue in prisoners, too, with recently introduced incentivised regimes which rely upon persuading inmates to adopt the desire to exploit the system for the betterment of their conditions. Incentivised regimes are a concerted attempt to move prisoners from passivity to a more goal-directed state. They must manipulate their responses to the system in order to achieve preferment, and they must manipulate their image in the eyes of the staff, so that the staff recognise their virtue and complicity with the regime. In a Weberian sense, manipulative behaviour, shorn of its pejorative undertones, is rational action that is directed toward a goal, and the widespread use of it is a hallmark of an advanced and complex society, where status and power are prime goals. So it is one of the many ironies of prison that prisoners can 'succeed' by being manipulative only as long as they are not labelled as such.

In 1999, HM Chief Inspector of Prisons published his thematic review of Suicide and Self Harm in Prison Service establishments in England and Wales, in response to a request made by the then Minister for Prisons in December 1997. It concluded that the current strategy (1994) did not pay sufficient attention to the differing needs of disparate groups of prisoners, such as females and young offenders. It re-stated particular concern with local prisons, and pointed to the clear failure in resourcing these establishments at levels which would allow full and purposeful regimes. Some serious failures in implementation of the current strategy were identified. In particular, the need for case reviews was often ignored, vital documentation was inadequately monitored, and staff were not adequately trained. Perhaps the two most significant indictments were that some senior managers had failed to take ownership of the strategy, and there were overwhelmingly negative cultures in some establishments. The thematic review stressed that healthy relationships between staff and prisoners are fundamental to any successful strategy, and these relationships should be based on professionalism, care and awareness of others. The phrase 'Healthy Prison' was used to describe prisons with positive cultures which managed to deliver successfully the Prison Service's Statement of Purpose. The Review also pointed to the more proactive part which prisoners can play, especially in local prisons, and the findings of this study endorse this claim and suggests some positive ways in which this could be implemented.

My Research Question

In order to formulate my own research question, I tried to empathise with the situation of prisoners by imagining that I myself was incarcerated. In this task of imagination, I was aided by personal accounts of prison, such as Serge (1970), as well as visits to prison both as a visitor and as a researcher. I asked myself what aspects of prison life I would find most intolerable and productive of despair. Underlying the myriad petty restrictions and compulsory aspects, which vary culturally and historically, I considered that there were defining aspects of prisons everywhere, which have a universal nature and which bear cruelly upon the human spirit's desire for physical and psychological freedom. These aspects concern the way in which, when the prison gates clang shut, the exercise of personal choice is ended, with regard to where one is, at any particular time. Prison seizes and manipulates the time-frame of prisoners, by which they have hitherto lived and planned their lives. Where this has been a theme in previous research, it has generally considered long-term prisoners. But this appropriation of personal time-frames is entailed by the nature of the prison place, and all prisoners, remanded untried, remanded awaiting sentence or convicted, whether serving a week, a year or a life, must adjust to this defining characteristic of the prison, and to the way it threatens personal autonomy. It is a long time since Sykes (1958) pointed out the importance of preserving opportunities for exercising control and choice in order to ameliorate the pains of imprisonment, and with the gradual improvement over time of some aspects of imprisonment, the deprivation of personal autonomy is a harsh reality that easily gets overlooked.

During a very preliminary stage of reflecting about the project, a prisoner said to me "The thing about prison is that, anytime, you gotta be where they say you gotta be". I was struck by the force of this terse universal truth, which was seemingly simple yet harboured infinite complexity. After a short silence, he spread his hands and added "That's it. That's all. It's hard". There was a long sigh, and his eyes filled with tears.

And so I formulated some prosaic questions which were attempts to tease out of prisoners their experience of dealing with the forcible removal of choice over where to be and with the seizure of their personal time. The remaining questions dealt with the personal self, and with the prisoners' perceptions of changes in the self-relation following incarceration. It is these three elements of time, place and self which inform the structure and nature of this qualitative project. These three sets of questions quite naturally produced talk about suicide in prison, about suicidal feelings and experiences which influence these feelings. Because I did not raise the subject, each prisoner brought it into the conversation when he wanted to, and talked about it in his own way and from his point of view. Once he had shown that he wanted to discuss it, I responded appropriately.

The interaction of prisoner and environment is a dynamic and dialectical process, which changes over time. Listening empathetically to prisoners situated at different stages of the process illuminates some of the ways in which they deal with the place they are in and the time they are doing, and how the manner of this dealing affects their sense of self and their preparedness or aversion to dealing with their predicament by resorting to suicidal actions. This illumination can be used to inform policy, not through quantitative justification, but through a qualitative appreciation of the prisoner's point of view.

The definitional problems involved in categorising the wide range of self-harming behaviours affect all research, all policy and the reality of day-to-day practice. Stengel's (1970:237) definitions are useful, in that a suicidal act is any act of deliberate self-damage, which the person committing the act could not be sure of surviving, and suicide is a self-inflicted death, which is 'usually accompanied by the intention of dying'. But even the experience of drawing my sample pointed up the fragility of defining suicidal acts and intentions in prison, because the institutional contexts, and the agendas of the prisoners and staff, complicate the process of assigning intention.

My sample was intended, for the purposes of contrast, to consist of a group of officially defined 'suicidal' prisoners and a group of 'copers'. The suicidal prisoners were identified by the establishment through open F2052SH documentation, which specified each as being 'at risk' or 'not-coping'. My group of 'copers' were again identified by the establishment, usually in practice by the wing manager. 'Poor copers' have previously been identified in research typologies (Dooley 1990, Liebling and Krarup 1993) and the distinction between poor and good copers has been a fruitful and useful one in previous prison research. But my pilot work quickly disclosed that clear-cut distinctions between 'poor' and 'good' copers, and between 'suicidal' and 'coping' prisoners can not be sustained across time and changing circumstances. Nor is the idea of a spectrum very useful, with 'coping' at one end, and 'not coping' at the other, for this would suppose that each prisoner could be positioned at some exact point on the spectrum.

There are other reasons why these definitions cannot be sustained. The F2052SH documentation is not used consistently on all locations: it can be a blunt categorisation, sometimes applied to the seriously suicidal, sometimes to the prisoner who suddenly self-harms in a non-serious way. Sometimes it is kept open for a long time, and in other cases it is peremptorily closed whilst officers are still expressing deep concern about the inmate.

Hal, who had been placed on F2052SH documentation because he persistently and repeatedly harmed himself, was one of the prisoners in my suicidal group. He was well-known in the prison, both on the wings and in the medical centre, and the subject of many amusing anecdotes. No one who had cared for him considered him to be at real risk of suicide, and yet he was classified as 'at risk' or 'non-coping' and in the same category as prisoners who had narrowly averted death by serious suicide attempts. The F2052SH documentation was, therefore, a 'belt and braces' approach for a prisoner who was difficult to categorise and manage. In interview, his behaviour was disclosed as a personal and strategic form of adaptation to prison, which was highly developed and long-standing. It pre-dated the prison setting and was regarded by the prisoner as having progressed from being a personal habit to an addiction, much like nail-biting or smoking.

The case of Hal points up the bluntness of a labelling system, which must logically and defensively define inmates as 'at risk of suicide', where their preferred or involuntary form of adaptation to prison life involves persistent but limited self-harm. For even where there is no overt and developed intention to commit suicide, the possibility always remains that this may be the outcome.

Conversely, the prisoners identified as 'copers', who had *never* been identified by the prison as being remotely at risk, sometimes disclosed to me secret resolve and intention about suicide, highly developed over a long period, if certain personal circumstances were to prevail. So the notion of a discrete group of suicidal prisoners, neatly balanced by a discrete control group of 'copers' may appear neat and methodologically desirable, but it would be a distortion of reality. Each prisoner moves in and out of stages of relative 'coping' at different times in his prison experience, and that 'coping' is relative to his usual frame of mind, which is naturally distinct from that of other people.

'Coping' classifications belong to the language of a psychiatric/pathology model, and can serve to neutralise the very real problems that all prisoners have in adapting to the prison environment. They obscure the fundamental recognition of the environment as essentially problematic. In practice, they legitimise awarding special attention to some prisoners and withholding it from others.

As a reminder of the fluid nature, therefore, of the coping process, I categorise my interviewees as Now 'coping', and Now 'not coping', and the presence of the inverted commas serve as a reminder that this is an official definition placed upon inmates, at that particular point in time. Even at the time of official definition, there is considerable overlap between the two categories. It is not a definition necessarily shared by the inmates themselves, their families or dispassionate observers, and it would not hold across time. It merely provides a useful organising principle for the two groups in my research.

The process of initial screening takes place during induction procedures. Prison rules state that all prisoners must be seen by a doctor within the first 24 hours of custody. It would be unrealistic to expect this defining moment to hold true all the way through the turmoil of adjustment to a highly stressful environment. Nevertheless, it is clear that this gate-keeping procedure is considered important and defining. Procedures for evaluating prisoners were variously referred to by staff as 'psychiatric screening', 'risk assessment', and 'mental health evaluation', and the use of such phraseology suggests a quite considered and thorough set of procedures. Upon further investigation, however, it would transpire that whilst some of these inmates had indeed been the object of a reasonably extensive set of procedures, others had merely been the object of a hurried encounter, and yet the terminology of screening, assessment and evaluation would still be applied.

This is a typical exchange on the subject of the reception and induction process with Ben, who is now 'coping' in the Induction unit. I ask him to tell me about everything that has happened in the 24 hours since he came into custody, and this is the part that is relevant to medical evaluation:

We're being called out, one by one, to see the doctor. Then they gave us something to eat. After that we were called round the corner to see prison officers, for photos and things. The doctor asked about medical history, any illnesses, this and that. And then took my blood pressure and said it was good, and said 'thank you very much', and that was it.

(Did he ask you about your psychological state?)

No, I don't remember him asking that, no.

(Did he ask you if you felt depressed?)

No (laughs).

(Perhaps (laughing) he sussed you out without asking?)

I don't know (laughs). I remember the medical questions, because he was just filling out a form, right in front of me, and he never took his eyes from the form. But nothing else, no.

HM Prisons Inspectorate has expressed disquiet about entry procedures, and assert that in busy prisons with large daily receptions, effective screening and medical examination are not possible, given current working patterns (Reed and Lyne 1997). So although it might be supposed that judgements about a prisoner being *suicidal* or *non-suicidal* are reached judiciously and carefully, it is more often the case that this categorisation is arrived at after a very cursory assessment, and may indeed be generated from the observation of inmates' general demeanour and overt responses to prison life. Given the prevailing pressures in local prisons, it is particularly in these prisons that assessment of inmates necessarily takes place in a rushed and superficial fashion. It is not always apparent to prisoners that these assessments and professional judgements have in fact taken place, and where they have, they may not be experienced by prisoners as beneficial to them in the sense of professional *care*. The issue of what constitutes *care* is a running subtext in the narratives, and will be addressed explicitly in the final chapter.

The Prison Place

Institutions and the force that they exert over individuals are of perennial interest to a social scientist who is sensitised to power, authority, and normalisation practices, and their capacity to affect self-identity. It was Goffman (1961) who stimulated my curiosity about the prison as the institutional context for the most extreme act of desperation any human can perform. The prison is an extraordinarily provocative institution, because it is the place to which persons are sent as punishment. Punishment is a complex social function (Foucault 1979); the range of effects it is capable of producing is large, and it is not reserved for the guilty, as the large population of untried prisoners testifies.

In the 1980s, the remand population increased by 165% compared with a 22% increase for the prison population as a whole (Crighton and Towl 1997). The majority of remand prisoners are not returned to prison at the conclusion of their cases. In 1995, for instance, 66% of remanded women and 53% of remanded men were subsequently found not guilty or were given non-custodial sentences after their case was settled (Home Office 1997). Nevertheless, they have been held in secure conditions, undergoing the same spatial and temporal deprivations, with slight variations, as convicted prisoners. Experientally, guilty or innocent, they undergo punishment.

The remand population is significant in terms of prison suicides. In the period 1972-1987, a disproportionately high number of successful suicides (47%) were by remand prisoners (Dooley 1990). An analysis of 60 self-inflicted deaths between January 1st 1994 and 31st March 1995 showed that 19 were by remanded inmates (SASU, Prison Service 1995). Previous international research has found remand prisoners consistently over-represented in prison suicide figures (Novick and Remmlinger 1978, Home Office 1984, Hatty and Walker 1986, Backett 1987, Dooley 1990). This persistent characteristic of prison suicide was first noted in research done in 1879 (Third Report of the Commissioners of Prisons 1880), as was the characteristically high dangerousness of the period immediately following entry into prison. About 10% of suicides occur within the first 24 hours of custody, and about 45% in the first month. About 60% of self-inflicted deaths occur in the first three months following arrival in an establishment (HM Chief Inspector 1999). Over time and across cultures, evidence points to the significance of the interaction of inmate with the prison *place* as a fruitful focus for investigation.

As already observed, one common concern in research has been the rate of suicide and its relationship to the suicide rate in the community (Lloyd 1990), and a second strand of research has consisted of valuable empirical studies which have retrospectively examined completed suicides (see Topp 1979, Phillips 1986, Dooley 1990). Much psychiatric, clinical and psychological research has in the past seemed ambivalent about the qualitative *place* aspects of prison. Instead of focusing on the characteristics of the place, and on the forced interaction of prisoners with prison, which prisoners identify as sources of stress and pain, such research often focuses on attempts to quantify particular psychological characteristics of the prisoners themselves, in order to measure their success or failure to cope with an environment which has not been methodologically recognised as qualitatively problematic.

Thus it has even been argued that prison is conducive to good health (Bonta and Gendreau 1990:357), or that it does not produce any long-term or overall bad effects upon cognitive, perceptual-motor or personality functioning (Banister 1973, Heskin et al., 1973, Sapsford 1978). Other psychological, psychiatric or clinical studies have tried to quantify the negative effects in terms of cognition, emotional well-being, relations with others, or psychosis (see for example Gunn et al. 1978). The capacity of the prison to produce stress and psychological harm in some prisoners has been recognised by more discursive approaches (see for example Toch 1992, Zamble and Porporino 1988), and the particular significance of the early phase of imprisonment has repeatedly been recognised (Toch and Adams 1989, Gunn et al. 1978, Backett 1987).

Some distinctive sociological studies, over a long period and in various settings, have recognised the extraordinary and subtle aspects of the institutional environment which prisoners or inmates find harmful in terms of well-being and personal identity (see for example Sykes 1958, Goffman 1961, Mathieson 1965, Cohen and Taylor 1972, Nagel 1976).

Despite widely varying theoretical approaches, and inconsistent methodological approaches which may have encumbered findings (Snow 2000), it is now generally recognised (Biggam and Power 1997) that stress and distress in prison have many facets, and there are physical, psychological and social factors which must be taken into account. Additionally, the subjective nature of these factors is recognised, and their dependence upon an individual's own perceptions of the situation, and the personal meanings attributed to his/her interaction with prison. It has become more common to take account of prisoners' individual perceptions and predicaments (see for example Liebling 1992, Power et al. 1997, Biggam and Power 1997). The Prisons Inspectorate and voluntary sector organisations have repeatedly attempted to address the issue of prisoners' own experiences. Liebling (1992) has emphasised that to understand the phenomenon, it is necessary to take the place of the prisoner and see what that prisoner feels. It follows then that any research into prison suicide that purports to be meaningful must include verbal accounts from prisoners (Liebling 1996:41).

Methodologically this study puts prisoners' verbal accounts of their experience at the heart of enquiry. It employs a stance of disciplined empathy, in the formulation of the research question, in the appreciation of the special research environment of prison, in the methodology employed, in the actual questions asked of prisoners and in the presentation and analysis of findings and their implications.

References

Backett, S. (1987), 'Suicide in Scottish Prisons', *British Journal of Psychiatry*, vol. 151, pp. 218-221.

Banister, P.A., Smith, F.V., Heskin, K.J., and Bolton, N. (1973), 'Psychological Correlates of Long-term Imprisonment: 1 Cognitive Variables', *British Journal of Criminology*, vol. 13, pp. 312-323.

Beck, A.T., Kovacs, M., and Weissman, A.S. (1979), 'Assessment of Suicidal Intention: the scale for suicide ideation', *Journal of Consulting and Clinical Psychology*, vol. 47, pp. 343-350.

Biggam, F.H. and Power, K.G. (1997), 'Social Support and Psychological Distress in a Group of Incarcerated Young Offenders', *International Journal of Offender Therapy and Comparative Criminology*, vol. 41 (3), pp. 213-230.

Bonta, J. and Gendreau, P. (1990), 'Re-examining the Cruel and Unusual Punishment of Prison Life', *Law and Human Behaviour*, vol. 14, pp. 437-472.

Chiswick, D., Spencer, A., Baldwin, P., Drummond, D., Henderson, A.D., Kreitman, N., Stark, R. and Younghohns, P. (1985), *Report of the Review of Suicide Precautions at HM Detention Centre and HM Young Offenders Institution, Glenochil*, Scottish Home and Health Department, HMSO, Edinburgh.

CIBA Foundation (1973), *Medical Care of Prisoners and Detainees*, Associated Scientific, Amsterdam.

Cohen, S., and Taylor, I. (1972), *Psychological Survival: The Experience of Long-term Imprisonment*, Penguin, Harmondsworth.

Council of Europe (1996) 'Final Response of the United Kingdom Government to the Report of the European Committee for the Prevention of Torture and Inhuman or Degrading Treatment or Punishment, on its visit to the UK from 15-31 May 1994.

Crighton, D. (1997), 'The Psychology of Suicide', in G.J. Towl (ed.), *Suicide and Self-Injury in Prisons, Issues in Criminological and Legal Psychology, 28*, British Psychological Society, Leicester.

Crighton, D. (2000), 'Suicide in Prisons: A Critique of UK Research', in G. Towl, L. Snow and M. McHugh (eds), *Suicide in Prison*, British Psychological Society, Leicester.

Crighton, D. and Towl, G. (1997), 'Self-Inflicted Deaths in Prison in England and Wales: An Analysis of the Data for 1988-90 and 1994-95', in G.J. Towl (ed.), *Suicide and Self-Injury in Prisons, Issues in Criminological and Legal Psychology, 28*, British Psychological Society, Leicester.

Dexter, P. and Towl, G.J. (1995), 'An Investigation into Suicidal Behaviours in Prison', in N.K. Clark and G.M. Stephenson (eds), *Criminal Behaviour: Perceptions, Attributions and Rationality, Issues in Criminological and Legal Psychology, 22*, British Psychological Society, Leicester.

Diekstra, R.F.W. and Hawton, K., (eds) (1987), *Suicide in Adolescence*, Martinus Nijhoff, Dordrecht.

Dooley, E. (1990), 'Prison Suicide in England and Wales, 1972-1987', *British Journal of Psychiatry*, vol. 156, pp. 40-45.

Douglas Grant, J. (1985), *Management of Conflict in Correctional Institutions*, Princeton University Press, Princeton.

Feeley, M. and Simon, J. (1994), 'Actuarial Justice: the Emerging New Criminal Law' in D. Nelken (ed.), *The Futures of Criminology*, Sage, London.

Foucault, M. (1979), *Discipline and Punish*, Penguin, Harmondsworth.

Garland, D., (1990), *Punishment and Modern Society: A Study in Social Theory*, Clarendon, Oxford.

Goffman, E. (1961), *Asylum*, Penguin, Harmondsworth.

Gunn, J., Robertson, G., Dell, S. and Way, C. (1978), *Psychiatric Aspects of Imprisonment*, Academic Press, London.

Hatty, E. and Walker, J.R. (1986), *A National Study of Deaths in Australian Prisons*, Australian Institute of Criminology, Canberra.

Heskin, K.J., Smith, F.V., Banister, P.A., and Bolton, N. (1973), 'Psychological Correlates of Long-term Imprisonment: II. Personality Variables', *British Journal of Criminology*, vol. 13, pp. 323-330.

HM Chief Inspector of Prisons for England and Wales (1990), *Review of Suicide and Self-Harm in Prison*, HMSO, Cm.1383, London.

HM Chief Inspector of Prison for England and Wales (1999), *Suicide is Everyone's Concern: A Thematic Review*, The Stationery Office, London.

HM Prison Service (1992), *Caring for Prisoners at Risk of Suicide and Self-Injury: The Way Forward*, Prison Service, London.

HM Prison Service (1993), *Caring for the Suicidal in Custody*, Prison Service, London.

Home Office (1984), *Suicide in Prisons: Report by Her Majesty's Chief Inspector of Prisons*, HMSO, London.

Home Office (1986), *Report of the Working Group on Suicide Prevention*, Home Office, London.

Home Office (1997), *The Prison Population in 1996: Statistical Bulletin 18/97*, Home Office, London.

Home Office (1998), *The Prison Population in 1997:Statistical Bulletin 5/98*, Home Office, London.

Howard League (2000), 'Suicide Rate Soars Amongst Prison Officers', in *Howard League Magazine*, vol. 18, no. 4, pp. 3 London.

Liebling, A. (1992), *Suicides in Prison*, London: Routledge, London.

Liebling, A. (ed.) (1996), *Deaths in Custody: Caring for People at Risk*, Whiting and Birch, London.

Liebling, A. and Krarup, H. (1993), *Suicide Attempts and Self-Injury in Male Prisons*, Home Office, London.

Livingston, M. (1997), 'A Review of the Literature on Self-Injurious Behaviour Amongst Prisoners', in G.J. Towl (ed.), *Suicide and Self-Injury in Prisons, Issues in Criminological and Legal Psychology, 28*, British Psychological Society, Leicester.

Lloyd, C. (1990), *Suicide and Self-Injury In Prison: A Literature Review*, HMSO, London.

Mathieson, T. (1965), *The Defences of the Weak: A Sociological Study of a Norwegian Correctional Institution*, Tavistock, London.

McDermott, K. and King, R.D. (1989), 'A Fresh Start: The Enhancement of Prison Regimes', *Howard Journal*, vol. 28, pp. 161-76.

McHugh, M. and L. Snow, L. (2000), 'Suicide Prevention: Policy and Practice', in G. Towl, L. Snow and M. McHugh (eds), *Suicide in Prison*, British Psychological Society, Leicester.

McHugh, M. and Towl, G. (1997), 'Organisational Reactions and Reflections on Suicide and Self-Injury' in G.J. Towl (ed.), *Suicide and Self-Injury in Prisons, Issues in Criminological and Legal Psychology, 28*, British Psychological Society, Leicester.

Nagel, W.G. (1976), 'Environmental Influences in Prison Violence', in A.K. Cohen, G.F. Cole and R.G. Bailey (eds), *Prison Violence*, Heath, Lexington Books, Lexington MA.

Novick, L. M. and E. Remmlinger, E. (1978), 'A Study of 128 Deaths in New York City Correctional facilities (1971-1976)', *Medical Care*, vol. 16, pp. 749-756.

Pattison, E.M. and Kahan, J. (1983), 'The Deliberate Self-Harm Syndrome' in *American Journal of Psychiatry*, vol. 140, pp. 867-872.

Phillips, M. (1986), 'A Study of Suicide and Attempted Suicide at HMP Brixton', *Department of Psychological Services Report*, Series I, 24, Prison Service, London.

Playfair, G. (1971), *The Punitive Obsession*, Gollancz, London.

Power, K., McElroy, J. and Swanson, V. (1997), 'Coping Abilities and Prisoners: Perception of Suicidal Risk Management, *The Howard Journal*, vol. 36 (4), pp.378-92.

Prison Reform Trust (1997), *The Rising Toll of Prison Suicide*, Prison Reform Trust, London.

Reed, J. and Lyne, M. (1997), 'The Quality of Health Care in Prison: Results of a Year's Programme of Semistructured Inspections', *British Medical Journal*, vol. 315, pp. 1420-1424.

Ryan, M. (1996), *Lobbying From Below - Inquest in defence of Civil Liberties*, UCL Press, London.

Sapsford, R. J. (1978), 'Life Sentence Prisoners: Psychological Change during Sentence', *British Journal of Criminology, vol.18, pp. 128-145.*

SASU (Suicide Awareness Support Unit), HM Prison Service (1995), *Review of Self-Inflicted Deaths conducted by the Suicide Awareness Support Unit*, Internal paper. Second Report of the Commissioners of Prisons, PP, 1878-9 (C.2442), xxxiv.

Serge, V. (1970), *Men In Prison*, Gollancz, London.

Snow, L. (2000), 'The Role of Formalised Peer-Group Support in Prisons' in G. Towl, L. Snow and M. McHugh (eds), *Suicide in Prison*, British Psychological Society, Leicester.

Stengel, M. (1970), 'Attempted Suicide' in *British Journal of Psychiatry*, vol. 116, pp. 237-238.

Sykes, G. (1958), *The Society of Captives*, Princeton University Press, Princeton.

Third Report of the Commissioners of Prisons, PP 1880, (C. 2733) xxxv, I.

Toch, H. (1992), *Living in Prison: The Ecology of Survival*, American Psychological Association, Washington.

Toch, H. and Adams, K. (1989), *Coping: Maladaptation In Prisons*, Transaction, New Brunswick, N.J.

Topp, D. O. (1979), 'Suicide In Prison', *British Journal of Psychiatry*, vol. 134, pp.24-27.

Towl, G.J. and Crighton, D. (2000), 'Risk Assessment and management' in G. Towl, L. Snow and M. McHugh (eds), *Suicide in Prison*, British Psychological Society, Leicester.

2 Theory and Method

Introduction

Suicide in prison is a problem where dominating modes of knowledge, in relation to policy, have tended toward a narrowly positivistic approach: it is unfortunate that there is an official resistance to other approaches. Prison, like other law and order issues, has been a highly politicised issue, used with particular cynicism during the Thatcherite years of 1979-1997. Prison continues to be a politicised phenomenon, used expediently by politicians of all parties, and the expectation that the Blair government might attempt some education of the general population with regard to the cost, lack of efficacy of prison, and the utility of other types of punishment has not been fulfilled.

Statistics are valued by policy makers, and treated as more significant than words in terms of assessing the problem and devising policy responses. Even penal reform groups with the best of intentions, such as the Howard League, fall into this trap when they publicise league tables of suicide rates in particular prisons. With regard to actual policy, there is a huge gap between words of intent, and full implementation. Performance targets remain largely numerical, and the official view exists that only statistical measures of success and failure are valid. This is patently disingenuous: a prison with an excellent culture of suicide awareness and support may be unlucky enough to suffer a cluster of suicides within a relatively short time, while a prison with a very low level of implementation may be lucky enough to sustain none.

One of the roots of this managerialism is a desire on the part of policy makers to seem to be efficient, and to do enough to ward off damaging opprobrium which could have some political fall-out. Another more serious root, however, is a disbelief in the full humanity of prisoners, and a disregard of their status as members of a moral community beset by self-inflicted harm and death. This resistance to accord prisoners the same worth as others permeates discourse at the highest level, and trickles down into practice. Cultures in particular prisons can be categorised as unhealthy, because of failures in standards of care and a fundamental lack of respect for others (HM Chief Inspector 1999). Government ministers and members of Parliament do not write about or speak of prisoners as if they were fellow citizens. Prisoners are part of the broad mass of otherness, to be reviled for their anti-social behaviour, and stigmatised during and after they pay the due penalty for their misdeeds. They are an extremely convenient and constant political target, called into play when needed, and permitted to strut the stage of populist bigotry as folk devils. As Garland (1990) points out, penal practice can be put to official use as a form of rhetoric.

Because of this stance, which is never too frankly spelt out but which reveals itself implicitly in resource allocation levels, documentation, training, institutional culture and practice, I intend a lengthy explanation of my particular approach, in which I draw on 'philosophical fragments put to work in a historical field of problems' (Foucault 1981:4). Compatible fragments in philosophy, philosophical hermeneutics, humanist geography and social theory are used in service of the goals of obtaining expression of suicidal feelings in prison, of understanding such expression through empathising with inmate experience, and in arguing that these feelings must be accorded value and attention as emanating from full human subjects. Some readers, either because they do not need to be convinced of these arguments, or because they do not intend to be convinced, will want to skip this chapter.

Critics might argue that my approach is over-elaborate, even pretentious. After all, is this study anything more than a prosaic account of prisoners talking aloud?

My answer would be to agree that the essence of it is, indeed, what prisoners have to say. This is a complex rather than a simple matter. When individuals talk about life, death, identity, survival and dignity, their utterances are multi-layered, and the task of not only hearing them, but listening to them, and analysing their talk in ways that show fidelity to the speakers, are complex tasks. When those individuals are prisoners speaking from a closed community, this process is even more complex. The resistance to allowing them to speak to the outside community has been fostered by successive governments and prison authorities. One contemporary example concerns the blocking and harassment surrounding the production and attempted circulation of the One Off documents by two prisoners, Andrzy Jakubczyk and Paul D. Ross, which detailed the ways in which potentially suicidal patients are treated in prison (see Horner and Stacey 1999 for a fuller account).

The general public is not accustomed to hearing from prisoners about the reality of prison. So, for the most part, unless they take a critical interest in penal affairs and justice, they do not have the ability to listen impartially and consider what prisoners have to say, and this inability may in part relate to an ideological climate which has tended to deny the full humanity of prisoners. It could be claimed that the widespread inability, both on the part of the general public and of special interest groups such as politicians and policy makers, to listen openly and impartially to what prisoners say, is part of a range of normalised responses in a society with ambivalent sensibilities toward punishment (Garland 1990). But because offenders are imprisoned in our name, and emanate from our moral community, and because in that sense 'they' are 'us', they have an absolute right to be heard without denigration and prior judgements about their moral worth. What they have done does not define what they are. If the term 'citizenship' has any purchase in our society, they are citizens (Medlicott 2000), temporarily disqualified from the community, but entitled to participate fully in the inner community in which they find themselves.

Beyond Positivism: The Need For A Qualitative Approach

The epistemological justification for using qualitative approaches in conjunction with other approaches lies in the nature of the prison as an institutional phenomenon within a liberal democracy. As such, it is a phenomenon about which we are entitled to know every detail of practical everyday experience, and the effects of this experience upon inmates. The quantitative enquiries, the official statistics, the growing tendency to use actuarial practices as the basis of policy (Feeley and Simon 1994) are all approaches which have their place in the government and governmental practices of a sophisticated post-industrial society at the end of the twentieth century. But the conviction that a positivistic approach will, of itself, eradicate uncomfortable functional glitches in the smooth operation of a complex organisation, may be more suited to organisations where the 'product' is not a human being, and where contradictory issues of punishment, containment and rehabilitation are not struggling against each other both in baseline purpose and in everyday practice.

It is not enough, therefore, to analyse either the workings of such institutions or the behavioural responses of inmates from the perspective of positivistic science alone. For it is in closed institutions such as the prison that positivistic science most clearly reveals itself as providing tools for enquiry that are incomplete and sometimes too blunt. Inmates are confined against their will, at the behest of the courts, and in the interests of a social order which can be enforced by the state when necessary. Yet, despite this forcible confinement, no modern prison can be run except by consent on the part of the inmates. They are partners, albeit unwilling ones, in the enterprise of running the prison community. This ambiguous relationship of compulsion/consent confers a deep political complexity on the phenomenon of imprisonment. But it establishes that prisoners' voices are a necessary ingredient in the running of that community.

In a liberal democracy, inmate experience is also of legitimate interest for the society at large, because inmates are representative members of the whole civil populace. Members of society who are not confined are entitled to enquire how the institution works, since it works on their behalf. Understanding how it works logically includes understanding inmate experience. Analysis of inmate experience is, therefore, a proper part of the overall field of enquiry, and a necessary precedent to any willed change. Such analysis, in order to be meaningful, has to examine the quality of prisoner experience, and it must do so in ways that demonstrate fidelity to the phenomenon under scrutiny. In this way, it can complement and enrich more positivistic approaches. In examining what prisoners say, this study then proceeds to provide an analysis of the body of material as a whole. In this analysis, how is the fidelity principle adhered to? What is the justification for my particular interpretations of prisoners' narratives?

Philosophical hermeneutics, and in particular the work of Wilhelm Dilthey (1833-1911), provide a fruitful and flexible base for my analysis, because the science of hermeneutics stresses the value of interpretation of texts and utterances, and of social phenomena *as if* they were texts (Dilthey 1978:10). Additionally, hermeneutic enquiry aims at an understanding which relates a complex whole to its parts, believing the former to be comprehensible in terms of the latter, and the latter meaningful only within the whole (Dilthey 1978:203, 259, 262). Thus, each prisoner's narrative is complex and meaningful in its own right, but it acquires more depth and meaning when considered as part of a body of narrative from many prisoners.

Like Kant, Dilthey took human experience as the foundational base for the human sciences. For both Kant and Dilthey, experience was the product of mental activity which shapes and structures the data it receives. Prisoner experience of daily reality in prison is an important part of the complex phenomenon of suicide in prison: it can be uttered and interpreted, in terms of the structures of the knowing mind, and this analytic can be productive of knowledge about social action in a particular setting.

This Kantian approach to the investigation of meaning has an important corollary in relation to the possibility of change. The institutions of human society, such as the prison, do not come into existence in a moral, political or cognitive vacuum. They are conceived and ordered in particular patterns by knowing minds with particular interests and purposes. Because of these interests, they can never be operated solely according to rational and scientific principles: there are always normalisation processes involved which work to mould and shape human action in particular ways. Sometimes such processes can transcend the original purposes behind them, and produce normalising effects which are unintended but persistent. In societal settings which remain responsive to changing politics, culture and belief, normalisation processes do not remain set in stone. It is one of the tasks of a responsible social science constantly to analyse and test them.

Dilthey took Kantian assumptions about the structures of the knowing mind somewhat further than Kant in relation to their usefulness for a human science. He agreed that the structures of the knowing mind are accessible to experience, for the knowing mind experiences human life as the product of mental activity which endlessly shapes and structures the data it receives. But he was critical of the cold model of knowing reason at the heart of Kantian consciousness, preferring instead to stress the categories of willing, feeling and imagining at the heart of the knowing human subject, for these are the distinctive bases of all human experience (Dilthey 1978:197, 201-2, 224). It is to the fidelity of these bases that this research project strives to adhere, for it is in prison, and in the phenomenon of prisoners forced to come to terms with the difficult environment of prison that these bases are expressed in such exemplary fashion. Additionally, it is through the willing, feeling and imagining of a researcher employing disciplined empathy that the interior experience of prisoners can be expressed, sorted and presented to policy makers.

However, it would not be adequate merely to discuss the problem of epistemological justification as if the sole task of the human sciences was to achieve explanatory understanding of the mental world. Human action is rarely discretely mental, and suicidal behaviour is no exception. Indeed, it is the physical manifestation of the phenomenon which presents such a challenge to the ordered and normalising routines of the closed institution. The essential inter-relatedness of the mental phenomenon of suicidal feelings with the physical acts of self-destructive behaviour present the human scientist with two partial problematics:

Viewed subjectively from within the knowing mind, suicidal behaviour is the outcome of complex, often inaccessible and anguished mental activity.

Viewed from an exterior vantage point, suicidal behaviour presents as a set of behavioural symptoms, theoretically amenable to measurement, prediction and control.

It is toward the second of these problematics that positivistic psychiatry, emboldened with its hegemonic successes in the 19th and early 20th century, has inclined. However, it is not sufficient to explain the problem from the perspective of one problematic only, nor to use that 'explanation' as the basis of changes in policy and practice. Recognition of the value of a positivistic approach must be accompanied by a recognition of the limitations of this approach. The exclusivity of a wholly positivistic attitude must be relinquished, for although science can dissect the causal order of nature, it has less success where human action is concerned. Human action is not essentially predictable: interests, motivations and affect trail from it, and 'willing, feeling and imagining' are constitutive elements. As such, these elements form a proper field for investigation. It is an extraordinary omission on the part of HM Prison Service that inmate experience has been comparatively neglected, but that omission is perhaps an indication of the official view of its worth.

Disciplined Empathy

Having established that inmate experience is an appropriate sphere of enquiry, the issue then arises as to what the appropriate investigative stance is to be, and how the richness of interior experience is to be accessed. It would be possible for a social scientist who espoused the unity of method thesis still to do qualitative research and yet to use a methodology modelled on the natural sciences. But she might discover that what is lost is that very richness of interiority and particularity that she had hoped to capture in the first place. This is not to suggest that the methodology of the natural sciences is being challenged in some way by a superior human science methodology, and found wanting. But it is to claim that the theoretical stance of hermeneutic inquiry is a valuable form of understanding with which to enlarge the modes of science which are essentially predictive in intention. Dilthey points out (Dilthey 1978:163) that the interdependence of scientific method with other methods is inescapable. For the bases of all mental facts are after all the conditions of nature and the physical world.

The larger question which I pose in this research revolves around the foundational categories of place and time. These abstract concepts live in everyday experience and identity with peculiar significance in the special place of prison, where prisoners must make some accommodation with forced confinement in a particular place, and relinquish all control over the timetable of their daily life. How is it that inmates make this accommodation in such a variety of ways, so that their experiences apparently range across a spectrum, with some experiencing seriously suicidal feelings and others managing an apparently unproblematic adjustment?

The appropriate investigative stance with which to approach this question is one of disciplined empathy. I presented myself to inmates as an open and non-judgemental listener, in order that they, in turn, would be open with me. I committed myself to the attempt to see the world that they saw, and try to understand that view. This empathetic task is partly imaginative, and involves putting oneself in the place and predicament of the other. Yet it is also a task of discipline and rigour, which involves screening out judgements which would compromise the empathy. Discipline is also involved in not allowing oneself to become overwhelmed by what one hears, and in not letting some aspects of a narrative dominate the overall interpretation. So disciplined empathy is not just a strategy to be used in the interview situation: as well as being significant in the way the research was carried out and analysed, it played a part in the choice of topic and the focus upon time, place and self.

In the interview situation, when a high level of disciplined empathy is achieved, one can often experience an intuition, in advance of the speaker, about the particular flavour of the response to an experience which he is about to relate. When this happens, it provides what natural scientists sometimes call the 'Ah ha' moment - a point at which one's methodology successfully produces an answer to one piece of the puzzle. In this case, it occurs because one has entered into the experience and feelings of the other, and understands perfectly why they are feeling what they feel. This is not, of course, the same as feeling what the other feels: it would be presumptuous to make that claim. But one can get alongside the experiences and feelings of others by drawing upon a philosophy of listening, using hermeneutic openness (Corradi Fiumara 1990). Listening sounds a mundane sort of activity, and openness is hard to define. But they can be dealt with together.

The development of the human sciences, as well as the construction of our social bonds, has been characterised more by the tradition of critical questioning than by elaborating solutions or answers (Corradi Fiumara 1990:35), and it is this tradition which has persisted, despite Tommaseo (1855) pointing out a long time ago that criticism is heard by many, but listened to by a few, understood by even fewer, and felt by the fewest of all.

Corradi Fiumara (1990:29) suggests that the problem of listening is a 'shadow-dimension of the epochal development of our culture'. The skills of question-posing, investigation, hypothesis-testing and experiment have, for instance, been highly valued, whereas listening attentively, as experience is narrated, has not.

But a human science which has room for the logic of critical questioning, but not for the logic of listening, must fail the test of logical adequacy.   For it suggests that human scientists will formulate their questions according only to what they are prepared to receive in reply. The questions posed will only be those that are evidently within acceptable parameters and which provide some cognitive security (Corradi Fiumara 1990:38). This may lead to a human science which perpetuates questions which have been asked many times before. Heidegger (1972:45) suggests that it would be useful 'to rid ourselves of the habit of hearing what we already understand', claiming

> The authentic attitude of thinking is not a putting of questions - rather it is listening to the grant, the promise of what is to be put in question... In order to perceive a clue, we must first be listening ahead into the sphere from which the clue comes.

The assumption that the human scientist can manage authentic and empathetic listening, and that this will aid the putting of questions, underpins the hermeneutic claim that the interactive attitude is not just an incidental bonus in enquiry, but a distinctive and indispensable means of grasping inter-subjectivity.

But it is important to stress that these theses of indispensability and distinctiveness are not making overarching claims to the superior nature of the attitude of enquiry adopted by the human sciences. The stance of this enquiry, drawing as it does upon philosophical hermeneutics, does not make any pretensions to superior, complete or absolute knowledge. It is intended to expand and enrich positivistic approaches, whilst at the same time taking them to task for their bluntness and crudity. This study is based on research at one particular establishment, with its own distinctive culture and practice, and on the narratives of a unique set of individuals. These factors imply some generalisability, in that confinement anywhere would produce narratives of the same order, but that generalisability is not complete, because each establishment has a unique culture which feeds into the range of interactions between prisoner (each of whom is unique also) and prison.

There are deeper reasons why this enquiry cannot make any essentialist 'knowledge' claims, and they lie at the deeper level of what can be termed 'epistemological modesty'. For what is uncovered is a group of experiential accounts still in the process of becoming. Each is a small part of the interviewee's life story. A life story exists at the interface between life as it is lived by the individual, and the story that is understood by the listener. Intrinsic to this interface are the social, economic and political times in which it is lived and told and understood. Thus individual experience and historical reality (Josselson and Lieblich 1993: xiii) are interwoven and told in the life story. In terms of this project, the subtext of this life story is the Me/Here/Now predicament, in which each individual, in answering my questions, implicitly asks of himself what sort of a place he is in, whether he can deal with his present situatedness and by what means. In doing so, he is laying out his personal resources, and pitting them against the experience which he is undergoing. The empathetic listener understands the monumental interior struggle involved, and treats the resultant disclosures with respect and recognition.

It is obviously important for researchers in the human sciences to acknowledge, with proper humility, the vulnerable nature of their knowledge, both at the epistemological level, and at the level of developing theory and research practices. For the mainsprings of human action are, in the last resort, unknowable to the same degree of certainty with which we 'know' that water will boil at a certain temperature. To acknowledge this is to acknowledge the qualitatively distinctive nature of the human objects of social enquiry. The complexity and essential unreachability of human action justify a wide range of epistemological approaches which, in turn, entail differing theoretical assumptions and methodological implications. To cling to one only, and to claim that that one alone can produce knowledge would be to embrace epistemological narrowness and an exclusive attachment, with all its attendant limitations, to one model of the world, and, more significantly, one model of man (Hollis 1977). So, although this study takes an interpretive stance, it acknowledges the value of other stances.

This necessary humility is part of the stance of fidelity to the sheer complexity of the object of scrutiny, and it should not be seen as apologetic or defensive. To endorse the thesis of ultimate unknowability is in no way to demean the value of qualitative research. Acknowledging the essential unknowability of a phenomenon and the limitations of hermeneutic enquiry does not mean embracing a position of scepticism. Kantian approaches to knowledge are non-sceptical: what there is to know, we can know (Kant:1929:A493) and there are no gods and angels which preclude us from full knowledge of human action. Yet knowing can never be fixed because of the process of empirical advance. What, after all, may seem 'real' or 'apparent' in any particular historical moment stands in necessary relatedness to our perceptions of current knowledge, and to the means at our disposal for empirical progress.

There now exists a growing body of statistical data and psychiatric/psychological research and evaluation on the problem of suicide in prison. But hermeneutic enquiry into social action and experience is lacking, and this deficit needs remedy in order to gain the fullest possible understanding of the phenomenon. Scientistic researchers may protest that 'stories' have no place in trying to uncover the 'reality' of prison suicide, but such protestations may expose a deficiency in the open-mindedness that necessarily precedes an overall picture of a phenomenon.

These accounts form a body of data that is amenable to qualitative analysis. The time-place context of prison is filled with routine, and structured apparently similarly for all inmates, and yet each prisoner has a social identity which is special and individual. So prison, as a social system, is not experienced in uniform ways, but as a series of interactions, some shared, some highly individual. Its structural characteristics are extreme and overt: for instance, the exercise of overt power is a factor which is built in as a founding characteristic of the prison as institution: it is not some afterthought grafted on as an optional extra. And yet, additionally, there are less visible and covert aspects to prison life, which, when thoroughly investigated from the prisoner perspective, also disclose the routine practice of power.

Despite the unassailable logic of the structure/action dialectic, there remains much official scepticism about the capacity of inmates to convey useful information about the experience of prison. Rather than being viewed as subject consumers of penal policy, they are viewed as its objects. The 'reality' of prison experience is often taken as residing wholly in official accounts, by staff, policy makers, government officials and statisticians. Historically, the voices of prisoners have not been acknowledged as significant in debates about justice, punishment, rehabilitation, sentencing, or prison regimes. Researchers like Joe Sim and Phil Scraton, (see for example Scraton, Sim & Skidmore 1991) whose work recognises and honours the experience of prisoners, tend in official circles to be regarded as suspiciously 'radical' when more properly their work should be central to the formation of ethical policy.

In drawing attention to the experiential accounts of prisoners, this study intends to assert that these are one part of the whole 'truth' about suicidal prisoners, which has been addressed in previous research (Liebling 1992), but which is still regarded as less 'scientific' than positivism. HM Prison Service cannot afford to ignore such research, for it is part of that much needed global picture of the working of the prison system, to which the HM Chief Inspector of Prisons (1991) referred in the Woolf Report, following the riots of April 1990. An awareness of the possibility of similar events in the future meant that, as the Report emphasised, a stance of listening and openness must henceforward be part of the overall system of monitoring and evaluating penal policy. Post Woolf, there is undoubtedly more listening and openness, especially in the area of suicide, for such listening and openness form a necessary part of any preventative strategy. However, there remains much to do, in relation to expressed inmate need, and the duty of care on the part of the Service.

Finally, it is worth pointing out that it is easy to find epistemological justification for *not* acknowledging the value of hermeneutic enquiry, and there is indeed much political comfort to be gained by taking refuge in the limited findings of positivism, and denying the validity of qualitative and social research on the grounds that it lacks 'scientific' credibility. As Jupp (1989:68) points out, '(q)ualitative research, and not just quantitative research, can contribute to policy-making although its credibility within the definitions and perceptions of policy-makers may not be as high'.

To cling to a position which dogmatically and uncritically asserts the negative worth of all qualitative research in turn amplifies its generalised lack of credibility, and may be extremely convenient for policy-makers. In some circumstances, it may be termed a 'politico-ethical refusal', for if the validity of all such research, regardless of its conduct and findings, can be established as worthless, then the policy and practice implications can be ignored. If, as is the case with my research, the findings appear to have a strong ethical dimension, rooted in universal human need, and therefore compelling on grounds of natural justice, and yet they suggest change which is uncomfortable and/or costly in terms of a costs/benefits analysis, it is particularly useful to be able to mount a wilful refusal to consider social analysis, on the grounds that it is non-scientific, lacks credibility and is difficult to replicate.

However, 'the social scientist is a communicator, introducing frames of meaning associated with certain contexts of social life to those in others' (Giddens 1984:285). In the case of the phenomenon of prison suicides, prisoners' frames of meaning have been a neglected issue, and their reality needs conveying to all those who are ignorant of them, and especially those with the power to relate that meaning to policy and practice.

The Telling Of Narrative

Narrative is the form in which the raw data in this research is received by the researcher-as-listener. The concept of narrative has been utilised in a variety of different ways both theoretically and methodologically, most of which are not fruitful in my chosen approach to the problem of prisoner suicides. In this research, the usage of philosophical hermeneutics is assumed, whereby narrative is a life-plot which serves the individual at the time that he/she is narrating it (Josselson and Lieblich 1993, Widdershoven 1993). It is an account of events and experiences which appear to the teller, at the time of narration, to possess contingency ranging from the strong to the barely attenuated. Narrating is one way in which individuals tell what they know of their identity. 'The fact that people believe they possess identities fundamentally depends on their capacity to relate fragmentary occurrences across temporal boundaries' (Gergen and Gergen 1983).

As a social action, the concept of narrating provides a bridge between Dilthey's theory of what the human sciences is and how it should investigate the social world, and the practice of life by individuals, and, in this research, in a particular institutional setting. It is the action of narrating which produces the raw yet immanent data which is to be shaped into a perspective on prisoner suicide. Narrative is the recounting of time-centred experience: as a way of ordering life experience, it is a key tool in minimising the level of unknowability about the life of the self and the life of others. By exploring it theoretically, it can be shown to serve as a bridge between theory and practice.

With its saturation in time structures, narrative as a concept is epistemologically appropriate to this enquiry. For the focus of this research is the situatedness of human actors who are confined in an institution whose prior purpose and responsibility (as directed by the courts) is to seize time, or, to coin a stereotypification, to force them to 'Do time'. This seizure thus obliges them to confront time as an enemy - time passing, time seeming to stand still, and the ways in which the content of past time has placed them where they are now (Medlicott 1999). The experience of 'doing time' casts a shadow over future time. All of these abstractions are painfully felt but hard to reflect upon and even harder to articulate.

In choosing to focus on prisoners' time consciousness, in a special place whose purpose is to seize time, I am focusing on not just one but two dimensions of existence, place and time. These are foundational categories of being-in-the-world: time, once it has ceased to be a philosophical abstraction, and is related to being in the world, can only be experienced in specific places. So my questions to prisoners are about how they interact with the prison place and prison time, and what this interaction does to their sense of identity.

Most of the interviewees in this study have, in the past, been the object of official or 'expert' discourses, perhaps medical, judicial and psychiatric. The expert may have 'read' the life-plot in a particular way, which 'explains' all previous errors, as if 'reading' a text, and claim that this is the true account of reality. The subject of the life-plot may, however, find this account wholly alien to his life experience (Medlicott 2001). Reading a text and reading actions in the past are both activities which are subject to hermeneutic principles (Ricoeur 1984), but the hermeneutic involved in reading the lives and experiences of others must be based on listening, openness and fidelity to the phenomenon under scrutiny. This mode of listening, which is discussed later, is much more intensive than the expert's, because it seeks to understand the life-plot from the vantage point of the speaker, rather than from a formalised expert discourse.

Intentionality is the characteristic which unites all mental acts of all narrators, be they telling of the past or of their own lives (Husserl 1964). Yet this principle of intentionality allows that mental acts are, in principle, fallible. To say that one has seen a unicorn at the door of one's cell does not entail a truth about the *existence* of an intentional object. The claim is not accessible to empirical observation, but it is accessible to phenomenological description and eidetic intuition. Thus for the claimant, it may be highly meaningful in terms of his 'truth', and for those to whom the claim is made, meaningful in terms of making sense of the claimant's life situation, from the claimant's point of view.

These intentional mental acts are all inherently time-conscious (Husserl 1964). Humans do not experience temporal reality as a chaotic jumble. The flow of time is not mute, unformed and meaningless: in its barest essence, it inevitably consists of birth, life and death. This universal template of human existence is filled out by experience, and every experience occurs against a backdrop of precedence and succession. The capacity to experience Now spans both the past and the future. This capacity is necessary to humans in order for them to make sense of the world. Its absence causes terrible suffering in the human agent and generally, in modernity, leads to that agent being categorised as mentally impaired, and that agency being compromised.

Each narrator in this research study is engaged on a task of inherent fragility. It is true that the self-narrative may be related in a retrospective way, but the action is still unfolding and the retrospection is constantly being re-shaped in order to fit in with present circumstances and purposes. The researcher who must then deal with these personal narratives must struggle to do so in ways that reflect the intentionality of the teller, conscious however that *her* own intentionality is entailed by *her* activity. Thus the fragility of the process is compounded.

In the case of seriously suicidal prisoners, it is striking that the life-plot which is related seems, on the one hand so full of suspense as they stand in the midst of experience, and yet on a path which seems, to the listener, to lead so inexorably toward suicide, because of the time-structuring and intentionality of the teller. The logic of this ending sometimes strikes the empathetic listener with an overwhelming and implacable inevitability, so that it becomes hard to remember that other endings to the story are indeed possible. For the narrator, the only ending is the one which is apparent now, because thus it is that meaning is bestowed through now-feeling, now-knowing. Kierkegaard's formula - that we live life forwards but understand it backwards - is a lucid aphorism for describing the heuristic service that personal narrative gives to the narrator. Narrative bestows present understanding on the rich confusion of lived experience for the self, just as the time-structured account of the historian does for others.

For prisoners, the initial impact of a prison sentence alters the near and far horizons so radically that the time-plan of the life-plot is overturned. In the period January 1st 1994 to March 31st 1995, for instance, one third of recorded prison suicides took place in the first 30 days of custody (H.M. Prison Service 1996). After the initial shock and chaos, which spans a varying duration in different individuals, the surviving self re-organises its picture of the future: the configuration that seemed to extend into the future is revised, and other stimuli are incorporated and absorbed into a new temporal configuration. In other words, the prisoner begins to re-write the narrative of his life to take account of his present situation. Without narrative, there would be no history and hence no self.

In this research, prisoners are listened to as they narrate the manner of their coping with prison. This task of coping may feel lonely, and yet the telling of an individual story is also a telling of the inter-subjective community within an institution, where the nature of the institution produces a certain kind of enforced community and bears upon each individual in a forceful yet individually unique way. Most significantly, I am inviting each to reflect upon the consequences of this in terms of his own self-picture. It would be patronising indeed to assume that prisoners can not perform this phenomenological task, and, although their thinking and verbal skills varied enormously, I encountered no-one who had not already undertaken this task during their time in prison at one level or another, and who could not communicate to me something of the nature of their discovery. This laying bare of individual subjectivity is essentially inter-subjective, since the 'I am' of the ego only exists insofar as it is reflected by others.

However, despite the employment of empathy, the quality of communication between inmate and researcher may be claimed to be necessarily limited. Some would claim that the truest communication may only occur between those who have known each other for eternity (Jaspers 1951). Yet the very longevity of a close relationship, its intimacy and all the accompanying dialectical baggage can actually prove a barrier to communication, particularly when the communication concerns shame, guilt, sorrow, regret and a desire for death. Prison pushes inmates into an abyss of solitude: the stranger who appears as an outsider, with no affiliation to prison, to governmental authority, to family or to friends, and, as a relief from this solitude, empathetically invites communication, may be good enough to be privileged with relatively authentic disclosures.

These disclosures are stories in themselves, and stories in the making. Each is unique to the teller, and is felt, willed and imagined in ways that can never quite be captured unequivocally in language. Methodologically my goal is to translate each individual interview in ways that show fidelity to the teller. In this first task, I am merely discovering the thread of narrative (Young 1989), by listening with hermeneutic openness.

However, this research goes further than this. From the body of interview data as a whole, I engage in the analytic task of imputing a common frame of meaning, and in this second task, I am applying, with intentionality, my structure of narrative to the phenomenon of suicidal feelings in prison, a structure which I hope remains faithful to the reality of prisoner experience.

Having discussed the nature of these tasks, it is now time to turn to the manner of carrying out these tasks.

The Gathering Of Narrative By The Researcher As Outsider

Personal narrative is a story about the process of becoming the self that one presently feels oneself to be. It is the representation of process, of a self having a conversation with itself and with its world over time (Josselson in Josselson and Lieblich 1995).

Feeling suicidal in a prison setting is an intense and particular kind of life experience, almost overloaded with meanings for the bearer. When a researcher invites personal narrative in this area of experience, she is brought more closely into the investigative process than if quantitative or statistical methods alone were used (Josselson and Lieblich 1995). In inviting personal narrative, I chose to employ the attitude of *disciplined empathy*.

The capacity of the human scientist to empathise with other human minds is a distinctive and indispensable capacity, which is not paralleled in natural science theory or methodology. This distinctively human capacity is an important epistemological justification for research such as mine, which uses the subjective accounts of prisoners as the raw data from which to generate concepts and recommendations for practice in the field of suicide awareness. By authentic listening, I refer to the open listening, discussed by Gadamer (1979:74):

> Anyone who listens is fundamentally (sic) open. Without this kind of openness to one another there is no genuine human relationship. Belonging together always also means being able to listen to one another.

Listening therefore is implicit in our social bonds, and it is this that we draw upon in order to achieve hermeneutic openness in research. It is after all part of the essence of language, and in the everyday practice of social action, we are all accustomed to demanding of those closest to us not just to hear us, but to *really listen*. Heidegger (1972:95) provides an invaluable methodological imperative for this study:

> Perhaps only a little can be said concerning proper hearing, which nevertheless concerns everyone directly. Here it is not so much a matter for research, but rather of *paying thoughtful attention* to simple things. (my italics).

In order to pay thoughtful attention to this multi-layered process, and to focus on it in a wholehearted and concentrated way, it was important firstly to define my role to myself. Having no affiliation, monetary or otherwise, to the Prison Service or to any other agency, gave me the status of an independent outsider. My green pass, worn at all times, announced to the prison staff and inmates alike that I was an outsider. The very label 'criminologist' seemed to invite interested responses on the part of both staff and prisoners, who often seem to share a fascination with the possibilities for them of study in that area, and posed questions in relation to their individual situations which often broke the ice, and additionally underlined that I was from a world wholly outside of Prison Service concerns.

Sociological studies of the prison which have been carried out over the past three decades have employed various stances (King and Elliott 1977), but rarely that of the single independent outsider. For instance, Morris et al. (1963), Bottoms and McClintock (1973), and Liebling (1992) had home office funding. Emery's (1970) study was officially sponsored. Cohen and Taylor (1972) employed an appreciative stance, and pursued research which arose out of teaching within the prison and which was mutually appealing to the inmates and researchers.

My independent status was valuable, in that (i) the assurance to prisoners of confidentiality and trust was watertight, since no-one else saw the raw data; (ii) the data was gathered solely in order to serve the research; (iii) no rules or structures pre-empted the disclosure of findings, except those of a responsible social scientist.

Staff in the prison, wishing to be helpful and also wishing to express some of the abrasion of their own encounters with particular inmates, would sometimes assure me that particular inmates were not to be trusted, and that the inmates would produce, in interviews, fantasies about themselves and their past lives, and attempt to manipulate me with regard to their alleged guilt. Such advice, if absorbed, could have contaminated the data. As an outsider, however, it was easier to bracket this off and, indeed, as time went on, to avoid receiving such disclosures altogether. It was difficult to withhold empathy - both as a fellow human being and as a researcher fascinated by institutions - from the plight of the prison officers, many of whom were obviously severely stressed by the exigencies of a demanding and emotionally draining work environment, exacerbated by too many inmates, too much rapid change and not enough support. But my outsider status made it easier to prevent this empathy from colouring my focus on prisoner experience.

Interviewing

There is a copious literature on interviewing as a qualitative methodological tool (Kvale 1996, Chirban 1996, Rubin and Rubin 1995). In the final analysis, however, the way that the interview is conducted flows out of the epistemological base, and out of the theoretical intentions and values of the researcher. Additionally, because an interview is a self-consciously staged rather than spontaneous event, for which the interviewer must take responsibility, there is also an ethical dimension. So for the researcher-as-outsider, the choice of research topic, the theoretical and methodological approaches, the balance of rigour and imagination, are not just intellectual approaches to a perceived problem. They are implicitly expressive of the values of the researcher, and in the interview situation, these values assume an explicit reality.

The acknowledgement of the value-laden nature of this research does not arise just because this is a qualitative study. Whatever problem and/or approach is chosen in social scientific research, it will involve an embeddedness in values. There are no immaculate descriptions or pure representations of research data (Glaser 1978), and to adhere to some specious fact/value distinction is mythic and unworkable. The social researcher, having analytically picked away at the fact/value distinction, must eventually just accept their reciprocity and pragmatically get on with the job in hand.

There were underlying assumptions which structured my approach to the interview as *event*. For the interviewer, the event is one of many, but for the interviewee, it is a strange interruption to the monotony of prison routine, a one-off event which may be extremely challenging. It is important to be open and non-deceiving about the research: Kelman (1967) points to this as a moral, as well as a methodological imperative.

A second such imperative is to construe the interviewee as a subject person, for only then is the epistemological position derived from Dilthey served with fidelity. It would be easier, in many cases, to treat the interviewee as an object person, for this is what he is used to in this particular institutional context. Additionally, this strategy might obviate some of the dissonance I described earlier, but it would negate the force of the theses of indispensability and distinctiveness. Nor would it properly access the knowing, willing, feeling subject.

Although my approach derives from philosophical hermeneutics, there are theoretical approaches deriving from psychology which emphasise the subjectivity of individuals as agents. Kelly's (1968) constructivist approach in Personal Construct Theory is a telling example, in that it casts doubt on the meaningfulness of 'objective reality', and emphasises the primacy of cognition, subjective experience and meaning. For these interviews strive to reach the subjective meanings narrated by interviewees, not the originating events or some supposedly neutral account of them. Personal meanings are the filter through which individuals process their experience. In such processing, individuals construct not just themselves, but also others and the shared social world. They make their own meanings, even of common structures such as rules and institutions:

> People are neither prisoners of their environment, nor victims of their biographies, but active individuals struggling to make sense of their

experiences and acting in accordance with the meaning they impose on those experiences (Kelly 1968:15).

Ironically, in this life-task of construing their narratives, individuals can construct their own imprisonment, in the way in which they construe the past. So my interviewees are prone to the pains of imprisonment on three levels (i) in the prison as institution, (ii) as the subject of their personally constructed narratives and (iii) as fatalistically propelled by their past.

Despite the usefulness of Kelly's (1968) recognition of personal agency, a counterbalancing principle of this research must be an awareness of the awesome power of some of the constraints operating in these life stories - the constraints of social structure, poverty, deprivation and abuse, all of which are exemplified in the prison population to a disproportionate degree in relation to the general population, and all of which are struggled against in various forms of resistance.

These layers of theoretical recognition underpin the interview as event, and produce ethical and political overtones and real consequences in terms of the conduct of the interview. If an interviewee begins to narrate a significant episode of childhood abuse, he cannot be interrupted and pulled back onto the desired interview plot. The interviewer must listen empathetically, respond when required to do so, and wait until the interviewee is ready to be turned back to the interviewer's concerns.

In research such as this, which centres interviewing as the means of gathering data, the pilot study is an essential part of the research, particularly when it takes place in a closed institution. It is true that each interview is unique in itself, but it is also true that the more one does, the 'better' and 'richer' the interviews become. The prison is a daunting environment: by the time the researcher-as-outsider sits down face-to-face with an interviewee, she will have had to pass through the security procedures of the main gate, stood by whilst many doors are unlocked and locked again, attempted to ingratiate herself with many levels of overworked and busy staff in order that they co-operate in selecting and accessing prisoners, and, most importantly, attempt to present an empathetic attitude to the inmate who is about to be interviewed. The pilot study was invaluable: the six lengthy interviews that were conducted and recorded could be listened to repeatedly in order to address some failures of empathy and to develop some principles of conduct for the main research, as well as some criteria for achievement of an acceptable level of empathy. From the pilot study, the following principles of conduct were adopted:

- Interviewees were given a short explanation of the project and asked for their consent.
- Interviewees were asked for their consent to the recording of the interview and given assurances of confidentiality. Their questions on what these assurances constituted were answered in full, and the status of the 'researcher-as-outsider' was explained.
- Interviewees were told that they could ignore any questions and terminate the interview at any time.
- Interviewees were given cues to indicate that they were in control of the encounter. For instance, they were always asked where they would like to sit.

At the end of the interview, the tape recorder was switched off and, if the interviewee wished, some time was spent in unrecorded conversation. After the interview, in response to officers' enquiries, it was always stressed that the prisoner had been co-operative and of much value to the research, in order to prevent diminishing a prisoner's standing in the eyes of the staff.

In deciding which interviews to include in this study, and which to reject, a key factor was whether or not an adequate level of empathy had been achieved between interviewer and interviewee. When sufficient empathy was present, the following characteristics prevailed:

- The interview included frequent and prolonged eye contact between interviewer and interviewee.
- The interviewee demonstrated relative psychological comfort by appropriate body language.
- The unrecorded chat at the end of the interview was 'of the same voice', with no abrupt disjunction in personal style from the preceding account.
- There was mutual listening, in that the interviewee responded directly to the interviewer, and vice versa.
- The interviewer maintained respect for the autonomy of the interviewee through the entire process of listening, transcribing, analysing and writing up.

The maintenance of respect entails a recognition of the subject status of the teller, and the affording of opportunities for him to express his autonomy. Sometimes it is the over-rehearsed personal narrative which generates the most fruitful concepts, in relation to suicidal feelings, and sometimes it is the split-second response to a question that no-one has ever previously asked. Listening sounds a mundane activity, but listening empathetically and attentively, waiting through long silences, holding back from making some banal comment or rushing onto the next question are all difficult in practice.   Some of the listening is to sounds that cannot, of course, be transcribed: the sigh, for instance, has an expressive force in these interviews that words cannot do justice to.   There were so many sighs in the data - of regret, pleasurable remembrance, hopelessness, grief, relief and helplessness.   Where relevant, sighs and pauses are noted in the transcribed extracts.   Sometimes the special quality of a silence, or a pause, or a sigh, is interpreted and noted, because the particular quality of it is so striking and asks for recognition.

It is necessary also to acknowledge that empathy has its limits, if the listener is not to be too crushed by the burden of narrated suffering, which she is powerless to alleviate.   *Disciplined* empathy means that the researcher in an area such as this must draw firm boundaries for herself in order not be overwhelmed by the plight of individuals, the process of doing the research and attempting the task of understanding the data.   One boundary is the recognition that she can do nothing to help individuals in the context of their offence, their guilt and the length of their sentence. She can however remind them of particular resources in the prison which could be appealed to for help with particular problems.

Another boundary is the acceptance that change in this policy area is incremental and slow, and that anger and impatience about the inhumanity of some aspects of the prison system are, of themselves, counter productive. These natural emotional responses can, however, be channelled into the analytics of the research endeavour in positive ways, remembering that the research will form one small strand in an ongoing dialogue intended to accelerate the process of positive change.

The narrative data of prisoners is always permeated with an inherent tension.   I have already mentioned the apparent inevitability, when the narrator re-tells his experience in the light of his understanding of Here and Now.   Behind his words, however, lie the shadowy possibilities of outcome, and the event of narration is itself one contributory variable in how the story will continue.   So the narratives are characterised by a tension between apparent inevitability and inescapable contingency, and the interviewer has no means of knowing what strand will be added to the on-going story because of the encounter, the telling, the listening and the responses provoked by the event.

Analysing The Narratives

The activity of being empathetic, which I described above, involves adopting a pre-reflective attitude. In contrast, understanding what is heard is a highly reflective activity. The interpretative task which is performed upon this narrative data must respect its natural tensions and not pull the material into either end of a spectrum merely to add weight to a generated concept. This is part of the hermeneutic responsibility, for 'only from a hermeneutic position are we poised to study the genesis and revision of people making sense of themselves' (Josselson in Foreword to Josselson and Lieblich 1995). 'People making sense of themselves' must remain the guiding principle for the activities of listening and translating: the translator must always resist the impulse to take control of the material and do the task of making-sense, on their behalf.

Interpretation must therefore come after the task of empathising with the narrator, and listening and drawing out the personal and latent meaning. Interpretation does not mean engaging in elaborate and overworked discourse analyses, or overworked comparisons with totally different accounts. Each narrative stands on its own, as the account of a human subject responding to a specific institutional setting that entails loss of personal autonomy. Each human subject makes his own adaptation, and renders this implicitly and explicitly in response to the questions. The hermeneutic task is to take this material and to make manifest the latent meanings, the half-drawn connections and significants, but to do so in terms of the subjectivity of the narrator which has been conveyed empathetically to the listener and grasped by the listener in authentic communication. The inter-subjectivity between narrator and listener is the space into which this communication drops:

> A story about life presents us life as it is lived, and as such, life is the foundation of the story. In presenting life, however, the story gives life a specific sense, and makes clear what it is about (Widdershoven 1993:6).

This process of 'making clear' is one that has an effect both upon the listener and the teller. The listener begins to translate and put disparate pieces back together, but the teller, too, may be hearing the story for the first time, and as he tells it, it shapes his own understanding of the story.

The story contains features of continuity and discontinuity, for some pieces adhere together with a good fit, whilst some are rough and inconsistent with the rest. Thus, for the teller, personal identity is being both told and created, for 'the articulation of the implicit unity of life in an explicit story is itself part of the process in which identity is created' (Widdershoven 1993:7). For the meaning of our experiences and actions change, as we tell our stories. Despite the constant change, it is the Me/Now relationship which stands for truth, at the time of narration.

I have said that each narrative stands on its own, and no treatment must distort that uniqueness. Nevertheless, each teller is at a different stage in his own incarceration, and in a sense each telling is a part of one long telling of the various stages that might be travelled by an abstract *Everyman*. Thus each story of individual experience contributes to a body of narrative told by an *Everyprisoner*, which, by virtue of being systematically obtained and analysed, provides the conditions of possibility for theoretical 'discovery' (Glaser and Strauss 1967). Common meanings emerge, as well as distinctive and disparate responses to common experiences, and these produce an overarching patterning, from which it is legitimate and fruitful to drawn theoretical inferences about the phenomenon of suicidal feelings in prison.

This generation of grounded theory (Glaser and Strauss 1967, Glaser 1978) from a rich data source is methodologically distinct from an approach which seeks to verify or test existing theory. Apart from aiming at consistency with the epistemology I outlined at the start of this chapter, it was also my theoretical intention to keep some space for the generation of new concepts, and to allow for the possibility of a relationship with future change.

This relationship with future change is an abstract possibility, since the direction of policy cannot be predicted. Suicide is a highly complex phenomenon: in a prison setting, it becomes ever more complex with political, philosophical and ethical dimensions. It is not possible to anticipate the attention and resources which future policy may devote to the problem. But whilst it remains true that the grounded theorist should be cautious in his promise to the reader (Glaser 1978), this caution should not prevent that theorist from linking the findings, the theoretical discoveries and the generated concepts from the possibility of policy or culture change. On one level, it is the optimistic belief in the possibilities of those links that sustain the impetus of independent research.

Nevertheless, suggestions for future change must be accompanied by a proper awareness of the implacability of the phenomenon under scrutiny, and the limited effects produced by changes in policy and practice. It is impossible to eradicate suicide in prison, and important to recognise the long list of potentially contributory factors to suicide, which resist solution.

Most of these cannot, realistically, be magically solved for particular individuals by any social or penal policy. The early socialisation experiences of prisoners, poverty, physical and sexual abuse in familial and institutional settings, incomplete and spasmodic school attendance, previous psychiatric treatment, personal addictions and parental deprivation were all factors that were described to me by the prisoners I met. Although the focus of this study is not on the contribution of prior social factors to suicidal feelings, these multi-factored aspects of causation cannot be ignored, for they all contribute to the huge challenge faced on a day-to-day basis by prison staff, who must deal fairly and professionally with the bearers of these complex social and psychological factors. Methodologically, such factors are a source of conflict within the interview situation, for the need to talk about them is overwhelming, and the opportunities to do so in the austere setting of prison are so limited, that it was difficult to deny the interviewees this basic human need.

In the prisoners I spoke with, such factors were ground into personal identity and hence into narrative. They could not be separated out, as if they were intervening variables that were not relevant to the task in hand. A narrative brings with it the inclusion of all life experience up until the point of telling, as well as the implicit hopes and dreams for the future. That these narratives contained so much telling by inmates of prior deprivation and exclusion renders the responsibility of the prison all the more significant. Because these factors are so prevalent in the prison population, the prison has a *special* responsibility to provide an environment which will mitigate rather than exacerbate the effects of these factors, if it is to take seriously its duty of helping them 'lead law-abiding lives in custody and after release', as the Prison Service statement of purpose claims. And yet the problem of overcrowding, identified by HM Chief Inspector (1991) in the Woolf Report as a canker which had soured industrial relations and prevented the necessary improvement of prison conditions, is even more acute at the start of the 21st century. Discussions for future change occur, therefore, against a backdrop of overcrowding and the arguably deficient management of resources in recent years (Morgan in Maguire et al. 1994).

The structural issue of gender is significant in this research, both in terms of the interview as event, and in terms of the boundaries of this study which only considers male prisoners. Gender and power are issues that must be addressed in the enterprise of imputing a common frame of meaning for the research as a whole.

The questions in the semi-structured interviews, which are presented at the end of the next chapter, are designed to elucidate how these male prisoners cope with the time-place of prison and the concomitant loss of control over their time and space. These issues are certainly germane to female prisoners, who suffer the same characteristics of the prison place. But there are specific cultural reasons why these experiential principles of autonomy over time and space are of special fascination to the female researcher in relation to males.

The issue of autonomy over personal time and space has been, historically and culturally in Western societies, primarily a male issue, for it is males who have had more of a monopoly on personal autonomy since the commencement of the Modern Age. Since the industrial revolution in particular, females have largely been socialised to cope with more constraints in relation to the exercise of personal autonomy over time and space than have males. Traditionally there have been widely differing expectations of girls and women in terms of (i) self-control over personal time and space, (ii) accountability to others for time spent and space occupied, (iii) responses to rules and constraints over the self-management of time and space, and (iv) the consequent aspects of personal identity.

This is not to say that females do not experience just as acutely the pains of imprisonment: it is, however, to claim that, because of social, economic and cultural conditioning, the pains of imprisonment may fall somewhat differently upon females. That this is so is suggested by the different maladaptive responses to imprisonment on the part of the numerically smaller female prison population, which presents patterns of repeated self-injury, drug dependency and depressive illness rather than a strong pattern of distinctively suicidal behaviour. It follows, therefore, that an enquiry into the narratives of female prisoners, if remaining true to the chosen epistemological position, might prioritise different questions as a starting point for eliciting meaningful narratives.

So far as the pains of imprisonment are concerned, it is a grounding assumption of my research that the loss of control over time and space is an acute pain for males, acculturated as they are to relatively greater freedom than females since the time of early childhood. In my view these place characteristics of prison render all men in prison *vulnerable*, in a conscious or unconscious grief at the loss of autonomy and male identity, on the one hand so taken-for-granted, and on the other so prized and celebrated by men of all ages in patriarchal cultures.

This vulnerability is largely unrecognised and unexplored in previous research. Vulnerability is traditionally viewed as an individual characteristic possessed by some, and not by others. There has been a recognition arising from recent research by Liebling (1992) that the prison population suffer disproportionate levels of vulnerability on account of the backgrounds and life experiences of so many prisoners. But this is still a quantitative approach, in that it is the numbers of prisoners with particular characteristics which are regarded as significant. The concept of vulnerability has also been considered useful in understanding why some prisoners attract unwelcome attention from other prisoners, and in this usage, vulnerable prisoners are defined in terms of particular social and/or psychological characteristics, such as 'sex offenders, prison debtors and those vulnerable for personal reasons such as appearance, hygiene, age/disability, or behaviour' (McGurk 1996).

But I began with the qualitative recognition that the very special place characteristics of the prison render all male prisoners socially vulnerable, because of the contrast with their prior status as males in a patriarchal culture, where they have been accustomed, to varying degrees and within the usual constraints of an advanced post-industrial society, to managing their own choices in relation to personal timeness and space. In terms of a policy of suicide awareness and prevention, it may be positively unhelpful to label selected prisoners as 'vulnerable', thereby implicitly categorising the rest as invulnerable.

In terms of the gender issue in relation to the conduct of the research, it is not so easy to make formal distinctions. Still less is it easy to relate the findings to the gender of the researcher. I have already referred to the value of being the outsider researcher. Is this value increased or diminished by being a female researcher in a male prison?

Although the chosen prison establishment contained female staff, it was quintessentially a male environment with a strong culture of *machismo*. Male officers exhibited displays of masculinity, both in their body language, in the way they handled their large bunches of keys, in their speech and in their personal dealings, in ways that had no equivalence in female officer behaviour. These displays of masculinity were, on the whole, confined to group behaviour, and were heavily overlaid with demonstrations of toughness and robust humour. The prison officer role is one where much of the job is carried out in group situations, and it is reasonable to suppose that the display behaviours I witnessed are a truthful demonstration of how some of the job gets done.

In on-to-one encounters, however, even the most overtly *macho* prison officers would talk seriously and sensitively about the phenomenon of prisoner suicide, and about the characteristics of the inmates. Without any empirical evidence, it was my impression that the flavour of these exchanges was aided by my gender. In an atmosphere where *machismo* dominates, there may not be too many opportunities for staff to speak authentically, in ways that do justice to seriously held views.

In dealings between prisoners and officers, on the landings and stairways, the same atmosphere of *machismo* predominated. There was generally a rough and good-humoured attitude towards prisoners, which could however become authoritarian at any minute. There was, however, a marked difference in atmosphere in different prison locations, and this difference would form an interesting topic for research, in terms of the relationship between levels of goodwill and behavioural outcomes.

It is from this atmosphere that the prisoner steps into an interview situation with a female researcher, who asks him to disclose aspects of himself which he is struggling to manage. In almost all cases, prisoners disclosed that they had never had such a conversation in prison previously. In many cases, prisoners admitted that *they had never before in their lives had such a conversation.* In the few cases where prisoners had had similarly intense conversations about their feelings, it had been with cell mates.

It is impossible to evaluate the 'interviewer effect', in terms of gender, age, social class or ethnicity. But it can be surmised that the female interviewer operates with a powerful advantage over her male counterpart, purely because of the novelty of a female listener who may be construed by the prisoner in traditional cultural ways. Of course, some prisoners may construe females as particularly contemptible, but it remains true that the interview is a departure from the monotonous *machismo* of prison life. The male/female encounter may induce greater frankness than a male/male one, and it is my view that this is more likely than that it induces greater reticence. Impressionistically, I considered that there was great advantage in my gender, in the encouragement of frankness, and the way in which disclosures were delivered. Prisoners felt able to express great anger, grief and savage humour: they were not ashamed to weep. They did not appear to feel inhibited about using crude and explicit language in order to express how they felt.

No consideration of the interview as event can escape considering the implicit dimension of power. Despite attempts, within the parameters of the research, to hand some control over to the tellers, it is undeniable that it is a staged event and the interviewer is the stage director. It is not fanciful to recognise that, whatever precautions are taken, the situation has some of the elements of rape (Reinharz 1983:95) and the interviewer becomes uncomfortably aware from time to time that, on the level of encouraging private confidences, she is the rapist. In this sense, the interviewer is reproducing, in the different guise of the face-to-face encounter, all the characteristics of the institution as a set of power relations.

Where prisoners are experiencing acute suffering, this power imbalance is all the more acute, and the researcher may become aware that the interviewee deserves protection from people like herself (Finch 1984:80). Frankness as to the nature of the research, and openness as to the method, does not prevent an acknowledgement that if an encounter has at least some potential for harm, social scientists must weigh the benefits of the encounter against the possible costs (Erikson 1967). All of my encounters with prisoners had a theoretical capacity for harm, since they revolved around highly personal and sensitive issues to do with the pains of imprisonment. But, on balance, the rarity of this valuable material in the literature on prison suicide, and its inestimable value in enriching present approaches to the phenomenon provided me with some justification for proceeding, mindful that 'the only safe way to avoid violating principles of professional ethics is to refrain from doing social research altogether' (Bronfenbrenner 1952:453).

For all prisoners, the power issue is ambiguous and complex, especially for those remanded or convicted for rape and other sexual and violent offences characterised by the exercise of power. In such encounters, the issues of power and gender hang in the ether, undeniably on occasion flavouring the quality of experience for the interviewee, and making the interviewer uncomfortably aware that there is no way analytically to capture this factor. It must stand as an inevitable part of the intersubjectivity of the interview, acknowledged but phenomenologically unavailable for extraction and analysis.

In the final analysis, however, power lies with the researcher, in that it is she who analyses and writes up the research. In terms of the selection, juxtaposing and generation of concepts, it is *my* version of their narratives which stands as a record of 'what happened' during the research. A theoretical space was kept for concepts which were grounded in the common meanings and tellings of the inmates themselves, and which could provide the basis of recommendations for change. These acts of identifying concepts grounded in the raw data (Glaser 1978) carry with them the responsibility which always accompanies the exercise and practice of power.

References

Bottoms, A.E. and McClintock, F.H. (1973), *Criminals Coming of Age*, Heinemann, London.

Bronfenbrenner, U. (1952), 'Principles of Professional Ethics: Cornell Studies' in Social Growth', *American Psychologist*, vol. 7:8 pp.452-5.

Chase, S.E. (1995), 'Taking Narrative Seriously: Consequences for Method and Theory in Interview Studies' in R. Josselson and A. Lieblich (eds), *Interpreting Experience: The Narrative Study of Lives*, Sage, London.

Chirban, J.T. (1996), *Interviewing in Depth: The Interactive-Relational Approach* Sage, London.

Cohen, S. and Taylor, I. (1972), *Psychological Survival: The Experience of Long-Term Imprisonment*, Penguin, Harmondsworth.

Corradi Fiumara, G. (1990), *The Other Side of Language: A Philosophy of Listening*, Routledge, London.

Dilthey, W. (1976), in W. Richman (ed. and trans.), *Selected Writings*, Cambridge University Press, Cambridge.

Emery, F.E. (1970), *Freedom And Justice Within Walls: The Bristol Prison Experiment*, Tavistock, London.

Erikson, K.T. (1967), 'A Comment on Disguised Observation in Sociology', *Social Problems*, vol. 14 (4), p.368.

Feeley, M. and Simon, J. (1994), 'Actuarial Justice: the Emerging New Criminal Law', in D. Nelken (ed.) *The Futures of Criminology*, Sage, London.

Finch, J. (1984), 'It's great to have someone to talk to' in C. Bell and H. Roberts (eds), *Social Researching: Politics, Problems, Practice*, Routledge, London.

Gadamer, H.G. (1979), *Truth and Method*, Sheed and Ward, London.

Garland, D. (1990), *Punishment and Modern Society*, Oxford University Press, Oxford.

Gergen M.M. and Gergen, K.J. (1993), 'Narratives of the Gendered Body in Popular Autobiography', in R. Josselson and A. Lieblich (eds), *The Narrative Study of Lives*, Sage, London.

Giddens, A. (1984), *The Constitution of Society*, Polity, Cambridge.

Glaser, B.G. (1978), *Advances in the Methodology of Grounded Theory*, Mill Valley: Sociology Press, Mill Valley.

Glaser, B.G. and Strauss, A.L. (1967), *The Discovery of Grounded Theory*, Aldine, New York.

Heidegger, M. (1972), *What is Called Thinking?*, Harper and Row, New York.

HM Chief Inspector of Prisons (1991), *The Woolf Report: Prison Disturbances*, HMSO, London.

Hollis, M. (1977), *Models of Man*, Cambridge University Press, Cambridge.

Horner, S. and Stacey, M. (eds) (1999), *Incareration Humane and Inhumane: Human Values and Health Care in British Prisons*, The Nuffield Trust, London.

Husserl, E. (1964), *Logical Investigations*, Routledge, London.

Jaspers, K. (1951), *Man in the Modern Age*, Routledge, London.

Josselson R. and Lieblich, A. (1993), *Interpreting Experience: The Narrative Study of Lives*, Sage, London.

Jupp, V. (1989), *Methods of Criminological Research*, Unwin Hyman, London.

Kant, I. (1929), *The Critique of Pure Reason*, MacMillan, Basingstoke.

Kelly, G.A. (1968), *The Psychology of Personal Constructs* Norton, New York.

Kelman, H.C. (1967), 'Human Uses of Human Subjects: The Problem of Deception in Social Psychological Experiments', *Psychological Bulletin* vol. 67, pp. 1-11.

Kvale, S. (1996), *InterViews: An Introduction to Qualitative Research Interviewing*, Sage, London.

Liebling, A. (1992), *Suicides in Prison*, Routledge, London.

McGurk, B. (1996), 'Experience and Perceptions of Integrated Regimes for Vulnerable and Non-Vulnerable Prisoners', *Home Office Research Bulletin* no. 38, Home Office, London.

Maguire, M., Morgan, R. and Reiner, R. (1994), *The Oxford Handbook of Criminology*, Clarendon, Oxford.

Medlicott, D. (1999), 'Surviving in the Time Machine', *Time and Society*, vol. 8 (2), pp. 211-230.

Medlicott, D. (2000), 'Citizenship and Prisoner Healthcare: Letting Prisoners into the Debate', *Citizenship and Crime*, Howard League, London.

Medlicott, D. (2001), 'Condemned to Artifice and Prevented from Being a Pirate: How Prisoners Convicted of Terrible Crimes Recognise Themselves in Discourse', in R. Hamilton (ed.), *This Thing of Darkness: Perspectives on Evil and Human Wickedness*, Rodopi, New York.

Morris, T.P., Morris, P. and Barbara Barer (1963), *Pentonville: A Sociological Study of an English Prison*, Routledge, London.

Reinharz, S. (1983), 'Experiential Analysis: A Contribution to Feminist Research' in G. Bowles and R. Klein (eds), *Theories of Women's Studies*, Routledge, London.

Ricoeur, P. (1984), *Time and Narrative Vol. 1*, (trans. K. McLaughlin and D. Pellaner), University of Chicago Press, Chicago.

Rubin, H.J. and Rubin, I.S. (1995), *Qualitative Interviewing: The Art of Hearing Data*, Sage, London.

Scraton, P., Sim, J. and Skidmore, P. (1991), *Prisons Under Protest*, Open University Press, Milton Keynes.

Strauss, A.L. (1987), *Qualitative Analysis for Social Scientists*, Cambridge University Press, Cambridge.

Tommasio, N. (1855), *Della Bellezza Educatrice. Pensieri*, Giovanni Pedone Lauriel Editore, Naples.

Widdershoven, G. (1993), 'The Story of Life: Hermeneutic Perspectives on the Relationship Between Narrative and Life History', in R. Josselson and A. Lieblich (eds), *The Narrative Study of Lives*, Sage, London.

Young, K. (1989), 'Narrative Embodiments: Enclaves of the Self in the Realm of Medicine', in J. Shotter and K. J. Gergen (eds), *Texts of Identity*, Sage, London.

3 Telling

The following summaries introduce the prisoners who provided the data for this study. I have given them fictitious names. From here on, I describe them as tellers, to emphasise that, as the subjects of an active verb, they carry subject status, in contrast with the term 'interviewee', which makes them the object of someone else's activity.

The first group of summaries concern the prisoners who were not 'coping' at the time of interview. They had expressed suicidal feelings and had been made the subjects of F2052SH documentation, because they were judged to be at an unacceptably high level of risk of suicide. Some of them had made persistent attempts to self-harm, and some an almost successful attempt at suicide. Some will go on subsequently to further attempts.

The second group are those who were offered to me as examples of 'coping' prisoners, and whom I define as '"coping" now', to underline the fact that prisoners move in and out of coping stages and that this is not a fixed state.

These selective summaries, with some significant aspects of each particular individual, demonstrate the huge variety of prisoner backgrounds, and the differing attitudes to their situations. This range of human detail is brief but wide-ranging and shows up the fallacy of hard categorisations. These are individuals whose uniqueness must be methodologically recognised, for, without distortion, they will not fit tidily into the taxonomies of medical and psychological textbooks. They do not even fit tidily into the extreme taxonomy of 'now "coping"' and 'now not "coping"'. Yet to break down the taxonomy even further, into 'persistent but not serious self harm', 'one-off serious suicide attempt' etc. would impose further positivistic rigidity for no good purpose.

My first summary concerns a prisoner whose narrative I have not used in this analysis. I begin by summarising this encounter and explaining why the resultant data could not be used.

BOBBY is 38 and received a life sentence with a recommendation to serve 20 years six months ago. He described himself as a saint who had never been involved with drugs, drink or violence. He professed not to remember his offence, only the events leading up to it.

He had been brought up in the UK from the age of 13 by his grandmother, who was religious and a strict disciplinarian. He had been culturally dislocated by the experience of coming to this country from the Caribbean, and for about two years he was utterly silent at school and did not interact with peers in any way. At length, his 'silence' attracted attention from the school psychological service. In interview, he was very controlled and calm, and presented himself as the main protagonist in a narrative of blameless purity. He radiated a kind of calm intensity, and his eyes never left mine. I asked him when the last time had been that he had lost control and become consumed by anger. He related an incident that had happened just after he had arrived in the UK. It appeared to be the start of his 'silence'.

Bobby refused to answer some of the questions about his identity. When the tape recorder was switched off, Bobby's calm demeanour changed, as did his voice and style of delivery. In a much less controlled manner than previously, he told me about his visions, which he considered had led up to the offence. These related to certain tests by God, and showed how fortunate he was in thus being selected for the ordeal of prison.

The interview as a whole failed my criteria (see Chapter 2), in relation either to the establishment of empathy or the conduct of the interview. In particular, the discontinuity of the post-interview self from the preceding account implied an extreme form of conscious impression management (Goffman 1959). A summary of the interview, however, demonstrates the reach and usefulness of having empathy criteria.

Not 'Coping' Now

The following twelve prisoners were interviewed in the Health Centre, or, in the case of Thomas only, on normal location on 'B' Wing. All had F2052SH documentation open and live, because they were considered to be at an unacceptable risk of suicide.

JIMMY is 31 and had been in the Health Centre for two weeks when I interviewed him. He had been on remand for eight months, three in this particular prison and five elsewhere, and was awaiting a re-trial. This period of remand is his first experience of prison, except for one night stays as a result of being drunk and disorderly. On the way back from a court appearance, he had surreptitiously cut deeply into his elbow and it was only through the luck of an unscheduled stop that this was spotted and his life was saved. He lost a great deal of blood.

Jimmy comes from a wealthy Roman Catholic background, and is one of eight children of a corporate lawyer. His childhood was one of constant flux, moving from town to town in America, Belgium and other parts of Europe. He describes it as 'affluent and privileged - plenty of books, space, resources and stimulation'. He attended nine primary schools before the age of 11. His secondary schooling was more stable in two different schools. He described himself as 'a high achiever but with no ambition'. He gave up a place at medical school to travel, and says of himself at this time that he was 'shallow, iconoclastic, hedonistic, a bon viveur...really a clown, just fooling around'. He has taken alcohol and drugs to excess, and has several times completed the Alcoholics Anonymous programme but without success.

A week after my interview with Jimmy, despite observation in a locked ward, he cut himself again seriously under the cover of his bedclothes in the early hours, when there was least chance of discovery. He was again seriously near death but his life was saved because someone spotted the dark pool of blood beneath his bed. Shortly after this, he cut his throat and arm in another serious attempt, and he was subsequently transferred to hospital under the terms of the 1983 Mental Health Act.

BRAD is 21, and a heroin addict. He has been on remand for six weeks for drugs offences. He has been in Young Offender Institutions and prisons previously. He has made previous attempts at suicide before he came to prison, in the form of overdoses, and has twice attempted to hang himself in this six week remand period. He grew up in care, and could not bear to talk about the time before he was taken into care, during which he was sexually abused. He only went to school until the age of 12, because after that he got heavily into drugs. He could not say whether or not he was treated well in care, because he did not feel he has had a comparative experience of good treatment with which to compare it. He has never in his life felt really safe. He is now awaiting transfer to a psychiatric hospital, where he expects to get help with his addiction and depression. 'If they'd have looked at me years ago, and given me that help years ago, I wouldn't be sitting here talking to you today'. Brad has become much more self-aware recently, and believes that, with help, he can change.

PRADEEP is 26 and is serving a 12 year sentence for fraud and conspiracy offences. He was on remand for nine months, and, following conviction, made a failed suicide attempt. He has an HND in Business and Finance and ran his own business. He has a wife and family, and prior to these offences has never been in trouble before. He describes himself in the past as 'highly motivated. I wanted to get somewhere in life. I wanted to give my family a good life, I wanted to be a caring loving child to my parents, and be a good husband, have my wife be fond of me. I had a lot of plans...but after that incident...it just changed everything'.

JOCK is 27 and is serving a three-month sentence for threatening behaviour. He has previously done long and short sentences numbering about 17 in all. He is covered in tattoos, including his face. He has cut himself many times, both in and out of prison. Whilst out of prison, he took drugs and sniffed glue. When not in prison, he goes looking for love. 'I'm a sucker for love'. He has aspirations but feels they are impossible to realise. 'I'd like to settle down and live normal like other people, but I'm covered in tattoos. I've got...I've been told by the teacher on the out that I could have been a professional artist if I'd kept it up, but I just ain't got the time for it, because I know that my future's bleak: it feels bleak in a way, you know?'

SEAN is 29 and serving 12 years for rape. Whilst on remand in another prison, he attempted suicide. He has served six weeks since conviction, two weeks in the health centre followed by some time on 'A' wing, where he seriously self-harmed himself. As a result of the injuries suffered in this attempt, he was in the Physical Care Unit in the Health Centre at the time of interview. Staff were particularly reluctant to leave me alone with this inmate, and I was asked to read a charge card detailing his violence and his violent connections, and then asked to sign confirmation that I still wished to interview him with no-one present. We were ushered to a small room, and I was advised to keep the door open. But the noise of jangling keys echoing down the corridors so obviously distressed Sean that I closed the door after a few minutes, and his distress visibly eased. But he remained in such bottled-up anguish that we had to talk slowly for a long time before I could pose the initial questions.

He is in a long-term relationship. Before this offence, he describes himself as a quiet person, 'law-abiding, you know. Never done anything like...just me and my girlfriend knew where we was going, like. I was working and we was saving for a house, you know what I mean'.

Sean had a very troubled childhood in Ireland. Money was scarce and he remembers times when they ate nothing but potatoes for long periods. His father left, and his mother brought up four boys and three girls on her own. She was violent. When any of the children wet the bed, she would bring them all downstairs and make them watch her beat the culprit with a stick that she kept in the cupboard. They all slept in fear, the boys holding their testicles to stop themselves from peeing, but when they fell asleep, they could not control their bladders. Eventually, when they got bigger and stronger, one of his brothers attacked his mother with a hatchet, and pushed her around. Sean stood up for his mother and stopped this attack, because 'even though I wished her dead, I didn't want to see her come to harm'.

Sean was sexually abused up to the age of 11 by an older boy. Then he acquired the strength to resist. He was befriended by an older man, who taught him about coin-collecting and playing draughts. He looked up to this man, and when he died, Sean 'went funny and started doing things to meself'. Whilst still in primary school, he witnessed an RUC shooting.

Although he talked to me in a flood of words that lasted two hours, Sean describes himself as a loner. He can't face exercise in the yard, because he can't think of anything to say to other people. When he sees two or three others chatting, he wonders what on earth they can find to chat about. He says he always feels self-conscious in front of others, and utterly tongue-tied.

About two weeks after our interview, Sean manages to climb up somewhere high and hurl himself down, head first onto the floor. Not long after this, he is taken to an outside hospital for a psychiatric assessment.

BUD is 27 and is serving a 19 month sentence for drugs offences. He has never been in trouble before. He is in a long-term relationship, but his partner is only 17, and he is very concerned about how he is coping with Bud's imprisonment. 'He's far too young to take this. He doesn't know how to react, he's off the wires completely'.

He had what he describes as a privileged upbringing with a good education at a boarding school. 'I was learning, I loved learning. I got on with a lot of the pupils, the care staff were good, and we had freedom to go out in the woods, the fields, the barns'. Before he came to prison, he describes himself as 'very effervescent, I talk to anyone and I'm lucky I have quite a good personality - very social'. He was a counsellor with young people living rough in central London.

Since his conviction one week ago, he has not eaten. A week after our interview, he is persuaded to abandon his fast. But he has been hoarding his medication with the intention of overdosing, and after a tip-off by another inmate, this stash is discovered. Some months later, I learn that he is successfully integrated on a wing.

HAL is 32, and has 37 days left of a three year sentence. He has done the majority of his sentence on the wings, but for the last two months he has been on the hospital wing because of persistent cutting of his arms with razor blades. He used to cut himself on the outside and also in his only other previous prison sentence. His cutting got really bad in 1990, and he went on sickness benefit then. A year ago, he received a *Dear John* letter from his wife: she had taken the children and found someone else.

Before I interviewed Hal, he was often suggested to me as a prime candidate for my research. The staff spoke of him somewhat affectionately, regarding him as a 'character', and a 'textbook cutter'. He was incorrigibly cheerful during our interview, and seemed touchingly proud of his reputation. He shows me his arm, lacerated from a self-inflicted wound by a paper clip, which he succeeded in pushing right up inside his arm. This was as a result of distress caused by witnessing Jimmy's last suicide attempt (see above). 'The paper clip was that long, and that wide, and I pushed it in, kind of like loading a gun with a cartridge, but I've never done that before. I've seen a gun loaded on television, but I've never done it'.

Hal says that anyone who saw his hospital records on the outside would be 'gobsmacked' to see what efforts he has made to try and kill himself. 'Like, with anti-depressants and bottles of Scotch. 60 tablets and plenty of Scotch - like I've been unconscious many a time for days or a week (laughs). I'm surprised I'm not brain dead!'

When I laughingly point out that he has been spectacularly unsuccessful in his efforts, he laughs again. 'Yes, I've always been found. Someone's always found me. Never mind! I'm still alive to see my thirty third birthday!'

Hal would like some proper psychiatric help when he gets out. He thinks he has a split personality, because one minute he feels perfectly normal 'and the next minute I can change like the weather. When I'm like this, I'm o.k., but when my mood change to something else, like changes to bad, my mind just goes totally blank and I end up cutting myself to pieces. And...deep cuts and that, trying to kill myself'.

When the talk turns to school, Hal becomes more monosyllabic. He was bullied, and as a result he truanted for up to three months at any one time. His father drank a lot and was violent. When Hal was about 13, he was sexually abused in a one-off incident by the school bus driver. He has only recently had proper recall of this incident, which he describes to me in detail. 'I forgot, and it went out of my mind completely. As if nothing had happened. But in a funny way it's always been at the back of my mind. It's disturbed me, mentally and emotionally. It's faded out completely...I've tried to commit suicide in many many ways in the last 16 years, and I...it's kind of like it vanished into thin air. The memory of it vanished into thin air, and I've never ever ever remembered it, up until last week'.

Hal describes himself as a loner and says he trusts nobody. But now that he has remembered this significant aspect of his childhood, he is optimistic that he can put himself right.

MARTY is 26 and is a few months into a five year sentence. He was a foreman on a building site until conviction and has never been in trouble before. He has attempted suicide a number of times on the outside, since the time in 1990 when he was raped. He has been in the health centre since a suicide attempt three weeks ago. Medication is readily dispensed to him, but he does not see this as helping him in his present predicament. He had a very ordinary life on the outside, and is engaged to be married. He would very much like some counselling or psychotherapy in order to come to terms with the rape and the subsequent depression.

BRENDAN is 29 and is serving a life sentence for multiple rape. He has been in prison for 14 months, but only five since conviction. He was on a wing, but was moved to the health centre as a result of cutting himself. Prior to this offence, he had just completed a 5 year sentence for armed robbery, and he had previous sentences prior to that. He is considered highly dangerous, and was escorted to meet me in a small administrative office with glass sides and door, where we could be constantly observed from several angles, but not overheard. In all his sentences he has harmed himself by cutting and by attempted hangings. He used to be a crack addict, and also took Ecstasy and Speed.

Brendan grew up in Liverpool in a background which he describes as 'poor, emotionally. Poor, materially, no, we got what we wanted, guitars and stuff'. He was sexually abused as a child, and was moved around a lot, 'a bit of care, a bit of family, a bit of grandma'.

He is hoping to find the internal resources with which to make changes in himself. 'You know, it's not something the system says, it's something that my heart says - 'it's time you left all that behind and changed'. And because I don't really know how to change, I'm looking for ways to help myself, improve myself'.

I found the interview with Brendan a particularly challenging experience. His definition of himself as 'evil' struck no particular chord, but as the interview proceeded, I felt that I was not achieving the same level of empathy as I had with others. The empathy criteria were met, but in some intangible way, the interview felt less 'warm' than the others. Because of my methodological commitment to empathy, I was prepared to jettison the interview. Study and transcription of the interview, however, countered this view. There was no evidence for the lack of empathy I had worried about. Brendan had indeed contributed 'willing, feeling and imagining' to the process: his voice was slow, emphatic in parts and very intense. There were expressions of pain. Additionally, I found that I was not justified in suspecting a lack of reciprocity in my own interview conduct. My responses and encouragement to him matched those with the other tellers. I concluded that two factors had contributed to my doubts: (i) the fact that it was conducted in such an invigilated setting, and (ii) that despite my attempts to sit down with as little prior knowledge as possible about Brendan, several officers had tried to tell me about him, and one had commented (with an interesting slant on his view of the interview as some sort of contest): 'Now that one's a textbook psychopath: you'll not get the better of him'.

This interview alone demonstrates the difficulty of doing qualitative research in prison with consistent bases, and how the interviewer must always struggle to reproduce the same receptivity, not just for very different tellers, but with highly individual prevailing conditions and in a wide variety of settings.

ALAN is 40 and is eight months into a life sentence for murder. When I arrived to talk to him in the health centre, he had a panic attack. He expressed great hostility toward me. The staff member on duty sat him down and talked to him patiently and considerately, and eventually he agreed to talk to me about my research and then decide for himself if he wanted to participate or not. I was allowed in to the locked ward, and I sat on his bed whilst we talked. When I had outlined the research project for him, and given him assurances that he would be in control at all times, he agreed to proceed, and we went into the kitchen at the back of the ward, which was the only available place with privacy. We were interrupted several times by officers, cleaners and a nun needing to use the kitchen.

Previously, Alan was serving six and a half years for armed robbery: he escaped from prison, and it was during this period at large that he incurred the additional charges for which he has now been convicted. He is married and has two children. He grew up on Moss Side and was sexually abused as a child. He joined the army at 16 and it afforded him great relief in taking him away from his violent home. He did a tour in Northern Ireland and got injured, but returned from that tour 'well-adjusted and with no problems'.

Then in 1983 he was sent to the Falklands and experienced some of the worst fighting there. He killed two men. He is haunted by the knowledge of what he did, wondering if those acts were qualitatively different from his subsequent crime, wondering if the two soldiers had wives and children, and where their remains are.

Upon return to England he was diagnosed as suffering from Post Traumatic Stress Syndrome and was discharged from the army. He then began to act wildly, irrationally and impulsively, in ways that he could never predict or control. It was during this period that he committed the armed robbery for which he first went to prison. He described his dreams, his waking flashbacks and other agonies which seem to suggest that he still suffers from post traumatic stress disorder. He spoke highly of the psychiatric help he was receiving in the health centre: he was the only prisoner I spoke to who reported having had a two-way conversation with a psychiatrist.

Alan knows that if he is to survive, he has to keep up his self-esteem, remind himself of how loved he is, and involve himself in education. A recent incident on the wing has proved to him that he can ask for help, and walk away from trouble.

PAULO is 43, and is fighting extradition to another European country in order to serve a 24 year sentence, which he has so far managed to evade for a murder he was convicted of 20 years ago. At the time of my first encounter with him, he has been in prison for only two months, and is on a F2052SH, and in an extremely vulnerable state. He weeps through most of the interview and expresses guilt and remorse for what he did 20 years ago. He accepts that he deserves punishment, but the length of sentence which faces him is too daunting for him to accept. He begs me to help him in his predicament. His misery swamps him completely. It is all the more of a shock to him because, since his evasion of the sentence 20 years ago, he has led a hardworking and law-abiding life, working his way up from nothing to the position of owning and running his own business. On my second encounter with him, he is still labile and vulnerable, but is regarded as coping (see below).

THOMAS has been sentenced to six life sentences and a sentence of 18 years to run concurrently, but he is still awaiting his Appeal. He was convicted four months ago. He had never been in prison or in trouble prior to his remand period, which lasted nearly two years. All his life, since he was a child, he has suffered from depression and has had periods in mental hospitals. He comes from a loving home. In his early twenties, he lived in a car on a grass verge, a hundred yards from his home, not because he was unwelcome there but because he had cracked up completely. He has had a lot of medication over the years.

Now 'Coping'

The following summaries concern twelve interviews with inmates regarded by the establishment as 'coping'. For some, although apparently 'coping' at the time of interview, it appears that, in the past, they have suffered difficult, even desperate times. For others, it is apparent that they are in a period described by Gerry (now 'coping' on 'A' Wing) as the 'dream time', where the reality of their situation has not yet been fully realised, and where they are fearful of admitting to themselves anything negative, either in their past or their present, because to do so might bring internal chaos. All that can be claimed, therefore, is that, at this particular point in their sentence, they are not overtly or consciously vulnerable to the risk of suicidal behaviour.

This group were drawn from a variety of locations. Ben, Tim and Ramon were on the Induction unit, in the first 24 hours of this particular prison experience, and for Tim, on remand, it was his first experience of prison. Gerry was well into his sentence, and integrated on 'A' Wing, which has 23 hours of cell-time out of 24, unless inmates have a job. George and Ken were interviewed on 'B' Wing, which has a few more hours out-of-cell time, with George waiting to hear his tariff, and Ken looking towards his Appeal. Bill, Mike and Alistair are on the relatively more relaxed 'C' Wing at the time of interview, where the cells are unlocked for more of the day. Paulo, Les and Tel are on 'B' Wing, and are three prisoners who are on the cusp of change: they have all had intensive and persistent suicidal feelings in the past but are positioned at the time of interview as either on the brink of change, or in the process of consolidating change.

BILL is 21 and serving a life sentence for murder. He has been in prison for ten months, five of which were on remand. He has been in custody previously. His background was 'perfectly satisfactory', and there was no poverty. His parents split up when he was four or five, but 'it didn't affect me', and he maintained a good enough relationship with his father. He started truanting in his last year at primary school, and never really attended secondary school in the conventional sense, because he was excluded after six weeks of attendance for assaulting the Head of Year. 'The work was too easy - that's really why I didn't attend'. He got little schooling for three years and then attended a special Centre. His demeanour could be described as deeply stoical. He professed to be coping very well, and consistently reiterated that his background, his past and his present situation were perfectly satisfactory. He was interviewed on 'C' Wing, where the officers regarded him as a good coper, never having given cause for concern. I wondered what change would come upon him, if this 'dream time' ever ended and he awoke to some different awareness of his situation.

ALISTAIR is 43, convicted and awaiting a sentence, which he expects to be around 12 years. He has been in and out of institutions since the age of 9, when he was first taken into care. After life in children's homes and approved schools, he started thieving and went to a borstal. Thereafter he has been either in prison or out committing offences of theft and robbery. He described six specific prison sentences to me, but admitted that he had probably missed out a few. There were very few periods in his life where he was not in one institution or another, so it was difficult to talk to him about home and outside settings: he did not really have any non-institutionalised settings after the age of nine, and could remember very little prior to that. He was determinedly cheerful, and yet with a blank, resigned and passive demeanour. Questions about the sorts of events that he used to look forward to outside of institutions were just not comprehensible to him: he professed to get on with whatever regime or timetable he was subject to, and did not reflect upon the emotional content of his life. He tried very hard to remember his childhood before institutional life took over, and this is what he came up with:

> I was the sort of kid that always messed about with things. We came out of Bermondsey, I used to go down and nick bread...that was one of the things we used to do...and I just carried on and didn't really ever stop! I suppose, as a child, you could say I didn't have much of a home life as such. Going as far back as I can remember, we lived in a block of flats, and the memories that come back...I can remember my mother shouting out of the window 'help, help, call the police', because my dad was drinking and that. I can't say if he beat her up, I suppose so but I can't remember. I can only remember my mother shouting out of the window, and things like that. He was drinking, he used to gamble and take pills. I don't remember my dad knocking me around or anything...I got put away so it didn't really affect me.
>
> When I was in the children's home, I found it quite easy. Life wasn't really hard in the home and that...no. The people was genuine people and seemed very helpful. I went from there to an approved school, it was pretty much the same in there, really. I suppose violence and abuse went on, but not much. If you did run away from one of them places, then you would get the cane or the slipper. It happened to me, but I wouldn't say it was violence that was dished out willy-nilly. There was rumours of sexual abuse in my one, there was one headmaster there and he had his pets, so I suppose, looking back on it now, you think well, was there something more sinister involved? But I wasn't aware at the time.

MIKE is 40, with a common-law wife and two children. He has served a life sentence and whilst out on license, has been charged with, but acquitted of, a serious offence. He is awaiting release. He was born in London of African parents who had just come to England to settle. Both his parents beat him as a child, his mother in a way which he described as 'reasonable, for things that deserved it', but his father in unreasonable and prolonged bouts of violence that would last up to an hour. When he was 8, a son of his father by a previous wife came to join their family, and assumed the place of eldest child. Mike began to truant from school at 14, because he found school boring and under-stimulating. When he was 16, his father died, and after that he began to get heavily involved in fighting. He was never involved in drug or alcohol abuse: it was his fighting which culminated in his life sentence.

Mike has reflected upon his home background a lot. At one level, he finds his father's violence toward him 'incomprehensible, because I look at my daughters and just cannot imagine wanting to hurt them. For them, for myself, I chose love, or it chose me, and I'd like to ask my father about the fact that he chose violence'.

At another level, however, he has come to realise just what his parents went through in order to come to England and start again. He realises the stresses and strains that this must have caused them, their anxiety that their children should succeed, and hence their strictness. His father beat all his brothers, except the youngest.

> He'd point at all the boys in turn, before he beat one of us, saying 'You're a man, you're a man...' and then he would point at the youngest and say 'and you're a grabskirt'.

Mike's demeanour was calm, humorous, intelligent and reflective. The story that he told was one of painful adjustment to a life sentence, and of a personal journey that was laboriously reflected upon and worked over.

KEN is 52 and has just been convicted through a private prosecution of a murder that took place 20 years ago. He has been married for 32 years, and has a grown up family and grandchildren. He has never been in trouble with the law in his life. He has never really worked, and his home life revolved around the television, his pets and his family. He is not a strong or robust person, and sees himself as 'just ordinary, really'. All the pleasures that he describes as having looked forward to, around which he has structured his life, are the ordinary and everyday events of a close family, leading a somewhat isolated and private life. He was in a state of shock and distress at his situation but at the same time was managing to cope with it, and looking forward to his Appeal.

GEORGE is 33 and is serving a life sentence for murder. He is still waiting to hear his tariff. He has not been in trouble before. He describes his upbringing as happy.

It was tough, but I've got a lot of fond memories of growing up. There was violence in there, but you learned to, like, deal with that and get around it. There's violence everywhere, really, isn't there? But you don't let it become a part of your life. You learn to sort of avoid it, or to deal with it in a positive way.

George is considered a good coper, and presents a positive and cheerful demeanour which appears perfectly natural and unforced. 'I think I am a strong person, I try hard to be. Ummm...it's alright to fail, but as long as you fail trying, then it's not a real failure. And if you keep trying, then you can turn a failure inside out, into a success. The trick is, never to give up'.

He attributes this strength to the way in which he was brought up:

I get a lot of it from my mum. Mum is a very strong person, who went through a hell of a lot of things, and managed to come through. And I think, if she can do it, well... She always taught us to be strong and to keep plugging away, and I think that helps me. If she can do it, and my family can do it, and my friends can do it, then I can do it.

BEN is 28 and is serving a 4 month sentence for theft. He had a prior and similar conviction a few years ago. I interviewed him on the Induction unit in his first 24 hours in prison. He was brought up in a large family, where the mother and all the children were battered. He and his two brothers were taken into care, subsequently living in four different children's homes, but his sisters remained with their mother. His mother was a religious woman and had high aspirations for her children. The violent father, a successful barrister, left them and returned home to Nigeria.

For most of his life, Ben has experienced great anger over his father's behaviour, and great empathetic suffering with his mother's situation. Recently, he managed to write a letter to his father that was not filled with anger - 'one that he could actually finish reading, you know. And eventually, he wrote back, and he was overjoyed, you know'. Ben has a wife and four children, with a fifth child on the way, and they live in a cramped flat. Their dire need for furniture provoked him into this offence. He had had a temporary job, but lost it. He is full of remorse and a sense of failure, and intends to use this sentence to 'try to draw near to the Lord, and try to do His will, and change my life, you know'. He radiates good health and an open and happy temperament, which seems incongruous in his present surroundings.

GERRY is 35, serving a seven-year sentence for corporate crimes. He has completed his first year and is in the process of being divorced. He was a highly successful businessman, moving in the world of corporate hospitality, company jets and limousines. He did a previous five-year sentence for similar offences some years ago. In Gerry's early teens, his father suffered a nervous breakdown. Gerry's brother was mentally ill, and although violent, was cared for in the home. Gerry frequently had to lock himself in his room to protect himself. When he was 24, he discovered that he was adopted. He is extremely insightful about the prison experience, and the stages that inmates go through in their struggle to cope. His current stance towards his sentence is a robust one: 'I fight to do my job efficiently, just as I always did outside. You take pride in this. It matters to me'.

TIM is 50, married with two children. He has always led a stable and steady life, revolving around a large extended and traditional East End family.   He is remanded on charges of handling stolen goods and conspiracy, and has never been in prison before. I talked to him on the Induction unit, during his first 24 hours in custody. He was clearly in a state of profound shock, and the words came haltingly and repetitively.

> I don't think you can prepare anyone for the reality and confinement of prison, unless they've experienced it in the past. I understood prison was very much as it actually is, but it's still a shock and a traumatic experience, to actually be confined.

RAMON is 25, and is on remand on charges of conspiracy. I talked to him on the Induction unit in his first 24 hours in custody. He has never been in trouble before. He expects to get bail very shortly, and does not expect an eventual conviction. He describes himself as 'a happy-go-lucky person', and thinks that 'you just make a joke out of being in prison. You can't look too deeply into it. No everyone's the same, obviously, but humour is the way I'd look at it.' He has already had a visit from his girlfriend and family, and his main concern was for them. 'I can't really say in what sense I'm shocked, or measure it. With my visitors, I tried to be happy and make them laugh, just to let them know that I'm o.k. and not let them worry too much about me'. Later, he comments that prison is a bit like going camping, except that you cannot go home when you are bored.

PAULO is the only prisoner to appear both in my 'not 'coping' now' group, (see above), and also in this group of copers. Our second encounter is on 'B' Wing, some months after our first. The F2052SH document has been closed, and he is regarded as no longer at risk because he is considered to be coping. He is receiving a great deal of support from officers on the wing, and is holding down a job. In interview, he is still highly labile, verging on utter despair, and the story he tells is one of extremely tenuous adjustment to his situation.

LES is 27 and has a two year sentence. Following charges, he got bail and so served no period of remand, and has never been in prison previously. His is therefore a particularly valuable narrative: as a prison 'virgin' he suffered acute suicidal feelings and spent many weeks in the Medical Centre on F2052SH documentation. He is now successfully integrated on 'B' Wing, where I interview him, and has now done 5 months since conviction. He has been married 7 years, and has one daughter. His narrative forms a major part of Chapter Six.

TEL is 36 and is serving a four year sentence for drugs offences. He spent some time on remand at another prison, which he found difficult, but not intolerable. He has been here for over a year, and for much of that time he has been on F2052SH documentation, which is now closed, because he is now 'coping'. He is integrated on 'B' Wing.

LES and TEL are special tellers in terms of this research project. They are prisoners who have been suicidal, and have been the subject of F2052SH documentation, which is now closed, because they are not deemed to be currently at risk. They are interviewed on 'B' Wing, where they feel well integrated and supported by particular officers whom they named with gratitude.

Their narratives indicate vital stages in the process of emerging from a suicidal frame of mind. Les has made some inner changes and is coping with those changes, and beginning to look forward. Tel has also made some significant inner changes, has coped with this change and consolidated it in a way which means he can now look forward to a very different future. Their narratives are considered in detail in Chapter 7.

The Questions

The questions posed in the interviews were springboards designed to elicit uninhibited responses. In most cases, they were not worked through in the order stated here. Rather, they served the interviewer as hooks, designed to prompt the inmates to speak of their relationship with prison time, prison as a place and their present view of their personal identity. After the planting of the initial hook, the conversation proceeded naturally, with the interviewer empathetically responding to the teller's concerns, whilst attempting to hold to the shape and direction of the interview plan. With some prisoners, one question only from each section was enough to elicit a stream of material which covered the questions that had not yet been asked. With other prisoners, many prompts and/or diversions were necessary in order to achieve an interview consistent with the overall pre-occupations of time, place and self.

Despite the prosaic nature of some of the questions, they are personal and troubling, and they nudge the tellers toward painful issues. They were designed to allow the interviewer to follow a strategy of weaving a circle of relevance, and approaching painful points in a flexible fashion, so that if the discomfort became too great, the interviewer could retreat from that point and return to it later in the interview when intimacy and trust were greater (Douglas 1985).

1. TIME

Before you came to prison, what sort of ordinary, everyday things did you look forward to?

Did you ever think about the future? Were you the sort of person who had dreams, made plans?

Do you still do that?

In terms of your everyday life here, what do you look forward to?

Does this help, with the situation that you find yourself in?

How full or empty is your time here?

And does time pass quickly for you, or slowly?

Do you have any tricks that help you with the passing of time?

Do you worry about time passing?

So what worries you the most?

2. PLACE AND SPACE

Looking back over your life, where and when did you feel most safe? Do you have a favourite place, in your memory?

And have there been times and places when you've felt very at risk...perhaps through fear of others...perhaps through fear of your own feelings?

Looking back over the last three days, can you tell me what different places in the prison you've been in? (Alternative question for prisoners in induction: Could you tell me everything that's happened to you since you arrived here?)

Were you in those places by choice? (Not asked of tellers in induction unit).

Do you ever choose where to go and what to do? (Not asked of tellers in induction unit).

Do you think that making choices is important for you here?

How important is it, in your present situation, that you feel safe, physically?...And in terms of your emotional well-being?

Is there anywhere here where you feel particularly safe...or particularly at risk?

Is there anywhere at all that you feel possessive about, because you think of it as your space?

So what sort of a place is prison, in your experience?

3. SELF

Do you think you've changed a lot as a person, since you first came to prison?...In what ways?

Have you learnt anything about the sort of person you are, since being in prison? (Positive? Negative?)

And which aspect matters the most to you?

So what do you see when you look in the mirror? (What sort of a person do you see?)

Do you like yourself?

Do you think it's important, to like yourself, in view of the situation you're in?

Do you ever talk to anyone about how you're feeling?

And will you be the same person when you leave prison, compared with when you first came in?

Telling

In the following chapters, I break the narrative responses down, so as to consider the body of responses firstly in relation to the questions about Place, and then in relation to the questions about Time. In the interview, the Time questions were presented first, because they gave the teller the opportunity to talk first about his prior life and self, and to become comfortable in the interview situation. Here, however, I present the Place responses first, because the prison place is the primary context, and the temporal constraints are one part of that context. The questions about Self were intended to produce some synthesis, in that here the tellers spoke of the spatial and temporal effects upon their sense of self, and Chapter 6 reflects this synthesis.

What inmates say is not presented here *as if* it mapped onto particular theories of mind or selfhood. Shotter (1985) points out that, in explaining human conduct, the only talk that is officially authorised is from a third-person, external observer point of view. This external objectivising of prisoners, and suicidal prisoners in particular, is apparent in most previous research. For centuries, we have been held captive by the Cartesian picture of man, which so embedded itself in language that we constantly repeated it to ourselves. The maintenance of this picture required that we observed events and ordered them to the mental schemas already in our possession. If we did so, scientifically, disinterestedly and systematically, using explicitly stated theories and hypotheses, then what we observed might attain the status of *knowledge*.

But to engage with inmates' own talk and to encourage expression of their sense of self is to access their self picture, and a different sort of knowledge. My tellers are using ordinary language, and they are in a sense engaging in accounting practices (Shotter 1985). In response to my prompting, each is indicating how he gets along with himself, in this peculiar institution where individuals are thrown sharply up against themselves.

In maintaining a non-judgemental openness, and suspending the notion of a fixed standpoint (Shotter 1985), my goal was that inmates experience my listening as utterly accepting of the person that they think they are. It is of course demanding for inmates to speak of this personal self, and it can be surmised that they will not do so if they are aware of any morally coercive overtones in the encounter. In trying to take the role of the other, I was attempting to see the world from his standpoint and to become an object in his field of vision. My outsider status aided this process, and made it easier for the teller to trust the listener as an object from the outside world. But ideal goals remain ideal, and pragmatically the limitations have to be accepted or the job would never get done.

References

Douglas, J. (1985), *Creative Interviewing*, Sage, Beverley Hills, California.
Goffman, E. (1959), *The Presentation of Self in Everyday Life*, Doubleday, New York.
Shotter, J. (1985), 'Social Accountability and Self-Specification' in K.J. Gergen and K.E. David (eds), *The Social Construction of the Person*, Springer Verlag, New York.

4 Place

Introduction

The concept of individual space has cultural, social, psychological and historical variability. For instance, American visitors to Latin American cultures commonly feel their personal space is invaded in public places, as people come too close, touch too often and crowd against adjacent bodies, whereas in England they experience people in similar contexts as cool and aloof (Hall 1966). Studies of introverts have shown that by choice they sit further away from other people than do extroverts, and keep a greater conversational distance (Williams 1963). Within the generalisations produced by such research on discretely defined groups of people, it is apparent that individual needs for space and personal distance vary enormously. Sommer (1969) quotes an obscure formula which seems to suggest that individuals in crowds need at least two square feet, but that a fat individual would need at least twice this amount of space.

Prison is a place where individual desires and needs in relation to space must be set aside by prisoners as belonging to the old freedom. In this sense, it is a place that obliterates the notion of personal space. Inmates have no control over the amount of space assigned to them, or the nature of that space. With no notice at all, they may be removed from the space assigned to them and put into another space. Most terrifying of all, they are locked into their assigned spaces, sometimes with a stranger, and this space, or cell, is an intentionally austere place of sensory deprivation, in which they have to eat, sleep, dream, excrete and pass time. At any time, staff may burst in, search that space, touch, scrutinise and roughly re-arrange or remove any items, however personal, in that cell.

How does this peculiar place compare with the places they have left behind?

In general terms, they have left places where the social conditions are partly determined by economic and social structures. The UK at the end of the 20th century experienced three or four decades of an ever-intensifying market economy, where the framing of policy revered not just the expansion of individual ownership but also the destruction of social ownership. The privatising of council housing, for instance, without an accompanying building programme, entailed a diminution in quantity and quality of the stock of social housing. Combined with low public spending and a hard core of some four million unemployed workers these conditions produced housing estates deserted by banks, building societies, shopping developments, community projects and those residents with anywhere else to go (Hutton 1996). These places, where notions of 'community' and 'citizenship' were alien notions, became trapped in self-perpetuating spirals of decline. In contrast, 'good' neighbourhoods attracted funding for education and health, and, tended and nurtured by residents, achieved self-reinforcing upward momentum (Hutton 1996:210).

The economic and social fate that befalls particular places and the people who dwell there may be historically specific to a particular moment in societal development. It is empirically verifiable by visiting so-called 'sink' estates and measuring them by standard indicators of social and economic deprivation. This kind of approach, however, useful though it is to planning, development and social policy measures, does not always convey the many and subtle ways in which particular places, where for want of other choices people are bound to dwell, become places of fear, deprivation and hopelessness. Nor can it catch and arrest the inevitable resentment felt by the inhabitants, who may endure some or all of the following - ongoing patterns of poor socialisation, relatively low status, poor life chances, ill health, zero employment opportunities and lack of adequate income (Hutton 1996).

A disproportionate number of the prison population come from these deprived places. Whatever the content of their socialisation it has occurred in places which they are powerless, on an individual level, to change and improve, and where social empathy levels are low, and resentment levels are high. Powerlessness coupled with a resentment of that powerlessness has often been an intrinsic part of their socialisation process. But that is not to say that these places entail criminality. For these places may be enriched in other ways, familial and circumstantial. There are no physical settings which are not also social, cultural and psychological (Proshansky 1978), and physical settings can lie and deceive (Bettelheim 1975:173). So the significance of place, in individual psychological and bodily experience, is so much more elusive than what is implied by social and economic indicators.

Bodies in Place

Place acquires its significance through being occupied by the human body. Embodiment can only occur in a place: no-one can exist, feel, think or will, unless their body is in one place or another. Through criminal justice, the bodies in prison, brought to that place from a huge variety of complex place settings, have been made the docile objects of social and penal control, which produce normalising and excluding consequences (Foucault 1979). For, as a result of a prison sentence, the ex-prisoner finds himself excluded from some places, and denied ordinary opportunities in housing, employment and other spheres. So social and economic divisions are thus engrained upon the body, and in this societal sense, as well as in the personal sense, history is written upon the body (Barthes 1977). The subject in and of the body will experience, through these societal divisions, both internal mental responses, and physical bodily responses. Stigmatisation of individuals (Goffman 1958) is lived by them in the body as well as in the mind, and when subjects experience shame, rejection and embarrassment, their bodily sensations are engaged. They blush, they cringe, they involuntarily hang their heads or slump.

It is a peculiar feature of prison life that, for the visiting outsider, the distinctiveness and fascination of embodiment is more consciously marked than in the outside world. The general environment inside a prison is sparse and austere: there is little that is pleasant upon which to rest the eye. Measures specifically designed to prevent suicide, such as stretched wire netting across galleries, have an impact upon the prison environment and culture (King and McDermott 1995). By virtue of being in this place of environmental desensitisation, the observational and discriminating capacities of the outsider are more intensely engaged with the myriad bodies of assorted shapes and sizes. Encountering prisoner after prisoner, there remain three primordial features of difference: the body, the demeanour, and the level of suffering. But the latter two features assume a level of relative uniformity, because they are amenable to self-control, and it is considered wise to control personal expression in prison. And so it is the body that is always so very noticeably individual.

When, in the previous chapter, I described the demeanour of Ben, a prisoner now 'coping', I remarked upon his conspicuous good health and cheerful temperament. It is no exaggeration to say that, in contrast, with those around him, he shone, both in terms of his demeanour and his attitude. He had not been in prison long enough to acquire the habitual head-hanging or droop of the body. He strode confidently into the room, he made immediate eye contact and throughout the interview he demonstrated a high level of trust. Because of his health, his self-respect and his respect for others, his was a beautiful body in an ugly place.

Nevertheless, the body often fails to 'speak for itself' (Gergen and Gergen 1993:197), and the bodily demeanours of other prisoners were often hard to read. Prison produces a non-communicative demeanour, and prisoners often remarked on how advisable it was to habitually conceal how they were feeling. A person may experience loss or damage to the body during physical illness, and such loss is hard to conceal. But the inner states that accompany such conditions are not objectively observable, and may even be considered as irrelevant. Inner states tend to be ignored or minimised where individuals are suffering merely because of the place they are in. But the body has subjective as well as objective aspects, and both dimensions are part of the experienced corporeal self (Mann 1991). The history of place is indeed written upon the body, but it is only through allowing it to speak that this history can be accessed. And because place, in prison, is uniform and the same for the whole population, it is not considered to be an especially significant determinant.

It is therefore hard for prisoners to speak of their own embodiment in place. They find it difficult to step mentally out of such an overwhelming and omni-present place, and make observations from some exterior vantage point about the nature of the place, and their placement in it. Additionally, their placement is shared by everyone, and, after their own initial adjustment to prison, place, as an abstract force, becomes 'commonplace', and other places cease to exist except in memory and dream.

But prison is not commonplace: it is a special place, whose chief function is to intensively control space so that escape is impossible and order is maintained (Sparks et al. 1996). Inmates occupy specific places within prison only because, at that particular time, they are required to be in those places and not permitted to be in other places. Routines are maintained through the slotting of individuals into institutionally ordered practices, which consist of special arrangements of place and time: it is the endless reproduction of these ordered practices which make the social relations of prison life so fascinating to social science (Giddens 1984). As a researcher in prison, one is initially struck by the extraordinary nature of prison, but as time goes on, even its most peculiar aspects acquire a taken-for-granted ordinariness. Yet, in a sense, the most extraordinary aspect of prison is that people live, work and move around this unreal world and treat it as banal and 'normal'. Prison humour is an interesting mechanism: it renders as amusing some horrible things, and, in doing so, perhaps it helps with the tension experienced by the mismatch of personal disbelief - as in 'I just cannot believe this place!' with 'but this is what it's really like!'

Bodies Communicating

The level of self-harm and self-inflicted deaths recorded in prisons each year is an objective measurement of one kind of behaviour of bodies in place. In this behaviour, individuals choose or are driven to inflict visible, painful and sometimes fatal damage upon their own bodies, demonstrating an ownership over self which is not felt to be demonstrable any other way (Mann 1991).

The recording of this behaviour should be comparatively easy: what is harder is to record the inward experience that accompanies this kind of affective behaviour. To reduce such behaviour to clinical observation is to lose its valuable capacities, one of which is to speak symbolically of the self in place. Recently attempts have been made to systematically record the thoughts and feelings of those who self-harm, and it is becoming more usual to recognise that this kind of action is communicative.

In a symbolic sense, prisoners have other bodies, of which they can speak. There is the free body, appropriated by the court and put into the care of HM Prison Service. This body becomes an object to be kept secure, and cared for in a physical sense, so that the decreed sentence may be served. The body which is the object of suicide prevention policy must not be allowed to escape - through the self-determination of death - this time and this place. There is also, as Barthes (1977) points out, the erotic body, and despite the natural reticence of prisoners on this subject, they could not always help themselves from alluding to this painful aspect of their present deprivation. Mostly it was to mourn.

In terms of Dilthey's categories of willing, feeling and imagining, I became aware, as the project went on, that I could do no more than recognise that the accounts of subjects incorporate a taken-for-granted embodiment which operates symbolically in varying temporal and spatial ways. I had not expected to feel such curiosity about 'the body in prison', but as more and more prisoners confided about the bodily discomforts of prison, and the relationship of these to feelings about personal identity, this aspect of the self in place began to seem more and more complex.

Reflection on it produced a realisation of some of the limits of empathy. I felt equipped to empathise with the pains of others on a psychological level. This capacity, though not always developed, is part of our imaginative selves, and helps us to live with relative harmony in organised societies.

But each of us only knows what it is to dwell in several versions of our own body: we lack the mental structure to be able to 'know' how the embodiment of others feels. So, in the following discussion of place identity, I am able to speak empathetically of place identity in the psychological sense, and to intuit the settings which prisoners describe, whilst recognising that my capacity to empathise with their bodies in place is necessarily circumscribed, partly because of the gender difference. When prisoners described physical deprivation, as I listened, I would find myself intuiting my female body into the experience. But this would naturally produce an empathetic distortion of what is being described. So there are natural limits to empathy, and an awareness of these is useful and necessary.

Place Identity

Despite the limitations of my research, I considered it important to make a space for recognition of embodiment in other places. Insofar as was possible in one deep interview, I struggled to prevent my knowledge of the inmates remaining restricted to the unfree body of prison life. The first few questions about place were attempts to access what prisoners had valued and enjoyed before they came into prison. In this way, I was able to establish that all prisoners, regardless of their background, have a sense of place, and this is thrown into crisis upon entry into prison.

What prisoners remembered, with painful nostalgia, of their embodiment in previous places, reached me empathetically, so that I could imagine the body of the prisoner in front of me as a free body, in different moods and different settings, laughing with friends, shouting at a football match, playing with children or talking in smoke-filled pubs. Additionally, such talk helped to develop the empathy which was so necessary to the rest of the interview.

Accessing such personal responses is difficult, because the prison environment encourages watchfulness and the erection of defences against self-disclosure. But encouraging talk of the places from which each prisoner had come, where he had grown up, and where he had had significant experiences, was theoretically necessary, because to empathise with each teller entailed recognising the significance of lost places. These lost places were woven into the 'story' of who they were, and how they came to be in the place of prison. They were being grieved over, in that elusive state of mind which our culture calls 'home-sickness'. As was noted in the 17th century, this 'illness' (called 'nostalgia') (Relph

(1976:41)) had a simple cure - to be returned home. The illness did not only afflict those who actively longed to be home: on the contrary, the symptoms of melancholia could involuntarily afflict those who were apparently glad to have left, and this indicates something of the complexity of the relationship between people and place.

The significance of place, as an inner experience, is hard to access in traditional social scientific research, since it is so peculiar to the individual. Yet it is a far more universal characteristic of human existence than the territoriality of capitalism would suggest. For all of human history, special places have been revered, preserved, protected and fought over by tribes, cultural, religious, national and international groups, and in elevating places as unique spheres of value, humans have practised an inner attachment, using the idea of place as a resource to define national, cultural, religious or tribal identity. In our culture, we speak emotively of 'a place of worship', or a 'place of safety' or a 'place of work', and the meaning of such phrases is powerful because of the strength of symbolism attached to them. Heidegger (1958) claimed that 'place' was a way of defining the human being, for it shows the external and internal boundaries of his existence and of his freedom and imaginative aspiration. This internal boundary of existence is a deeply complex dimension of the way that man experiences his self in the world, and humanist geography shows us that 'to be human is to live in a world that is filled with significant places: to be human is to have and to know *your* place' (Relph 1976:1 (his italics)).

But individuals' sense of place is an elusive phenomenon to identify and grasp, especially when the place is a specified and institutional place in which they must dwell for a certain time, and which forcibly removes them from their places of attachment in the outside world. As a place, the prison is a building of bricks and mortar, generally grim and austere looking, but sharing many characteristics with schools, hospitals and factories. As an apparatus for transforming individuals (Foucault 1979:233) the prison houses a unique set of ideas and purposes quite unlike any other. It provokes a multitude of symbolic meanings.

In the literature on self-identity, due weight is given to the social and cultural processes that are involved in the development of self-identity. Indeed the constitutive activity of socialisation processes is a major theme in the discipline of sociology. The fact that all such processes occur in places and spaces, and may be shaped by interaction with these places, is however a neglected theme.

For psychology, a major theme is self-development through the recognition of self as separate from others, and, from infancy onwards, particularly significant others. Again, it is worth stressing that this theme generally neglects the fact that this dialectical development occurs in particular settings.   The loving home is self-evidently a qualitatively different setting from the violent and abusive home, or the large institution. The 'place' and 'setting' characteristics carry lifelong consequences for the inner self, just as much as the level of nurture or the efficacy of transmitted values, because of the intentionality of the active mind in the experiencing self. For the experiencing self does not just functionally 'use' settings as backdrops for social action: in complex conscious and unconscious ways, the self and its setting become dialectically inter-related, so that the setting has lasting significance for the experiencing self.

Thus each individual has an 'environmental past', a past that consists of places, spaces and their properties which have served instrumentally in the satisfaction of the person's biological, psychological, social and cultural needs (Proshansky et al. 1983). This past becomes embedded in the self, as 'a sub structure of the self-identity consisting of cognitions about the physical world' (Proshansky et al. 1983). This sub-structure, or 'place-identity' is unique and individual, since each person records and retains memories in different ways. Each has needs and desires that are different, and that are gratified to varying extents in different settings. So the acquisition of a place-identity is not a uniform process, more a 'potpourri of memories, conceptions, interpretations, ideas and related feelings about specific physical settings as well as types of settings' (Proshansky et al. 1983).

This place-identity is not merely acquired cognitively: it is a form of attachment which has significant meanings which far outstrip the functions and attributes of places. The following exchange with an inmate makes clear the complexity and ambiguity of affective-evaluative dimensions which connect individuals to specific settings (Proshansky et al 1983), and at the same time points up the sheer elusiveness of these dimensions:

(What was your home like, where you grew up?)

   Oh, perfect, perfect.

(So was it a loving home?)

   Yeah. My mum and dad were perfect. (Long pause) Well, my Dad, my dad
   is a drunk, he's always getting drunk. My mum, we're like that, I'm very
   close with my mum. My dad is just a...well...he drinks every day.

(Is he a violent sort of man?)

> When I was a kid, he was. He'd hit me with anything, (starts to stammer),...lump of wood...the last time he hit me was when I was...I think I was 15, he whacked me across the legs, the kneecaps, with a ring spanner. He done me in with a ring spanner, a big one like that (gestures).

(When you were very little, do you think he was violent?)

> Oh of course he was. He used to use anything on us. Like something he used to call a boiling stick, like, they used to use it for pushing the washing down in those old washing machines in the Seventies, and he used to hit us with that, or he had a big brown leath...leath...leather belt, and...er... (stammers profoundly) or he'd use a plimsoll, he'd use anything that he... could get his hands on.

We talk about other things and his stammer vanishes. Towards the end of the two hour interview, I return to the subject of his father:

(You've told me a bit about your dad: do you think that relationship has helped to make you the person you are, or are there other more significant influences?)

Hal replies in an urgent unstoppable flow of words without pause for thought:

> Well I'm not angry about what my dad used to do every Christmas when he bought us our toys, little tanks and Tonka toys and stuff, and then if we played up, he threw them in the fire, and then we'd have to wait until next Christmas before we got anything, yeah (laughs) he used to sit there with my little green remote-controlled tank, moving it back and forwards, and if me and one of me brothers or me and my sisters had a fight he'd pick 'em up and throw 'em in the fire. (Long pause). Yeah (reflectively). Right rotten ratbag he was.

(And you say you are not angry about that?)

> Nah (incredulously). I've grown up, I don't need toys any more (laughs).

(Well, I suppose you could be angry, on behalf of that little boy?)

> Nah (incredulously). I don't hold grudges, me.

This interesting exchange began by Hal claiming that his home life was perfect, with a loving mum and dad. Without any direct questions which would lead the teller self-consciously to consider his place identity, nevertheless it is elusively disclosed via the homely details of a washing machine, fireside and toys. All the detritus of home-life is present, but in actuality the homely setting is the arena of maltreatment, and the everyday items are instrumental in the suffering inflicted. The man sitting by the fire at Christmas time, moving a little green tank back and forth, waiting for an excuse to throw it in the fire, is a powerful visual image, out of the potpourri of his remembered past. It is a specific physical setting, and it is unique to Hal, for it is impregnated with the flavour of specific parental treatment. He carries it with him still, and still denies its importance. My suggestion, that he could feel anger on behalf of himself as a child, was understood instantly, and that too was denied. And when I asked Hal if he had ever tried to talk to his father about the past, such was the stress and tension of his terse reply, that I was made fully aware of his recognition of the dark significance of the vignette he had related:

We have. He doesn't want to know.

This was one of the shortest responses in the whole interview, yet its clipped intensity, in conjunction with the previously related anecdote, encapsulates a central tension to do with place identity. This is the tension between expectations grounded in common knowledge, and affective-evaluation of experience. Hal, like other inmates, knows that home is supposed to be a loving place: indeed, he describes it as 'perfect' in that respect. And yet, through experience, he knows it to be a place where he was tormented and treated badly, and, though he would like to persuade his tormentor to reflectively re-visit it with him, he cannot. There remains this tension in his place-identity, between what he normatively expects of a home setting, and the painful reality. Many other inmates related far worse occurrences in their home setting, and yet they simultaneously clung to blanket claims of the perfect place.

Some inmates pull other memories out of the potpourri of memories and interpretations, and can separate out the affective responses to different aspects of place settings. Bud (not now 'coping', Medical Centre) remembers unhappy school-days, but in a good and caring setting:

I was very privileged, it was a good school, a boarding school. I didn't enjoy school, but I never approached the degree of unhappiness I have now. I was learning. I loved learning. I got on with lots of other pupils, and the care staff were good. We had the freedom to go out in the woods, the fields, the barns... and my parents could visit whenever they wanted.

The variety of originating settings, and the infinite range of interpretations of them are a research subject in themselves. Research has established links between prisoner populations and abusive family environments (Livingston 1997), maternal deficits (Rieger 1971), childhoods in care (Livingston 1994), familial physical and/or sexual abuse (Lester 1991; Wilkins and Coid 1991; Coid et al., 1992; Liebling 1991). It was not the purpose of my research to investigate in detail the early socialisation of my tellers. But I note in passing that eight out of my ten copers told long and painful stories of physical and/or sexual abuse in childhood, and seven out of my nine non-copers. These stories were not solicited, and the absence of them in the other respondents does not imply that this feature of early life was absent.

Such abuse is not only some abstract social scientific indicator, presaging a troubled life. It is a set of memories, indelibly attached to the places and settings in which it occurred. Stepping into similar places will always stimulate, consciously or unconsciously, reminders and recall of those memories. Each socialisation process was entirely distinctive, not just because of the physical life settings, or the events that occurred, but primarily because of the individual interpretations and symbolic meanings put on all social and individual experience which had occurred in a variety of place settings. Each teller had an individual place identity. To hear even briefly of this interpretation helped me to acquire an empathetic identification with the teller, both as an object in my consciousness and as the subject of their story. When they could relax and speak unguardedly of their memories and interpretations, they were entrusting me with 'largely unselfconscious intentionality' in relation to their place identity:

> The basic meaning of place, its essence, does not therefore come from locations, nor from the trivial functions that places serve, nor from the community that occupies it, nor from superficial and mundane experiences - though these are all common and perhaps necessary aspects of places. The essence of place lies in the largely unselfconscious intentionality that defines places as profound centres of human existence (Relph 1976:43).

Of course, during infancy and childhood, it would be realistic to stress the unselfconsciousness of this intentionality:

There is for everyone a deep association with and consciousness of the places where we were born and grew up, where we live now, or where we have had particularly moving experiences (Relph 1976:43).

Following childhood, or the first departure from a significant place, this deep association can never be so unselfconscious again. For once one has left either a beloved or a hated place, and moved on to other places, one acquires a more self-conscious awareness of the losses and gains associated with particular places:

> This association seems to constitute a vital source of both individual and cultural identity and security, a point of departure from which we orient ourselves in the world (Relph 1976:43).

It is likely that the first departure from a significant place, and all subsequent departures, become part of the reflexive cognitive processes (Mead 1934) through which a person defines him/herself as an object to him/herself as subject. But of course these processes are not merely cognitive, for place is a source of emotional attachment also. The Here-and-Now place for my tellers is a very special place, in that it is incarcerating them and preventing each one from returning to past places, except in thought. Past places are thought about, and grieved over.

It is clear that the past socialisation processes remembered by prisoners are highly varied. Some of them may strike the listener as unenviable. Nevertheless, socialised somehow, the self moves forward into adulthood and, prior to incarceration, has managed 'a round of experience that confirm(s) a tolerable conception of self' (Goffman 1961:2). In order to empathise fully, I wanted some access to this tolerable conception of the adult self, before prison, who got up, ate meals, laughed, yawned and lay down to sleep. So I asked each inmate to tell me what ordinary, everyday things they used to look forward to, when they were free. The answers were prosaic in form, but individual and distinctive in content and meaning.

Jimmy especially remembers weekends, and looking forward to parties, which were wild and hedonistic. Brad's days on the outside were structured by his heroin addiction, so he would rise early to 'have a hit', and then have to go out to get money. Paulo used to work a 16 hour day in the cafe he owned. Alan remembers playing football with his kids and going to soccer matches. Brendan's days began by taking some crack. Martin used to look forward each day to coming home from the building site where he worked, and doing the cooking. Bud remembers getting together with family and friends, and going out. Walking down Old

Compton Street in London always took 'forever', because he would bump into so many friends, and stop to chat.   He remembers lying in bed, watching videos, and spontaneously deciding to get up and go for a pizza. George remembers particular anniversaries and birthdays and

> ...a specific time one Christmas a few years ago, which I spent abroad, and which I remember as...(laughs), yeah, I'd say that was pretty good at being happy. Well it seems a million miles away now, sometimes, but...(laughs).   At least I've got that memory, I suppose.

Each of these pasts helped me to achieve an empathy with the individual who had been torn from it and placed in prison.   Putting together a life-history is a life-task: the storyteller's jobs of revision and editing continue from quite early on until the end, so the listener is always receiving fragments that are provisional and shifting.   They are all tantalising glimpses of the self in other places and other times.   They provide a fascinating kaleidoscope of images as a background to the present place of prison.

Expectations and Fears

It is difficult to prompt individuals to describe what they thought the prison would be like, before they ever entered through the gate.   The expectation becomes so very quickly overlaid with the reality.   The concept of 'prison' is so heavily over-loaded, due to its varied cultural usage in a variety of ways over hundreds of years, in plays, operas, novels, poetry, films, comics, and documentaries.   It is an emblematic word, carrying connotations of 'a bad place'.   So the expectation has been vividly formed by cultural and social processes, but these are quickly overlaid with the reality.   And the reality is not vivid, in the way in which media images are: the humorous and dramatic incidents fictionalised in the mass media do not occur every five minutes in prison, if ever: in reality, it is drab, monotonous and boring.   And yet, the prison place is highly significant, for more than 10% of self-inflicted deaths occur within 24 hours of arrival at an establishment, and 45% within one month (Crighton and Towl 1997).

Those who were in the early stages of their first experience of prison were able to reflect upon their expectations and compare these with the reality. Ramon, now 'coping' in the Induction unit, adopted a matter-of-fact attitude:

My only knowledge of prisons before I came in was from the telly, really, 'Porridge' and things like that. And I've seen documentaries on prisons. So I had a rough idea. I think you've just got to think of the worst possible things, before you come in, and the worst time, and if it's better, it's bonus. I think this Induction bit's got to be the worst bit, 'cos you're locked up pretty much 24 hours a day. I wasn't nervous about coming in, but I wasn't looking forward to it.

Tim, also in the Induction unit and now 'coping', is not as successful at maintaining an insouciant approach, and is more soberly reflective on the inability of the reality to match, experientially, the expectation.

I've been to visit people in prisons, and I have thought about it prior to coming in. But of course that's no preparation for the reality of it. Because when you can go in, and then leave, it's totally different to being locked in a very confined space for long periods. I don't think you can prepare anyone for the reality and the confinement of prison. I understood prison was very much as it actually is, but it's still a shock and a traumatic experience, to actually be confined.

Intelligent preparation, however strongly motivated, makes no difference, as Gerry (now 'coping' on A Wing) points out:

In my first sentence I was dropped into this environment from a very different environment. I was a high flyer, company jets and limousines, - and then I was dropped into Beirut, for want of a better word! I mean, I was lucky: I was three and a half years on bail while the Serious Fraud Office investigated. So I had three and a half years to prepare to come into jail, and yet I still wasn't prepared for that moment when I walked through the door.

Because of his prior sentence, Gerry has first-hand knowledge of the stigma of prison, and a clear idea of what sort of a place it is:

Prison is a very tough place, very grim, very violent. And the most important thing to realise about it is that it doesn't work. Not because of what happens inside. Because of what happens when you get out. You're not allowed to start again with a clean slate.

The most fearful expectation confronting those in prison for the first time seemed to revolve around a fear of other prisoners, particularly 'the other' with whom one would be obliged to share a cell. Being locked up with a stranger taps is a terrifying prospect. Even the insouciant Ramon admitted to worries:

Who you share a cell with has got to be one of the biggest worries, because there's a lot of people who are out of it on drugs, just scummy people.

Tim was just as apprehensive: his companion of the night before had gone to court, and he did not know if he would return or if another stranger would be put into his cell:

Someone might come along to share the cell who's quite cheerful, quite a carefree sort of guy. But it's the unknown, really, which is the worst of it. Because you don't know what you're trying to cope with. Until you're faced with it. So it's like everything in life, it's the unknown that is worrying.

Reality

There are many different ways to conceptualise the prison as place, and the range of conceptualisations is exemplified by accounts ranging from Sykes' (1958) structural-functionalist approach to Cohen and Taylor's (1972) more subjectivist conception. Others writers have taken the prison to be one of many 'total institutions' (Goffman 1961). There is broad agreement that it is a specialised institution, and 'when society constructs special institutions for classes of non-persons, the idea of Utopia is not very relevant' (Sommer 1969:150).

At the structural level, prison is a place predicated upon the power of the state, and internally, the maintenance of the prison as a place of order and secure containment hinges upon the everyday operation by staff of power relations, where 'power refers to the realisation of one's will even if others resist' (Wright Mills 1959). But ironically, this production of intended effects can only occur by consent, because the staff (609 at the time of my research) are spread throughout the prison and the prisoners (averaging 598 during my research) are placed in denser concentrations. Recent history has shown that if substantial numbers of prisoners combine in revolt, the results are far-reaching. The operation of power relations must, therefore, be cloaked in an institutional attempt at a civil society.

The prison as a place with form and function is a very shaped environment, with its wings, landings and cells. But that does not mean that it is designed with human spatial needs and behaviour as the prime rationale. 'For the most part these institutions are designed with society's interests in mind rather than the individuals' (Sommer 1969:150). The overall societal goals are order and containment: large numbers of potentially volatile people must be managed in a mass and yet with appropriate segregation. Because of the urgency of these goals, it is a depressing aspect of the prison environment that human spatial needs are inevitably neglected, adding to the overall stress for staff and inmates. The concept of personal space, or portable territory, in the sense of the maintenance around a person of some individual distance (Sommer 1969) almost disappears in the prison, because of crowding and overcrowding. Nevertheless, since space represents a human need, it remains something that inmates are able to reflect upon.

However the individual's particular need for personal space has been acquired, it is apparent that the prison environment involves a dislocation of this need, and the individual is powerless to change the setting in any major structural way. These two aspects, the lack of space and the powerlessness to change this, are aspects that prisoners are quickly sensitised to in their first taste of prison. Tim recalled his shock:

> I got into my cell about 8 p.m. my first night. When I saw the cell, I was shocked at how small it was. I would think they are cells for one person. Sleep was obviously very difficult: I found the cell very claustrophobic for two people.

Ramon could formulate rational criticism, but almost instantly realised that this had no purchase in this particular place:

> It's a small room - I wouldn't want to be in one much smaller. I don't think the rooms are well thought out: there's no desk to sit down at and write a letter. There's no window to look out of. (Laughs, spreads his hands). But obviously, you are in prison! They're not thinking about design and comfort!

For a first-timer like Pradeep (not 'coping' in the Medical Centre) the smallness of the cell was a jolt that they can hardly put into words:

> You start realising how small the cell is, and how long you might be doing in it. That's when it all hits you. If I'd been remanded before, or been in a police cell, I might have been able to handle it, but the first time you come inside...I cannot even begin to tell you...(weeps) it's just such a big shock.

For prisoners undergoing strong suicidal feelings, like Paulo (not 'coping' in the Medical Centre), this response is long-lasting and becomes something of a preoccupation:

You keep on thinking of the years you have to do, in this little space...you are in it for 23 hours a day...well, you can imagine for yourself...(weeps). Trying to survive is a problem...it's not possible (weeps).

It is not just the lack of space which causes surprise: it is the uses to which the available space must be put. Ramon is still preoccupied with design features:

I didn't think the cell would be that small. It was quite a shock. I thought it would be a little bit bigger, and there'd be more of a private toilet.

Tim also feels strongly about this aspect:

There's a toilet in the cell, it's very basic and obviously if you use it other than for urine, it's quite embarrassing because you've got your inmate with you.

The lack of privacy, described in a matter-of-fact tone by a 'coper' as 'quite embarrassing', is suffered far more acutely by non-copers, and Pradeep describes much more emotively and vehemently, weeping as he does so:

You tend to feel like an animal, the way they treat you in here.

Copers like Ramon sometimes use humour to take the edge off the discomfort:

It's a little bit like camping, but you can't go home when you're bored!

There are physical limitations to what one can do in a cell, if one's cellmate is present, and Tim is trying to think of ways to deal with these:

This morning I had a wash-down of me body, because me cell-mate was gone to Court. But that might be difficult tomorrow. I don't think there would be the room if someone's in the cell. I'll have to adapt to the lack of privacy. I think all of it's going to be hard.

For prisoners used to prison life, the experience of a single cell can be compared with sharing, and reflected upon. Alistair, coping on the relatively relaxed C Wing, has been institutionalised since the age of 9:

He's got his locker, and I've got mine. He's got his own personal things in his locker, and I've got my personal things in my locker. I personally wouldn't dream of going into his locker without asking him. Likewise, the same with him.

Other than that...bear in mind that this is a situation where I'm on remand and you've got to be two to a cell. If you do a sentence, like I done many a time, you're in a single cell. Looking back on the sentences I've done, really and truthfully you are better off being in with someone. I've done a 6, I've done a 5, I've done a 4: you know that, when the cell door bangs shut, if you want a game of cards, a conversation, you can't have it.

I've gone into a cell on my own, pushed the door shut, sat down like this...and sighed 'Oh. Oh.'

(Alistair sighs heavily, sits motionless and passive for a moment, looking utterly forlorn and alone. Then his face returns to his customary blank). I suppose that's what it's like really.

Others echoed the feeling that sharing was preferable. Mike, also coping on C Wing, has served 16 years in various prisons, and much prefers a shared cell, although he has had many spells in single cells and likes his own company:

When you're put in your cell at 5 p.m., and banged up till the next morning, sharing seems infinitely preferable.

Mike went on to say that, never in all the years he has served, has he needed to spell out the respect for each other's space in a cell. It has, in his experience, always been tacitly understood that he does not touch his cellmate's locker or bed, and vice versa. But everything else is always shared.

Gerry echoed this respect for each other's beds:

We don't touch other people's beds, no. If you had a lot of people in the cell, you might sit on them. But apart from that no. We share tapes or books, things like that. But I'd always ask first. You've still got that common ground, where you ask. It's prison, but you have your own property.

Gerry was reflective about this respect for each other's space, and saw it as a healthy adjustment, rather than a capitulation, to prison:

I suppose, if you think about it, deep down, that's important, because it's part of not being institutionalised, isn't it? It's like the way that lots of people don't like giving up their own clothes and wearing prison clothes. It's that

last bastion of personal property, your clothes. I mean, I carry a handkerchief on me that's been my personal handkerchief (from years ago).
I've got prison glasses as spares, but I won't use them, I always stick to my own pair. So when you think about it, there are things that you do keep, and they are important.

Several inmates echoed this distinction between sharing everything that can be shared, and keeping private only highly personal items. This sophisticated life management of the tiny cell seems to consists of respect for the other's space, and a best use of resources, as Bill (now 'coping' on C Wing, spells out succinctly:

In the cell, you share everything. It's that simple. It's the only way to get on.

Coping convicted inmates like Gerry, go to great pains to create their own space in single cells as a much needed source of comfort:

I mean, your cell's your home, you don't like anyone else going in there. It *becomes* your home. When you're banged up, I suppose that's safety...it's more of a relief to you when you're banged up, because you put your feet up and listen to the radio for a couple of hours.

This grounding of oneself in a kind of 'home' is all the more necessary for a lifer like George, now 'coping' on B Wing:

Yes, it feels like my space, and that matters to me. When you start to get a few bits and pieces, and when you get your own radio, a few tapes, some books, and some pictures on the wall, it then develops into your little sanctuary, as it were. There'll be times when you're out on the wing, when you just, like, you can't cope with it, you just can't get on with anything and I'll just go in my cell.

And I feel comfortable knowing I can do that, and just pull my door to, and lie on my bed and kip for an hour or read. Most people know that once you've gone to your cell and shut the door, you kind of want to be alone. Maybe a few friends'll pop their head in the door and see if I'm alright. I'll say 'Yeah I just want to chill out for a while', and they say 'Cool, no problem'. And off they'll go.

This sensitivity on the part of inmates to other inmate's needs was often related to me by the 'copers'. They were appreciative of spatial needs in themselves and in others, and this spatial sensitivity was an important social aspect of the necessary adaptation process on the part of these copers. In such a peculiar environment, which combines extremes of overcrowding with extremes of segregation, spatial sensitivity to others is an important aspect of support and encouragement, and it is readily apparent on a wing if officers, too, encourage and nurture it. It helps in the formation of a community of mutual aid and reciprocity. Rumours of new regulations appear to threaten spatial sensitivity:

> I get on with anyone who's banged up with me, but obviously...I don't know if you've read about it, but they're going to start bugging people's cells, and things like that now. So obviously it makes you want to trust other people even less, really. Obviously, it'll take a friendship that you have with someone away, and make you even more wary of people now.

The increasing likelihood of having to share with someone with a drug problem is also a threat to this adaptation process:

> You share everything with your cellmate, and you work on the system that if your cellmate sees you've gone quiet, then he knows you're either thinking or reading, and he'll leave you alone. But unfortunately, if you've got somebody in with you who's coming off drugs, or something like that, you've really got to stamp your mark on your own area. I've had to do that once or twice, when I've had people playing music until three or four o'clock in the morning. I've said 'Now this is unreasonable: some of us want to get some sleep now'. And that's it. I suppose I can be a bit forceful if I have to be.

'Being forceful' is no problem for Gerry, an exceptionally big man. But for many people, the issue of an irrational or dangerous cell-mate is part of a cluster of fears about coming into the prison place. The prevalence of drugs in prison and the necessary policy measures used to fight the spread of them are seen by prisoners as threatening to their privacy. When I asked Ken ('coping', 'B' Wing) if his cell felt like his own space, he replied in an unstoppable flow:

> Well, yes it does seem like my own space. The only thing...I think, what is humiliating for me, I don't know about the rest, I can't speak for the rest, I can only talk for myself. Um, for a start off, I've never been on drugs, I've never tasted drugs. And what does get me feeling embarrassed and makes me feel dirty is when they come round and when they do a cell search.

> Because they stand you, and they make you strip off, and you take your underwear off, and then they make you bend over. One officer in front and one officer behind. And I think it's degrading, and, what's the word, I can't think

of the word...it's humiliating. I mean, you wouldn't even do that to your own child.

But I mean, whether it's a man doing it or a woman, it's so degrading. It's terrible...I've had it happen twice in a month. I mean, they say talk to an officer about it, and Mr. C...is very very good to me. But sometimes if you talk to an officer, they tend to use a phrase, they say you're paranoid. Which to my mind is...well, you're not paranoid, you want privacy.

Several prisoners made the point that these drug searches were entirely counter-productive to the attempt to create a community. It is hard for the searcher and the searched to build social relations when they are forced to participate in such dividing practices.

When I was doing my pilot study, I spoke to some ex-inmates, and some of them described prison as a 'holiday camp', and yet, upon close questioning, they admitted that, during their time inside, they had periods of profound feelings of loneliness, frustration, despair and suicidal impulses. They still held to their original description, however, and were not able to explain the dissonance of the two views. It was as if they were implicitly acknowledging that those profound feelings were their own fault and responsibility, and that if they had been well-adjusted, they would have maintained a proper holiday-camp demeanour throughout. Amongst my interviews, prisoners who were undergoing painful suffering would nevertheless claim that prison was not as bad as they had thought it was going to be.

The mismatch between expectations and reality points to the emblematic power of the prison place, and the work done by the imagination in construing prison as a place where one is reviled, insulted, assaulted and locked in windowless small spaces. This attitude is aided by the institutional environment and the prevailing ideology, but in an implicit rather than an explicit way. Many feelings about the place are only partly due to experience, because 'prison' as the term for a generalised 'place' is heavily loaded, not just in the cultural ways described above, but in personal ways. Individuals build it up in their imagination - perhaps reinforced by parental and teacher threats in early childhood - as a place of terror, pain and brutality. Upon entry, then, it can seem ordinarily bleak and austere, not extraordinarily so, for the over-riding impression is often one of blankness and emptiness. So the puzzle to the self is that it is so mundane, and yet so hard to bear.

For instance, it can seem a relief that prison officers speak to one in relatively normal, brusque tones. As I was interviewing a prisoner on the Induction unit, and he was agonising over feelings of guilt, an officer burst into the room so loudly and so suddenly that the crash of the door hitting the table and the following exchange were captured on tape:

> Excuse me he's got to finish now (to me). (Without a pause) Could you come and get your tea (to the prisoner in the tone not of a question, but of an order). (Sound of scraping chair as prisoner immediately rises to comply with the instruction) (Simultaneously, without waiting, in a raised and threatening tone, the officer says) 'Now please'.

This manner of address is common: it is blameless in terms of content, but in manner it represents the kind of aggressive speech that one would want to take issue with, if experienced on the outside. For prisoners, however, it is probably an agreeable contrast to their fears and expectations. But, whatever the reality, prevailing power relations (Foucault 1979) do not allow inmates to take issue with officers, without the risk of unpleasant consequences. So 'not minding' must become part of the inmate's psychological make-up. The problem is, of course, that when inmates are intensely vulnerable, their senses are acutely raw, so that sensitivity to this kind of address may be more highly developed than usual. This heightened sensitivity can produce intensely-felt descriptions of the reality of prison. Jimmy, not now 'coping' in the Medical Centre, described it vividly:

> The worst thing is the enforced idleness, the enforced uselessness. Like so many human beings in a lava honeycomb, you know, and the cacophony, the stench, the resounding doors banging, and this and that...the 'Feet Off The Bed!' - it's never-ending, you know.

Prison has very powerful environmental affects, but prisoners manage to innovate, if they are coping, in a variety of individual ways. The following response from George began by me asking him out of curiosity how he coped without anything beautiful to look at:

> It's hard to know how to answer that really, because everywhere you look, it is a bleak environment really...I suppose I try to keep myself occupied, as it were, so that I don't really feel the environment. I feel what's going on, instead. If there's a bit of activity on the landings, I try to concentrate on that rather than on the grim surroundings. There's enough negativity about, so you try and focus on a good thing - you might get out at exercise, and see someone from another wing, and you focus on talking to him. Or you just enjoy being in the air, and feeling the sun in the sky, or whatever.

The issue of the grim environment is a difficult one, resonant with political considerations, and critical attention has been paid to the historical and architectural aspects of prisons (Foucault 1979, Evans 1983, Ignatieff 1978). The principle of austerity, so much a feature of penal policy in recent years, seems also to imply a need for an aesthetics of bleakness, not just in the architecture of prisons but in their interiors, and this is expressive of penal policy values. For a design problem is a value problem: and the solution depends on whose interests are to be served (Sommer 1969:171).

The rigours of design and the enforcement of place are so often considered in the literature in relation to the security and control aspects of holding large numbers for long periods (see for example King 1987). The issue of the shock of place, in which prisoners experience an assault upon their sense of place immediately upon entry into prison, is more elusive. The tellers in this research show how inexorably human activity is tied to place. Even a 'pleasant' prison environment will remain the instrument of incarceration (Canter 1987:214), for that is the nature of the prison place. 'The long-range question is not so much what sort of environment we want, but what sort of man we want' (Sommer 1969:172).

There is a harsh irony inbuilt in the prison environment, that whilst the system revolves around 'security', in the sense of making sure the inmates remain confined, feelings of security or safety are widely lacking in the inmates themselves. The prison is not experienced as a safe place of comfortable routine, except by those who are profoundly institutionalised like Alistair:

> I come to prison, I don't do nothing except stay in me cell all the time. So when the cell doors are open, I'm normally stayed sitting in me cell. I don't really associate with people much, to be honest. There's no hardship about prison, prison ain't hard...more importantly, the people out there are suffering more than what we're suffering. To be honest, it's a holiday camp really, it's not hard. The out is much harder.

A Place within a Place: the Medical Centre

The Medical Centre consisted of a Physical Care Unit, an Acute Care Unit and two wards. The Acute Care Unit had nine rooms with integral sanitation, and one unfurnished room without integral sanitation, which was used rarely (cited in a full inspection report by the Prisons Inspectorate). The wards housed a mixture of those suffering from diagnosed psychiatric illnesses and those suffering from suicidal feelings, who were supervised from a small glazed observation office with a communicating door to the ward which is usually kept locked. In the wards, the beds were arranged around the edge of the room with the head of the bed toward the wall. Inmates were not allowed on their beds between 7.30 a.m. and 8 p.m. Beside the bed was a chair, in which they may sit during the day, and a locker for personal possessions. In the middle space of the ward, there was a snooker table, and overhead a television.

Prisoners sharply differentiated between location on a normal wing, and location in the medical unit, which they variously referred to as 'hospital', 'health care', the 'medical wing' and Fraggle Rock. Paulo was typical of the suicidal prisoners whom I interviewed in the Medical Centre, in resisting relocation onto a wing. He was full of fear about the prospect of being confined in a cell. Other suicidal prisoners, like Bud, were terrified about the physical risks of being integrated on a wing, and their denial of the fear was often a not very successful mask:

> I don't feel physically unsafe here on this ward, but in the prison in general, yes. I couldn't give a toss about physically - if they want to beat me up just because I'm gay, let them beat me up. (Long pause) But I do feel unsafe, scared - I've never been so petrified of anything in my life. I'm not scared, I'm petrified and it's a horrible feeling. Very daunting to have such a heightened feeling, it really is.

This fear of the physical and psychological risks of being bullied on the wings is often associated with the nature of an inmate's offence, and, in view of the treatment sometimes meted out by other prisoners, is an eminently rational fear which, nevertheless, is often denied by men who would regard fear in themselves as a failure of masculinity. The quickness of Sean's response to being asked if he had felt unsafe on 'A' Wing, before he came to the Medical Centre, was quite telling:

> It's not the other inmates you know (emphatically). I'm not afraid of standing up for myself. It's just environment, the balconies, the bars, the keys, the rattling.

Sean is being nursed on the Physical Care Unit as a result of injuries he inflicted on himself on A Wing. In the following remark, he again refers obliquely to the physical reprisals he fears on the wing, when he refers to the age of others on the Unit, who are much older, less active, and suffer a variety of chronic physical conditions:

The nursing staff's O.K. I feel more comfortable here than on the wing. On the wing, I feel like I'm going to hurt myself, you know. This way here, I'm safe and the people in here are older, and I feel more comfortable here you know.

Many prisoners integrated on the wings told me that those who self-harm persistently do so in order to avoid life on the wings. For those successfully integrated, avoiding life on the wings in order to be put in the Medical Centre seems utterly misguided. Gerry ought to be in the Medical Centre because of a heart condition, but he goes to enormous pains to remain on A wing, even though it is a restricted regime:

I've had to be over on the PCU once or twice (for a heart condition) but I've come straight back. I've slept there, but I couldn't put up with that type of environment. I think you are cut off, and you are isolated. And I think that it's a more difficult environment to come from, back into the mainstream of prison.

I think that one of the problems that a lot of prisoners have is that, when they are suicidal, they are moved off to the hospital, which is a completely different environment to here on the Wing. When they do come back here, they have more of a problem integrating back in to the system. At least there's more going on here, you can make friends here, there's a lot of activity, even if you're just banged up.

He echoed the feelings of a lot of prisoners when he said:

It's a strange atmosphere in the hospital: the staff are not properly trained, psychiatrically, I don't think. The medical service in the whole of the prison service is terrible.

He went on to say, out of his own experience,

If you are over in the medical unit, one of the worst things you can do is persuade yourself that you are in hospital, not in prison. It's a denial, a shutting off.

Brendan, (not now 'coping', Medical Centre), is suffering visibly at the time of our interview from a pent-up yet suppressed anguish, and exemplifies the understandable longing for the comfort of this denial:

As far as I'm concerned, at the moment I'm in hospital. I'm not in prison. It's when I go back to my cell again, and it's when you get your bottom bunk and your top bunk, you're pissing and doing your dirties in the toilet with another person, and you can't cry...you want to cry sometimes but you can't you know what I mean? (Gets so upset that I long for him to weep, but again he appears absolutely unable to. There is a long pause, and we sit quietly, with the endless noise of bunches of keys and clanging doors in the background.)

George's remarks about his time on a ward, which he described as 'terrible', make the point that the wards by their open nature offer no protection, in terms of spatial segregation:

It's like everything that goes on there is right in your face. If there's a fight happening, it's right on you.

Because every event is 'right in your face', when inmates do behave as if they were alone, the behaviour comes to seem somewhat like a performance, to be harshly judged by others. Hal (ambivalently 'coping', Medical Centre) grieving over a son killed very recently, often sits quietly for long periods: this need in himself has not, however, made him tolerant of others:

Since the guys were taken to court and so on, and given life sentences and that, I often think about my son, and I sit there quietly, like, in honour of my little boy. And I've mentioned that quite often to my doctor, and he said 'Well you've got every right to do that.' (Later, Hal says contemptuously, 'Most of them sit around and wallow in self-pity. Me, I ain't got no time for that').

To be the close witness of a fight or a self-harming incident, to be unable to go away into another room, to have to watch the incident being dealt with, and the mess being cleared up, is profoundly disturbing for others on the ward. It can lead to further guilt, suffering and possibly more self-harming behaviour. Hal witnessed one of Jimmy's suicide attempts:

And he cut his throat and his arm, and I see the blood spurting out of them. He's still alive, he's downstairs on the A.C.U. But I witnessed it, and for the first time in 17 months since I've been in prison I broke down and cried like a baby. Because that was my mate that cut his throat, we were really good friends and I felt close to him. I felt really bad, cos. I was in the recess with him just 60 seconds before he done it. And I felt as if I could have stopped him, so I felt guilty.

That's the reason I done this last week. (Hal points to his bandages, referring to the incident in which he drove a paper clip up his arm).

For the suicidal, this lack of privacy is felt all the more acutely, because their need for privacy is so much greater by virtue of them being suicidal and feeling vulnerable. In this frame of mind, the 'ordinary' indignities of prison are magnified for Marty:

> What I've found is that you tend to lose your sense of dignity, there's no privacy. The toilet doors only go so high up...I'm not saying that any other prison's different, mind.

Additionally, the vulnerable have specific needs, such as the need for private space in which to weep. This need, and the suffering it induces, has no equal in privacy issues on the outside, Bud points out:

> I didn't get much privacy because I lived with my partner in one room, but that's completely different to this. You're choosing to be with that person. And if I did need time and space, he'd go out and leave me on my own. Or I'd go out. Till I met him I lived on my own for a while, so I do like my time and space. So I do miss space a hell of a lot. The other day I was crying, and I had nowhere to do it in private, and it's horrible, you know, it really is. Degrading.

Privacy is a basic human spatial need, and the vulnerable obviously feel the lack of it acutely. It does not just encompass personal need for space, but the opportunity to keep personal possessions private from others. The lockers on the wards are vulnerable: if the ward contains people who will not respect the privacy of others' lockers, it puts inmates into a double bind. Marty tearfully claims:

> At this stage I don't care any more about my locker, my things...they're going round the whole time on the ward robbing each other...I don't care.

It was very obvious from his agitation, however, that he did care, and this was the nature of the double bind: it had become apparent to him that there was no gain in caring, so he was trying not to care. The aggression of others, the response of the staff and the prison culture ensured that there would be no satisfactory outcome:

> The bigger fellows, they go around, like the guy in the bed next to me, he's really quiet, kind of timid. It's his first time in, and if the dessert is some cream or something, they go up and take it off him. He put in one complaint about

them already...they do that, they come over for fags, and if you don't give them fags, they say Yeah well, see what happens when you're asleep tonight. So you have to kind of sleep with one eye open...it's either that or you give them a roll-up. And if you see them at your locker, taking your tobacco, you just have to leave it at that. It's just too much (weeps).

If you report it, one of them...well it happened last week, the staff come in and say in front of everyone Don't do that again, stay down in your own corner. Then everyone hassles you because you've grassed someone up, so you're making things worse for yourself. You just can't win.

Hal, ambivalently coping through constant cutting, was quite clear about the privacy boundaries in relation to his bed and his locker:

I'm very possessive about my locker, because I've got 37 tapes in there with 600 title tracks, and no-one's going to touch them, because there's a lot of stuff there going to bring back a lot of memories. Not only that, I've got me cards on top of me locker, what I've made, and I've got personal effects and so on inside the locker, so I'm very possessive about it, yeah.

My bed - well, so long as no one sleeps in it, I don't mind them sitting on it. I don't mind them sitting in my chair, next to my bed, that doesn't bother me, just as long as they don't go down my cupboard and that.

Hal was quite exceptional, in that he was the only inmate I spoke with in the Medical Centre who spoke with a fierce sense of possession about his own property. He had, however, relinquished any possessive sense of 'place' about his space on the ward or even about his bed. It was as if his energy had been condensed to focus on the possessions that were essentially 'him', and which he could defend, if necessary. The greetings cards he referred to were items he made himself, and he dwelt on their importance to him at some length.

Bud's sense of private property too had dwindled to focus on his most personal possessions, about which he spoke apathetically. He lacked any feeling for the space assigned to him in the ward:

I've got photos of my partner, and my diary: my writing stuff is very personal, but the rest I couldn't give a toss about, my Gameboy and stuff. I don't feel territorial about my locker, it doesn't feel like 'mine', and if people want to come and sit on my bed, I don't mind.

But the problems of finding some private space in the Medical Centre impressed themselves on everyone's mind. Gerry spoke for many of the inmates when he said bluntly:

Suicidal prisoners shouldn't be shipped into hospital. They shouldn't be slipped the liquid cosh as a substitute for care. That just encourages them to use the 2052 as a crutch. The threat of suicide gets used as a crutch, or the label of 'predicted at-risk of suicide'.

Gerry had thought about what ought to be done with suicidal prisoners, and the problem of integrating them back into prison life after the difficult experience of life in the Medical Centre, and he was equally forthright with his recommendations:

The suicidal should be kept on the wing. If people are suffering, talk to them. Talk to them in proper terms. Help them to get out of it. Tell them that we are ALL here to understand. By 'we', I mean all of us on the wing. Keep a suite of cells for suicidals if you must, but keep them integrated on the wing.

It was clear that Gerry's notion of 'care' was of the common-sense, down-to-earth variety, involving empathy, frankness and friendly support. Although he had never been classified as requiring F2052SH documentation, like most prisoners, he had experienced a painful adaptation to prison, and still has times of acute suffering:

I still have my bad days - I go very quiet. We all have those, and we have to learn to leave each other alone then.

Like many prisoners, Gerry knew that this experience, and learning to give each other space, was a valuable resource, just going to waste, unless prisoners have more opportunities to help each other. He showed an instinctive awareness of the dangers of the dividing practice of medicalising the problem:

If you ship them into hospital, you're shipping them to Fraggle Rock. It just leads to an us and them mentality. Us who cope, them who don't. Those who don't, they cluster together in hospital, and the suicidal thing is catching. There's lots of fraggles all together, and self-harm becomes a show thing, something you do to demonstrate to 'them' what a hard time you're having.

Gerry has no doubt that enabling prisoners to help in the provision of care for the suicidal would be beneficial, and he had a succinct rationalisation to justify his claim:

> The best comforters are those that have gone through the experience themselves.

Those inmates presently coping were able to describe quite calmly their worries and fears.   But when I asked the suicidal tellers questions about their expectations of prison, on the whole they could not recall them.   These had been long swamped by the reality, which was often so overwhelming that they would fall silent for a while, sigh or weep, and then try, like Bud, to convey the reality as they were experiencing it:

> Prison's so oppressing. People say ' Oh you'll find Cat. C quite bearable', but prison's prison. No matter where you are, even in you're in Ford, you're still oppressed. You're still degradated. It's very degrading, you know. They treat you like a piece of shit, excuse my French. Go here, do this, do that.

Prisoners are aware that terrible things can happen in prison, and Jimmy feels that awareness will never leave him:

> I will carry away thoughts about man's inhumanity to man. And, certainly, the question of who guards the guards?   Because some of the greatest traducers of laws I've seen are the ones who are supposed to be guarding us here.

But these things do not occur every day, and are the exception rather than the rule.   Prisoners look around: it is not too extreme, too brutal, too demeaning.   Therefore the profound feelings of sadness and grief must be, by definition, due to their own weakness.   Thus is the burden of suicidal feelings translated into an extra weight upon the already demoralised self. The inmates I spoke to struggled to describe the ambience of prison as a place, with its free-floating atmosphere of unease. Bud puts it like this:

> If it was just the unhappiness of the place, you could cope with it, but again, the word that springs to mind is oppression, isolation.

Another characteristic of the place which inmates often referred to was the loss of control.   This was exacerbated in the Medical Centre, where several inmates spoke of feeling infantilised.   Marty (not now 'coping' in the Medical Centre) was typical in his expression of this feeling:

It's as if you don't have anything to do with your own life in here...the simplest decisions...anything you want to do, any information you want, in the morning, you have to fill out an application form. If you want certain books, if you want to speak to someone...I mean, children don't even have to do what we have to do in here.

Marty echoed others in finding the emptiness of life on the ward very debilitating. The days seemed to consist of getting out of bed and sitting in the chair:

Before, at home, I'd always be clearing up, and on the go. In here, there's just nothing. It's just getting up, sit down, get into bed and go to sleep. Get up, sit down, get into bed and go to sleep, over and over again....

On the whole, the suicidal inmates that I spoke to felt only a relative degree of safety whilst in medical care, safer than they would on the wing, but still extremely sensitive to the extraordinary nature of the place. Often their state of mind did not allow them to feel safe, and their histories had not given them a bedrock of safety in childhood, upon which they could draw. These feelings of non-safety can analytically be broken down into safety in relation to others, and safety in relation to oneself, but the experiencing self feels them inter-mingled.

Brendan (not now 'coping', Medical Centre), like many other inmates who were sexually abused as a child, does not have a bedrock of security in childhood upon which to draw, and does not know what it is to feel safety in relation to others:

(Did you ever feel safe as a child?)

No, not really. And my childhood is something which is good, bad, very bad, and...if I can call it a childhood. I don't really think I had a childhood, but I grew up, from a baby to man of course. But whether that was a childhood, or just a growing process, I'm not too sure.

This failure to achieve a sense of safety rooted in the self has, by their own admissions, led many of these inmates to look frantically and obsessively for security in others, and it is often linked to their own fear of their offending behaviour, and their inability to experience safety in relation to oneself. Brendan went on to talk about the failure of the prison itself to make him feel safe, echoing many prisoners' feelings about the current state of flux and change affecting the system:

I'm very good at looking after myself, physically. I don't feel threatened by any inmate or any member of staff. I don't want to be violent but if I need to be, I can be. I feel more...that makes me feel safe in a way, but because of the system as it is, that's what I don't feel safe with. Because I know, every time I think I know something, they've moved the goal post a bit wider, so that's where I don't feel safe.

It's what they can do to me in the long term, not the short term, that's where I'm scared. People who have big power can create big problems...that's what I feel.

Pradeep, (not now 'coping', Medical Centre) who did manage a degree of security on the outside, referred to the connection between feeling unsafe and lacking all social status as a prisoner:

When I had my own business, my house and my family, I was safe and secure. I wanted to become extra safe, you know?

But I've never really felt safe here - safety is when you become something. That's when safety and security come. When you're nobody, you're not safe.

I don't care where they put me. I have no hope, no hope at all. When you have nothing left in life, you don't have no fear.

The following exchange with Brad, a very young man who had had the worst kind of start in life, shows the agonising extremes of feeling unsafe in prison yet with a strong impulse toward self-protection:

(Have you ever in your life felt really safe?)

(Sighs). No.

(How safe or unsafe do you feel in here?)

I still feel vulnerable, because I've...prison, it's a university of crime, and when you come to prison, it opens up other avenues for you, but most of them are on the wrong side of the law. And...I don't want to be looking over my shoulder for the rest of my life. I want to be able to do something constructive and be proud of myself, and live my life, not survive it.

(I guess this feeling of being safe or unsafe...it's related to other people?)

You're ready 24 hours a day, you're alert, your instincts. It's not your feelings, it's instincts. Instinct takes over, it's a natural instinct to want to protect yourself.

But for many, the feeling of insecurity is not linked to others: it is rooted in what is known and glimpsed in the self. Brendan (not now 'coping', Medical Centre) had been explaining to me his ability to defend himself from others in the physical sense, and there followed this reflection:

I'm not a small guy so I don't really get much pressure. So that's a certain kind of safety. But emotionally I'm not safe. Mentally I don't think I'm safe. I'm no good at protecting my mind or my feelings. I can protect my body, but the rest I can't protect.

Sometimes, however, an inmate is able to receive help for the kinds of internal insecurity being experienced. Alan (not now 'coping', Medical Centre) had been integrated on a wing, but he received a knock-back in the form of a failed appeal. He fell apart, to use his own words, and found that in this state he was not sure that he could control his aggression toward some known child sex offenders on the wing. He asked for help to control his temper, and in response they moved him to the health centre and put him on F2052SH documentation. He was grateful, and received reassurance that the act of asking for help was a significant step forward.

In my days in the Medical Centre, staff and inmates were unfailingly pleasant to me, but I was always struck by the weight of unexpressed suffering in everyone I spoke to. The staff would sometimes joke with me, asking if I would like to listen to their suicidal feelings for a change. Sometimes, however, they would go on to explain how impossible it would be for them to be frank. The system only functioned, it was claimed, on the basis that most feelings were suppressed for most of the time. The longer I was there, the more I appreciated that this suppression of feelings was one aspect which made visits to the medical unit such a fatiguing experience, and contributed to the lack of safety felt by inmates. If feelings are expressed on the wings, inmates may get ridiculed, or perhaps physically assaulted. But in the Medical Centre, the response to feelings, long suppressed until they burst out, is more likely to be pharmacological.

Some of the inmates who had had experience of the Medical Centre and gained some distance from it also spoke of the sense of bottled up stress pervading the place to a greater degree than the rest of the prison. It was widely felt, as far as the inmates were concerned, that medication was a key factor in the suppression of feelings that really needed to be released. Gerry commented:

> One of the things I think they tend to do in the medical wing is, they tend to suppress feelings, the feelings of those that are psychiatrically ill, by giving them the liquid cosh, Largactil and other things. And there's no real study into it, or help. They are just left.

Marty struggled to express his feelings of frustration, knowing that he desperately needed to talk to someone about his experience as a rape victim. He has tried to raise the issue of the rape and his subsequent depression but he cannot find anyone to listen. He went to the observation hatch on the ward in a quiet time one evening, and tried to talk to about it to the member of staff on duty, who made a crude joke out of it and told another member of staff about it in a loud voice, so that the whole ward could hear. Marty felt very humiliated:

> They say on the hospital ward that they're here to help you. But they're not helping you. All they do is, if you've got a complaint, they put your name down to see the doctor, and the doctor writes out tablets for you. It's like...the answer to everything is a tablet. It's not right.

This was not the first time that Marty had tried to get some help in relation to his past trauma:

> When I came in, I told them I was depressed on account of I was raped in 1990. He didn't even look at me, he just said he'd give me something to help me sleep. Nothing bothers them, they don't care what you've been through. If you're desperate, the doctors come up and see you for two minutes - that's it, you're on a tablet.

All the suicidal prisoners that I spoke to were fearful of the effects of medication, and resisted it when possible as the following exchange with Brendan shows:

(Are you on medication?)

> (Proudly) Nope.

(Do you regard that as an important aspect of control?)

(Emphatically) Yes I do. I've been through medication before, to a stage where I didn't really know what day it was. And that's when people started to take advantage of the situation, in a medical aspect. And when I take medication, I feel it weakens my spirits. It also weakens my body, as well as my mind. And I'm open to all sorts of horrible nasty things.

Jimmy puts his finger on a real issue of civil liberties in prison, and asked rhetorically if inmates ought to be given medication against their wishes, in a place where they are able to freely express those wishes. He knew the question was rhetorical, because the issue of inmates' wishes is not something that in practice carries much weight:

They try and give me medication: I spit it out when they've gone. I did enough blurring as a teenager, I prefer my thoughts chemically untampered with. I've often been advised in my life to take Lithium but I don't like life if it's flattened into grey. Sure I lose the lows, but I lose the highs, the bolts of joy and rapture.

When I interviewed Pradeep, he had been on constant medication for some time:

(Do you know what date it is?)

No...I think it's the 10th, it's Saturday today. (It was Tuesday the 12th)

Life on the wing is a contrast to life in the Medical Centre, as it presents more opportunities for inmates to attempt manipulation of the environment in ways that make them feel safer, as the following exchange with a coping prisoner demonstrates:

(How safe do you feel in prison?)

That's quite a question, because I think you try to surround yourself with safety things. For me, those are personal objects, such as my own spectacles, which represent safety to me. But I mean, there's the odd occasion where you might lose your rag, or you say something, and you realise just how close you were to a dangerous situation.

Ummm...I feel safe-ish. The job we're in is a dangerous job, because cons don't like you when you're serving out food, you know, they all want more and they can't have more. There's 200 to feed on the wings. And you get it from the screws because you're in the middle of the cons. So you tread a delicate, fine line sometimes.

I'm lucky, I think I can handle most people with talking to them face to face, and trying to avoid confrontation.

Conclusion

In its essence, a place is a focused centre, where the social and individual action of life is coloured and given its meaning. Distinguishing between different places is distinguishing between different intentions, attitudes, purposes and experience. A sense of place bestows coherence, for '(p)laces are indeed a fundamental aspect of most existence in the world...they are sources of security and identity for individuals and groups of people' (Relph 1976:42).

All prisoners, whatever their background, come into prison with a place identity, which is put under assault by the prison. For the predicament of being in prison means a self-evident and enforced exclusion from the places to which there has been deep attachment. This deep attachment or rootedness may live on in the mind, but it cannot be nourished by being in the place of attachment. And this is an important but seldom recognised deprivation of prison. Nearly all prisoners are grieving for the places to which they were attached. These places gave them a vantage point from which to experience the world, a sense of their own positioning or 'placement' in the world and a set of spiritual, social and psychological attachments to a particular place. The capacity and expression of rootedness in place provides an abstract home, that profound internalised centre of human existence which is the foundation both of individual identity and of membership in the community.

It is clear that the coping inmates, such as George, put considerable emotional work into making a pale imitation of an actual home, and succeed insofar as this is possible, given the constraints. George's cell, by his own efforts and investment, is turned into something that can serve his individual sense of self. Gerry demonstrates that there exists amongst copers the attempt to sustain the reality of living in a property-owning democracy, where the principle of private property is enshrined, and other people's property is not touched without prior requests. The irony of this, in an institution which confines large numbers of people precisely because they have not been able to recognise this principle, is not lost on prisoners. Thrown back upon the basics of survival, however, they recognise the need to cling to this vestige of self-identity and nurture it. Many prisoners spoke of the objects of former places, such as spectacles, which seem invested with their own identity and are therefore highly valued and fiercely guarded.

So the cell, seemingly so cramped, seems to offer prisoners what the wards in the Medical Centre can never offer, a chance to make a significant space for the self: thus the cell serves to maintain and exercise the sense of place. Victor Serge was a libertarian Russian revolutionary, imprisoned in Paris from 1912-1917, and he too experienced the sense of place that cells can offer, including even the condemned cell:

> I have changed cells several times. It has never been without feeling a certain sadness at having to leave walls which could speak, whose every secret I knew, between which I had spent such hours of plenitude. My memory of an iron-gray death cell - despite an infinite fifteen-day nightmare - contains an element of authentic clarity (Serge 1970:67).

This central place of significance and meaning may not resemble in any sense the originating home from which the inmate comes, and yet, for the coping inmate, it comes to provide a grounding in the prison world, from which all other places visited in the prison exist relationally. Enclosure is not always a negative experience for the private self (Prost and Vincent 1995). For many, like Alistair, the enclosed space of a cell is experienced as a form of protection, from which he does not want to emerge. It is a place from which the prison becomes known and endured, and to which inmates return, often in relief from the harshness of institutional life. It is a 'here' out of which prisoners come at the start of the day, and can carry in their minds as a 'there', to which they must return for the long overnight bang-up. However confining, it is a set of walls which enclose a space for the self to nurture itself as best it can. Where shared, it comprises a place where the social characteristics of respect for others' property and space remain live and practised, keeping the semblance of social identity going.

So the cell has two essential characteristics, firstly, that as generalised place, the cell enforces compulsory confinement, and secondly, that it is a particular place which encloses the body and, through boundary and enclosure, offers possibilities of authentic experience. In the case of the latter characteristics, it offers much more than the Medical Centre can offer to the vulnerable, with its uneasy common space on invigilated wards, characterised by a lack of privacy and a failure in governance which results in feelings of non-safety in relation to the behaviour of others.

These characteristics of cells are synthesised by 'coping' prisoners in such a way as to provide the grounds for their coping. A true home is one to which persons return voluntarily: the cell is an imitative and constituted home, because the return to it and the confinement in it are compulsory. The home-making, then, is a constitutive act on the part of the coping inmate, involving emotional and cognitive work. The cell, meagre and badly designed though it is, offers just enough to enable this constitutive work to be begun. Despite the lack of space, the compelled sharing of it with an unknown and/or feared companion, the lack of privacy, and the enforced humiliations, the cell offers inmates the chance to 'do' place for themselves.

'Doing' place in prison is part of the acceptance process of the system of boundary and enclosure. For each, the acceptance process is an individual and possibly heroic journey, fraught with advances and setbacks, and never fully complete. For those fully institutionalised like Alistair, who acquires an exaggerated place attachment to his cell, the process is always inherently painful, as the compulsion to stay safe in the holiday camp of 'no decisions' fights with the inevitable anticipation of freedom, albeit an anticipation accompanied by an awareness that freedom will produce more suffering and begin again the endless round of offending, conviction and imprisonment.

Doing and making place in prison appears, from the evidence of these narratives, to be a significant aspect of the process of acceptance and adaptation. It is a requirement shared by all the inmates in this study, despite the variety of the cultural and social settings from which inmates are drawn. Viewed historically, the 20th century was one of Diaspora, where the threats posed by war, famine, and other global catastrophes have become implacable forces which move unimaginably large numbers of people against their will and turn their lives upside down. Rootedness in one place has not been valued in industrial and post-industrial societies, where attachment to place is a drag upon the necessary mobility of labour.

But Relph (1976) points out that location or position are not necessary or sufficient conditions of place identity. Mobility or nomadism do not necessarily preclude an attachment to place, and he gives the example of the Bororo people of Brazil, who demolish their villages every three years and rebuild again, never however losing strong home-ties. In Western society, mobility may be on the increase, but when transience is freely chosen and/or part of a cultural inheritance, it need not entail a rise in rootlessness. Individuals in relatively stable cultures often have a peripatetic life-style in early years which never results in much consecutive time in any one place. But peripatetic people may form quick attachments to many places, or to types of places. Professional travellers, such as travel writers for example, combine the characteristics of never settling in one place with an acute and developed sense of place.

We have seen the growing specialisation of space in this century, particularly social spaces, as the coupling of living space with workplace has become rarer. This specialisation of space has been accompanied by a greater spatial differentiation. The principle of private space is currently vigorously and increasingly asserted (Prost and Vincent 1995:142), and it may well be that the current fashion for asserting this principle has a relationship with the prior failure to value place identity. The micro processes of place identity refer to a personal and individual need which may, historically, have been so sorely tested on a macro level that we have forgotten its significance on the humble scale of individual need, and failed historically to nurture it as a prime constituent of the stable self.

The prison population contains relatively large numbers of people whose lives have been characterised by 'disorganisation' in the economic and social sense. Nevertheless, from their socialisation processes, they have extracted the means with which to fashion for themselves an awareness of the significance of place. They have private places, favourite places and forbidden places. All the inmates in my study, except for Alistair, could remember a favourite place, be it an area or street or building where they had lived, or the pub where they drank, or the ground where they watched football. They could remember schools and the places where their friends lived. In short, they had a 'sense of place' which performed important symbolic service in the maintenance of identity. The exception was Alistair, socialised in one institution after another: he exhibited no active attachment to previous places, and a passive attachment to his prison cell. He could not discuss the significance of being in one place as opposed to another. This deficit seemed paradoxically both to make him 'suitable' for the prison place and yet to heighten his vulnerability there.

All the other prisoners spoke of that 17th century illness of 'nostalgia', but not all had grasped that they will not be returned home as a cure. They have not fully realised the compulsory nature of prison, and they have not accepted that they themselves are in prison. Like Sean (not now 'coping' in the physical care unit of the Medical Centre), trying to convince himself that he is in hospital rather than prison, they will grasp at anything which relieves them from acceptance of this intolerable truth. Perhaps, deep down, there is the feeling that if they show enough of their pain and non-acceptance, someone will relent and let them go home to their proper place.

But prison life is relentless: whatever the suffering self experiences, it must begin by recognising the compulsory nature of the prison place. This entails suffering the drudgery of place (Relph 1976), where the body inexorably tied to a particular place, and must learn to accept the restrictions which go with the place. Each must accept tedious tasks, if these are imposed, or enforced idleness. Each must learn to live with daily humiliation and the constant worries over physical safety and mental stability. And each must do this mental work in isolation, perhaps taking advice from others, but learning the hard way how to do it for the self.

When the prison does not provide the conditions of possibility for a sense of place to be expressed or developed, a sense of alienation in both the self and the community is produced. In all the suicidal inmates interviewed in the Medical Centre, a sense of present place was absent, because there were not the opportunities for them to self-constitute their place, in the form of an enclosed space, with boundaries separating it from the space of others. They were confined in an extraordinary environment, a 'place within a place'. Despite their claims to feel comparative safety in the medial centre, it was apparent that these claims arose out of their fears regarding life on normal location. They had to work hard to maintain their contradictory levels of awareness: on one level, they spoke of the frightening and oppressive nature of the Medical Centre, the total lack of privacy there, the enforced witnessing of violent and desperate events, the deficits in governance which meant that their belongings were never safe. On another level they clung desperately to the notion that life on the wings would be worse. The intensity of this double-bind provoked more suffering for themselves.

Hal, interviewed in the Medical Centre and on a F2052SH although no-one could be found who would actually define him as 'suicidal', was the only prisoner who had managed a limited attachment to the things in place. But the space assigned to him in the ward meant nothing to him and gave him no feeling for place.

Those integrated on the wings recognised the horror of this environment, and the power of the double-bind described above. Gerry (now 'coping' on A Wing) had never been suicidal, and he had visited the Medical Centre for reasons purely to do with a serious heart condition. He found it isolating, strange and difficult, a place where feelings are suppressed, and where comfort is mainly of the pharmacological variety. Prisoners successfully integrated on the wings, even though suicidal, have a fund of expertise regarding the power of the Medical Centre double-bind: they are able to look back upon it and see that their crippling fear of life on the wings was misplaced. This expertise should be used appropriately in a policy of through-care for those prisoners, like Bud and Marty, who are immobilised by their fear of life on the wings and obliged to demonstrate, often in desperate ways, their continued eligibility to remain in the Medical Centre.

The wards did not offer prisoners any opportunity to experience enclosure and boundaries: as well as the lack of private places, prisoners had to endure constant invigilation from the observation hatch. They were unable to maintain control over their personal property, or ensure their physical safety. In these senses, the defining principles of a property owning democracy were removed. The combined features of the environment exacerbate the internal and lived suffering of inmates who are failing to adjust to prison. The place itself is an integral part of their despair, loneliness and disorientation.

Looked at from the prisoner perspective, it is appropriate to describe the Medical Centre as a 'placeless' environment, and the inmates there as suffering from placelessness. Placelessness describes both an environment without significant places and the underlying attitude which does not acknowledge significance in places (Relph 1976:143). Placelessness involves severing roots, denuding symbols of their meaning, imposing uniform order upon experience and diversity (Relph 1976:143). For geographers, this topophilia is an aspect of modern landscape and industrial development, where the driving rational goal is efficiency. The prison is the paradigm institution where those driving managerialist goals of security, efficiency and order seem to operate at the expense of humanity

Nowhere are these goals more visible than in the Medical Centre. The wards are designed and arranged to maximise placelessness. All inmates on a ward at any one time must be visible from the observation window. This is a place which requires docile bodies (Foucault 1979): it is a small-scale example, with maximum effect, of a Benthamite Panopticon (Foucault 1979), where control and discipline are maintained by constant invigilation and routine pharmacology. It is precisely because it is a place where self-evidently people are suffering, that the pursuit of these rational goals is so visible and so striking to the outsider. It is as if, to the punishment of being sent to the place that is prison, suicidal prisoners must be further punished, by having those aspects of life on the wing and in the cell which confer a sense of place, removed. A moral technology is thus constructed, which is characterised not by inhumanity, but, on the contrary, by the sensible use of knowledge and power (Foucault 1979). There may only be one officer on duty at the observation hatch, but, together with the use of medication, this is enough to achieve an economy of suspended rights (Foucault 1979:11). The horrible irony is that this moral technology constructs a vacuum for prisoners, as the hours pass and they fail to do much more than sit in a chair beside a bed on the edge of a large ward, staring into the middle space.

It is perhaps partly because of the placelessness of the environment that inmates such as Marty (not now 'coping', Medical Centre) sometimes experience inappropriate responses when they try to talk to a member of staff about deeply personal issues. 'Vulnerable' prisoners, (defined earlier as sex offenders, prison debtors and those vulnerable for personal reasons such as appearance, hygiene, age/disability, or behaviour) are most likely to be threatened or abused by other prisoners (McGurk et al. 1996).

But staff too respond unevenly to different categories of prisoner. One aspect of this may well be because placelessness, and the underlying attitude which accompanies it, affects staff as well, and leads to the inconsistency of their responses to the inmates in their care. If the place characteristics of a particular setting are not such as to encourage uniformly humane and empathetic care, it is not surprising if staff fall back on the tried-and-tested formula of deservedness, responding positively only to those prisoners who present themselves as deserving of attention. The declaration of the French philosopher Gabriel Marcel that an individual is not distinct from his place; he is that place (cited in Matore 1966:6) has even more force in the workplace, where identification with the nature of that place is inevitable. So it is not surprising if staff lose recognition of the distinction between professional and unprofessional behaviour, as Marty's experience demonstrates, and instead operate according to the distinction between deservedness and undeservedness.

The fact that these suicidal prisoners were confined in an environment that seemed designed to prevent them from maintaining a sense of place has an important corollary. Because they had been prevented from having a space of their own to claim and to maintain, they could not develop the spatial sensitivity toward others, which Gerry and the others on the wings displayed. It is not the case that suicidal prisoners are unable to develop a sense of place precisely because they are suicidal and/or 'depressed'. The narratives in Chapter Six demonstrate that even though prisoners may be suicidal, they may still have the capacity to develop and/or maintain a sense of place. They may then act in reciprocal ways towards other prisoners, recognising their spatial needs.

Organisationally, the prison attempts to manage the principles of population density combined with spatial segregation in a palpably overcrowded situation. This produces profound feelings of non-safety. Ironically, these feelings often lead to the removal of the inmate from the wing to the Medical Centre, where the failure to develop spatial sensitivity toward others is fostered by the characteristics of the location. So the inmate who was made psychologically vulnerable by feelings of insecurity goes to a place which encourages him to remain locked in this mind-set. Non-copers consistently reiterated how unsafe they felt in the Medical Centre, but they still remained fearful of being sent back to the wing.

All prisoners stressed over and over again that 'you have to look out for number one', and protecting the self is, as Brad said, a constant and instinctive response. So demanding a task is this in a placeless environment like the Medical Centre that there is often no energy left to develop that social awareness toward the needs of others for space and privacy which is such a significant indication of triumphant adaptation. It is self-evidently an adaptive response to the environment which brings comfort and ease with it, as George (now 'coping', 'B' Wing) demonstrates.

But what is most significant is this: in a place where comfortable and easy interaction with others is not a predominant characteristic because of the nature of the institution and the composition of the inhabiting population, spatial sensitivity to others is one of only a few possible avenues for expression of the social self. It entails reciprocity, awareness of others, and a transactional pay-off for the self. For, in displaying sensitivity toward others' needs, each demonstrates to himself that he is still capable of 'good faith' in human relations, despite the apparent intention of institutional life to degrade and humiliate him. There is, with this demonstration to the private self of the survival of social 'good faith', a concomitant and inevitable rise in self-esteem.

When coping prisoners such as Gerry said that there was still common ground amongst inmates, even though they were in prison, there was pride and self-respect in the tone of voice. There are few opportunities in prison for the social self to express itself: when these opportunities are offered, the hungry social self seizes them. Giving prisoners the opportunity to develop a sense of place is, then, a decisive factor in moving inmates through the suicidal period and on into a self-developmental period of adaptation to their situation. On the wing, the social aspects of community are kept alive in small ways, despite the tendency of the prison place to break its population into atomised individuals, and the inmates themselves attest to the value of this. On the wards in the Medical Centre, however, the placelessness of the environment does not allow expression of these social capacities to flourish.

In summary, this exploration of prisoners' experience shows that the assignment of positivistic labels such as 'non coping' to prisoners does not help explanatorily to understand the subtlety of their adjustment to the prison place. Prisoners enter prison with a highly developed sense of place, and, if given appropriate opportunities, can apply this to their predicament, develop and express a sense of place. They can do this in civil ways which contribute to the formation of a community. Their accounts show that the Medical Centre does not provide them with appropriate opportunities to maintain and develop a sense of place. It induces a more acute form of placelessness than the wings, and the experience of being placed and confined there can damage the capacity to form social bonds.

The development of the capacity to form social bonds is significant in accepting and adapting to the reality of prison life: the fact that this place of 'care' does not develop this capacity in ways which are relevant to prisoners' needs is a serious deficiency, and one which will receive further attention.

References

Barthes, R. (1977), *Roland Barthes*, New York, Hill and Way.

Bettelheim, B. (1975), *A Home for the Heart*, New York, Bantam.

Canter, D. (1987), 'Implications for "New Generation" Prisons of Existing Psychological Research into Prison Design and Use', in A. Bottoms and R. Light (eds), *Problems of Long Term Imprisonment*, Aldershot, Gower.

Cohen, S. and Taylor, S. (1992), *Psychological Survival - The Experience of Long-term Imprisonment*, Harmondsworth, Penguin.

Coid, J., Wilkins, J., Coid, B. and Everitt, B. (1992), 'Self-mutilation in female remanded prisoners II' in *Criminal Behaviour and Mental Health*, vol. 2, pp. 1-14.

Crighton, D. and Towl, G. (1997), 'Self-inflicted Deaths in Prison in England and Wales: An Analysis of the Data for 1988-90 and 1994-95' in G. Towl (ed.), *Suicide and Self Injury in Prisons* 28, British Psychological Society, Leicester.

Evans, R. (1982), *The Fabrication of Virtue: English Prison Architecture 1750-1840*, Cambridge University Press, Cambridge.

Foucault, M. (1979), *Discipline and Punish*, Penguin, Harmondsworth.

Gergen, M.M. and Gergen, K.J. (1993), 'Narratives of the Gendered Body in Popular Autobiography' in R. Josselson and A. Lieblich (eds) *The Narrative Study of Lives*, Sage, London.

Giddens, A. (1984), *The Constitution of Society*, Polity, Cambridge.

Goffman, E. (1958), *Stigma*, Penguin, Harmondsworth.

Goffman, E. (1961), *Asylums*, Penguin, Harmondsworth.

Heidegger, M. (1958) 'An Ontological Consideration of Place' in *The Question of Being*, Twayne, New York.

Hutton, W. (1996), *The State We're In*, London, Vintage

Ignatieff, M. (1978), *A Just Measure of Pain*, MacMillan, London.

King, R.D. (1987), 'New Generation Prisons, the Building Programme and The Future of the Dispersal Policy' in A.E. Bottoms and R. Light (eds) *Problems of Long Term Imprisonment*, Aldershot, Gower

King, R.D. and McDermott, K. (1995), *The State of Our Prisons*, Oxford University Press, Oxford.

Lester, D. (1991), 'Physical Abuse and Physical Punishment as Precursors of Suicidal Behaviour' in *Stress Medicine*, vol. 7, pp. 255-256.

Liebling, A. (1991), Suicide and Self-Injury amongst Young Offenders in Custody *Unpublished Ph.D. thesis*, University of Cambridge

Livingston, M. (1997) 'A Review of the Literature on Self-Injurious Behaviour Amongst Prisoners' in *Suicide and Self-Injury in Prisons*, ed. G. Towl, ICLP 28, Leicester: British Psychological Society

Mann D.W. (1991), 'Ownership: A Pathography of the Self' in *British Journal of Medical Psychology*, vol. 64, pp. 211-223.

Matore, G. (1966) 'Existential Space' in *Landscape*, 15 (3) 5-6

McGurk, B. (1996), 'Experience and Perceptions of Integrated Regimes for Vulnerable and Non-Vulnerable Prisoners', in *Home Office Research Bulletin*, no. 38, London.

Mead, G.H. (1934), *Mind, Self and Society*, Chicago University Press, Chicago.

Proshansky, H.M. (1978), 'The City and self-identity' in *Environment and Behaviour*, vol.10, no.2, June 1978.

Harold M. Proshansky, Abbe K. Fabian and Robert Kaminoff (1983) 'Physical World Socialisation of the Self' in *Journal of Environment Psychology*, vol. 3, pp. 57-83.

Prost, A. and Vincent, G. (1995), 'Riddles of Identity in Modern Times', Vol. V. in *A History of Private Life*, Belknap/Harvard, London.

Relph, E. (1976), *Place and Placelessness*, Pion, London.

Rieger, W. (1971), 'Suicide Attempts in a Federal Prison' in *Archives of General Psychiatry*, vol. 24, pp. 532-535.

Serge, V. (1970), *Men in Prison*, Gollancz, London.

Sim, J. (1990), *Medical Power in Prison: The Prison Medical Service in England 1774-1989*, Open University: Milton Keynes.

Sommer, R. (1969), *Personal Space: The Behaviour basis of Design*, Prentice-Hall, Eaglewood Cliffs, N.J.

Sparks, R., Bottoms, A. and Hay, W. (1996), *Prisons and the Problem of Order*, Clarendon, Oxford.

Sykes, G. (1958), *The Society of Captives*, Princeton University Press, Princeton.

Wilkins, J. and Coid, J. (1991), 'Self-mutilation in Female Remanded Prisoners: I. An Indicator of Severe Psychopathology' in *Criminal Behaviour and Mental Health*, vol. I, pp. 247-267.

Williams, J.L. (1963), Personal Space and Its Relation to Extroversion-Introversion *Master's Thesis*, University of Alberta.

Wright Mills, C. (1959), *The Sociological Imagination*, Oxford University Press, New York.

5 Time

Introduction

One of the lasting gifts of great literature such as Virginia Woolf's Mrs. Dalloway is to celebrate with special intensity the ways in which time is integrally and internally bound up with our sense of identity (Medlicott 1995). Psychological definitions of personal identity, such as *I am all that I inherited as well as all I have acquired* (Mann 1991) are always propositions about the importance of time in identity formation and development. We can only organise events in our experience through two principles, that certain phenomena repeat, and that life change is irreversible (Leach 1961).

The force of these principles in prison is monolithic. The tellers in this study attest to the power of prison time as a social and punitive force that constrains, and produces a range of effects in infinitely subtle ways for all those confined in prison, either on remand or for a specified term, be it short or long.

Culturally and historically, experience of the form of temporal reality is open to subtle change. After Huygens had invented the pendulum clock in the seventeenth century, and all sorts of instruments to measure time began to proliferate, perceptions of time inevitably altered. Linear perceptions, with past, present and future lying on a continuum, gathered credence. Perceptions of time are naturally highly subjective and unreliable, and Einstein captured these qualities when he observed that sitting with a beautiful girl for two hours may seem like two minutes, whereas sitting on a hot stove for two minutes can seem like two hours.

Time itself was enlisted as a tool in the structural power/knowledge relations (Foucault 1979) of industrial capitalism, in the form of time-tables and ritually ordered time. The time-discipline of emerging capitalism (Thompson 1967) produced a range of cultural and social effects, one of which was to facilitate ideas of progress and development within the concept of linear time, ideas with which we are all acculturated and which we implicitly build into the fabric of our lives.

Within the prison, the subjective experience of time as specifically linear produces pain and suffering. The linear view breeds ideas of passage and development, but the experience of a prison sentence is painful precisely because the passage and development of one's life are irrevocably arrested, and frozen in non-movement. Serge (1970:30) describes the resulting relationship of unreality with the landscape of time:

> Here I am back in a cell. Alone. Minutes, hours, days slip away with terrifying insubstantiality. Months will pass away like this, and years. Life! The problem of time is everything. Nothing distinguishes one hour from the next: the minutes and hours fall slowly, torturously. Once past, they vanish into near nothingness. The present minute is infinite. But time does not exist.

It was Serge's (1970) depiction of time that struck the prisoners in Cohen and Taylor's (1972) study of a maximum security wing as the most accurate in relation to time and their fears of deterioration over the passage of their life sentence. The painful problem of time for lifers has been long recognised (e.g. Sapsford 1983). But this recognition is implicitly predicated on the assumption that it is only the length of sentence which produces a painful relationship with the passage of time. My research, however, focuses on the cruel and unusual pain which results from the nature of prison time itself: time itself is a source of pain because the linear view that has been implicit in the socialisation patters of prisoners is not relevant in prison. Whether an inmate is in prison for a month or for life, the horrible mismatch of one's internal time consciousness and the reality of prison time produces painful dissonance. As Serge (1970) pointed out, there are swift hours and very long seconds. 'Past time is void. There is *no chronology of events* to mark it; *external duration no longer exists*' (my italics).

Of course there are events in prison, but it is the eventlessness of prison life which produces discomfort, stress and enforced passivity (Toch 1992:28). Time in prison seems to consist of endless repetition: events either repeat endlessly, or, just when inmates have come to rely upon them, fail to repeat because staff are too hard-pressed. So the personal management of time is the principal challenge. But the external duration of each life has been brought to an end: henceforward the prisoners must live to prison time, unable to choose freely how to spend any second of time inside, and unable to participate in the chronology of events that made up their life on the outside and helped to construct and maintain their identity. Family birthdays, wedding anniversaries, religious feast days, leaving parties for work colleagues - all the chronology of birth, life and death flows on outside the prison, and the prisoner remains bitterly aware of it whilst forcibly restrained from participation in it. Liberal theorists may assert that people are sent to prison as punishment, and not for punishment. But the fracture of their time-sense is an ongoing and punitive experience for the entire duration of their stay in prison.

Life in prison is actually better suited to the internalised adoption of a cyclical, rather than a linear, view of time, because of the capacity of prison to produce repetitive experience and enforce normalisation practices (Foucault 1979). Cyclical views of time were widespread before the invention of clocks. They still flourish in consciousness, alongside more linear representations, particularly for those who live and work in rural communities, where the repetition of sunrise, sunset, and the four seasons, so celebrated in centuries of art and literature, provide the grounds for economic and social survival. Repetition, renewal, habit and routine are valued in such communities and duly celebrated in festivals. Consciousness of the value and pleasure of repetition encourages the acceptance of the habitual and the routine.

In prison, however, the routine is compulsively thrust upon inmates. The time-table itself is a structural practice (Foucault 1979) with historical roots in rational and Enlightenment views on the achievement of order and discipline. The fixed rigidity of timetables, the preoccupation with counting and observing prisoners, the compilation of personal files, are all disciplinary measures seemingly designed to produce psychological effects in inmates (Scraton, Sim and Skidmore 1991).

Confronting the Enemy

On the level of regret for the crime or event which has brought inmates into prison, reflection on time proves a great source of suffering. Many prisoners speak obsessively about turning the clock back to a time prior to their offence. This is particularly true of those who have committed crimes of impulsivity. 'If only...' is a stream of thought which produces its own form of torture, especially for lifers. But even those with a few weeks to face speak of the implacable enemy of time. This enemy is central to individual fate, for each has been sentenced to either a known or unknown slice of time, and yet it is an enemy too elusive for inmates to grasp in thought.

Only when the allotted time has elapsed, can each inmate resume his life. So inmates want the time to pass. But they know that thinking about time and willing it to pass only produces the strange illusion of time moving even more slowly. So they try not to think about it. Over and over again, I would hear denials that time was something that was ever thought about. If I then waited, invariably the denial would be followed by further reflective remarks. Denying the enemy in this way seemed to be one of the most painful aspects of prison for the non-copers. Bud (not now 'coping', Medical Centre) voices a typical denial, which he cannot sustain:

> With the issue of time, the only thing you can do is shut your mind off from it, and just get on with it.

After a pause for reflection, the same speaker continues:

> Everyone deals with the thing differently: my way is to shut myself off from the time. If I looked at my sentence, I'd probably be in awe of it, and totally daunted. But I'm not expecting to be here too long, I'm hoping to die, so it's easier.

There are several circuitous ironies here: Bud is avoiding looking at the issue of the 'time' he has to serve, in case he is 'totally daunted'. But he is on his twelfth day of hunger strike, and as he goes on to demonstrate in our interview, it is precisely the issue of time which is so distressing to him and which he thinks and talk about obsessively. Here he speaks of the pains of 'empty' time:

> My time here is so very empty. I've used my mind all my life, but all I can do in here is write. You can only write so much, and read, and you can only read so much before you get bored. I listen to music, I play Gameboy, and that's it. When I first came in, I wrote about six letters a day, but there's only so much you can say in a letter, and only so many people you can write to. I tend to spend a lot more of my time thinking now.

In complete contrast to the claim that he has shut himself off from time, he goes on to say with great intensity:

> Time passes extremely slowly. I've been in 12 days, and it seems like four weeks. Time just doesn't go. It was the same situation on the wings, when I was on remand.

Bud's sentence is only 19 months, and it was a light sentence for his offence. Friends cannot understand his inability to accept the time that must pass before his release:

They say Are you a bit touched or something? - but to me, it seems that nineteen months is a hell of a long time to be separated from the life you're used to. To be separated from your family, your partner, your friends...that length of time...well... (extremely articulate, Bud cannot find words to express his response to the sentence time, and stares down at his hands).

Later, he returns to the struggle to express the unhappiness he associates with the length of time he has to serve:

I can't do 19 months. I could probably just touch on nine months or a year, with it doing me in completely. But 19 months...No. No hope. I'm strong enough mentally to know what I'm capable of withstanding, and I just can't address 19 months. I can't keep myself going. It'd just break me down. I know they will.

I've experienced unhappiness before (when a relationship broke up)...but that unhappiness didn't even begin to touch this, because this is like...although it sounds like a year and a half isn't that long, when you are in here it is, it's a tremendously long time. It's too frightening.

Although by his own admission, Bud is 'petrified by fear' and utterly degraded by the routines of prison, his daily life in prison in prison is marked by some things worth anticipating. But the time he has to serve appears to him, a young man, as long-term, and whilst he could bear short-term suffering, he cannot face what appears to him long-term suffering:

On a day to day basis, there's different things, speaking to my partner or my family on the phone. But on a long term basis, all I look forward to is dying. That's it, it ends there.

Sean (not now 'coping', medical centre) echoed Bud in finding the emptiness of time a source of acute suffering. Despite their best attempts to fill the time, they both fall victim to the grip of empty time in which destructive thoughts can get a hold:

Most of the time when I try to read, you just can't focus on the books, you know what I mean? So you spend most of the day daydreaming, thinking things, things you shouldn't think.

I spend most of the time sitting by myself, looking into the distance, you know. There's nothing. Empty. Nothing.

This retreat into oneself is partly forced upon inmates who do not necessarily feel themselves to have much in common with the surrounding talk:

> You try to talk to people, but when you talk to people in here, all they want to do is talk about crimes, you know. I can't really talk about them sort of things...they are always effing, swearing and blinding you know. Talking about what they are going to do when they do get out. Them's the things I don't want to know about, you know.

Like Bud, Sean tried not to think about the years ahead, but inevitably found that the subject he most tried to avoid, was in fact the one he thought about constantly:

> You don't lose track of time, no matter how you try. You just keep thinking of the years ahead. You just take each day as it comes, but the date's always in your mind, the years ahead you know. Each day that goes by, you're one day closer to getting out, that's the way you do think about it, all the time, you know.

Sean looks forward to sleep, but not to waking up. The nights are painful for him, because he expects the time to pass in a flash, and yet, because he cannot sleep properly, it drags as slowly as the day. He marks the passing of the time in the night by a series of regular noises:

> When you go to sleep at night, you hate waking up in the morning, you know. Every morning I hear one noise first, and that's the noise of a plane going up, so I know it's half-four in the morning. Then the noise I wait for after that is the noise of keys. So that's what I wait for every morning. The noise of the plane and then the noise of the keys. You keep thinking Oh let me go to sleep again. I want to go to sleep again, but you can't, you know. So you only get four hours sleep a night.

> Makes the days even longer, you look at your watch and it's six o'clock and you try your best to go down and sleep again, but you still keep thinking of how you're waiting for the keys, you know, so you end up staying awake.

He does not find anything else to look forward to, on a daily basis, except the television being put on in the ward:

> I wait for the TV, at 12 or 1.30. Then again, at 4 o'clock, it's on again. Then, once it goes out, you're lost. You might play a game of dominoes or draughts, but people aren't into that, you know, you just can't focus on things you know.

But one of the problems with looking forward to supposedly regular occurrences, such as the TV, is that they cannot be relied on, as Marty (not now 'coping', medical centre) explains:

> I look forward to the television going on in the evening from 4 till 8, because it makes the time go a little bit quicker. But if someone doesn't get out of bed in the morning at half seven, then they turn it off an hour earlier. And if it happens twice in a row, it'll be two hours, and so on.

So even these time-markers are precarious and cannot be relied upon. But Marty, like the others who are not coping, gets over-involved in present time and the slowness with which it moves. Like many, he is trying hard not to think of the time ahead:

> I try not to think about the future ...if I do think about it, it gets me thinking about all the things I could be doing, and it knocks me back, and I end up feeling very depressed and contemplating suicide. Time just drags...one day seems like three days. Like I say, I can't deal with time, even a day seems too long

Jimmy (not now 'coping', medical centre) is a person who has never thought of the future. With intense highs and lows of mood, he says ruefully 'The present has always been abundant enough for me'. But he experiences the passing of time acutely painfully:

> It's just like a matter of waiting for the end of waiting, you know. Killing time before time kills you. Like I say, I am able to retreat into an inner world. And I do write a bit...sometimes I'll just sit there, still, for three or four hours...I'm self-contained in a way.

Speaking of his feelings in his last, almost-successful suicide attempt, Jimmy tries to express the torture he suffered, and the part played by his internal time-sense:

> I was tormented, I was so stretched. There are no words to describe how I felt...in those dark days...you feel tortured, your spirit feels like it's stuck in sticky pitch blackness. But imagery...like inky crows and blind men's dreams...none of it comes even close to a description. Literally, the seconds ticking away, that's the Chinese water torture of what it's like.

The long periods of empty time, which Jimmy refers to as enforced idleness, are harmful for inmates whose mental state is very precarious. It can sometimes lead to lost time, where the thinker retreats entirely into another world. Time can even seem to speed up, as Pradeep's remarks show:

> It's so terrible here...there's nothing to do. I can be sitting on my chair thinking about a lot of things in life, and before you know it, time has just gone. Time just flies past, I don't really know it and it's dark again.

That this kind of 'speeding up' is not healthy is illustrated when Pradeep (not now 'coping', medical centre) goes on to say:

> One thing I do when I'm sitting, I've got a few pictures of my wife, and sometimes when I'm while, she actually starts talking to me. Sometimes I snap out of this place, and I see people walking around, sitting next to me, and I actually talk back to them.

The phenomenon of time seeming to be utterly empty and yet moving too fast seemed to be something that many inmates experienced from time to time, when they were in extreme distress. This has happened to Jock (not now 'coping, Medical Centre), several times:

> Sometimes when I've been on the wing, it's just too fast, you can't think to yourself, you just can't think. You lie there, you want to think, people go past your door, keys clanging. You want to concentrate on one thing, but you can't, with keys jangling, steps going past, everything too fast. It makes me angry.

Pradeep, like the other non-copers, cannot bear to contemplate the length of his sentence, but that is just what his mind returns to again and again. The thought of what will happen to loved ones, and being powerless to help is an agony that many cannot help reflecting on:

> If I was to walk out of here tomorrow, I'd have a chance of pulling my life back - but when I think of the time ahead, the 12 years, I just slip into depression. I start thinking of all the possibilities of things that could happen in that time, what will happen to my parents. And what could have happened if I'd been outside...I just can't seem to get out of that.

An additional pain suffered by the non-coping prisoners is the knowledge that, along with the placelessness they suffer, the space they occupy and the time they spend is in no sense their own, because they are observed all the time. Pradeep experiences this pain intensely:

I just feel suicidal, I'm being observed all the time. I am being watched and watched and watched. It's been over a month they've watched me, sitting in that chair.

The lack of a private space and a private time mean that inmates on the wards are deterred from requesting a visit from a Samaritan. Their perception is that this encounter would take place in full view of all. Marty longs to have someone to talk to about his feelings, but says vehemently:

Who wants a Samaritan walking across the ward and sitting down beside you, with everyone watching? If you talk to them, you're going to cry - it's like being in a goldfish bowl.

Lifers must cope with the pains of the present, and accept that the future means more of the same pains. Brendan (not now 'coping', medical centre), is a lifer who has served time previously, and he finds an added pain in that there is no point in looking forward in this sentence, and this contrasts bitterly with past times in prison:

In my first sentence, I used to look forward to going home and being with my girlfriend. And music - I'm a musician and I'd look forward to hanging round with my friends, and being loved in a physical sense. It kept me going. But in a life sentence, there's absolutely nothing to look forward to. There's visits, letters, phone calls, canteen - that's about it. No future.

He describes his time as empty, and slow-moving, but tries to cheer himself up by mentioning markers which, ironically, could only be relevant in a cheering sense if he were free:

Time's slow, yes it is. Since I got sentenced. You know...maybe it's just because it's the tail end of the year that passes slowly for me. Because once Christmas is gone, I'm sure Christmas will be round again before I know it. Then my birthday, my wife's birthday, Christmas, New Year. Yeah (grimaces bitterly) - those are all points in time.

Brendan has not yet received his tariff, but already he is learning to block out thoughts about the length of sentence:

I don't think about it. I'm numb. If I think about it, it gets me down, so I stop. I black it out. Most of the time I try numbing myself. I'm quite...Oh, well! It might be 18, it might be 20 years!

It's just a number, you know. I don't know whether I'm ever going to be released, so it's not exactly something I can look forward to.

Of the non-copers, Brad (not now 'coping', medical centre) was the only one who was managing to confront the future. He had attempted suicide many times, in overdoses on the outside, and two attempted hangings in this six week remand period. He was in visibly bad shape: his eyes drooped involuntarily, his speech was slurred and he could not control the movements of his mouth. He was aware that he could not control his suicidal impulses, and needed an enormous amount of help. But an extraordinary spirit blazed from him, although he spoke slowly and with difficulty. There were long pauses between every sentence, and he concentrated hard to say exactly what he meant:

I still take things one day at a time, but I do look ahead now. Yeah. I've got time on my hands so, - how can I put it - instead of putting my energies into destructive ways, I will put 'em into constructive ways, I hope. I'm expecting to go to hospital and get psychological help for my past, because I'm a manic, I'm...I get depressed a lot, and that's why I take drugs. I think about the future a lot. I think about what I want to do with myself.

But it is only the thought of constructive help which is giving him something to hold onto:

My time here is just wasted, and wasting. I'm wasting time being here, I'm wasting time. I just sit around, or sleep. It's a waste of my time. I talk to the others, sometimes we have a laugh. But we're just wasting away.

Brad has done time before, and never achieved this impulse toward a positive relationship with time that he is now experiencing:

I've realised a lot. I've done a lot of thinking, like I always do when I come into prison. I do a lot of thinking. But I kept on coming out with the attitude that I've done my bird, and it was nothing, and I can do it again. But now, I look at it now as wasted time.

So Brad is changing his internal time-awareness: he is becoming aware of a future with possibilities. He is also realising that future time could contain very different experiences from the horrific ones of his life so far. In the light of the terrible abuse he suffered as a child, I ask him if he will ever trust anyone again. There is a very long pause:

Umm...maybe. (Pause) In time. Maybe. And time is a great healer. (Sighs). Maybe I will, maybe I won't. Maybe I'll always keep certain barriers up, so I can't get hurt like that again. But, maybe I will trust someone again, I don't know, I can't answer that question fully as a yes or a no. That's a maybe.

Living with the Enemy

The three tellers in Induction had only been in prison for roughly 24 hours, and their reactions were wholly focused on prison as a place. They had not yet made their time-sense into an internal enemy.

The other copers did not have as much to say about their sense of time as the 'non-copers'. Hal (ambivalently not 'coping', medical centre) was subject to the life of the ward which the other non-copers found so difficult to adjust to. But, in contrast to them, he described himself as always busy.

I make my greeting cards, I've got nine of them up on my locker unit, what I've made, and I sold one this morning.

(When you were on the wing, were you busy like that?)

Nah (proudly) - I got into so much trouble on the wings, I was always getting done it. I got bashed up on B Wing, I got bashed up on C Wing. On A Wing I was on my way (a beaming smile) to being smashed up and bashed up, so...and I feel a lot better on here, 'cos. there's staff around me.

But Hal is into the home straight now:

Time goes slowly, yes. But I've only got four to five weeks left to do, and next Thursday, I'll have exactly 28 days to do. And believe me, the further it goes down, the more happier I feel! I feel happier getting out, but of course when I do get out...I just don't want the problems I had last year when I got out.

The relationship that the now-copers had with their internal time-sense was qualitatively different. They had far less to say about the phenomenon of time: it was not something they were hyper-conscious of. Somehow, they had learned to put it into the general perspective of their prison experience, or alternatively it had just dropped into their consciousness in a less obsessive way than with the non-copers. Some, like Ken, had improvised their own personal time-sense:

I telephone the wife every day, and twice at weekends. We get up at 5 a.m. and write to each other. Then we have a cup of tea together at about 8 o'clock. She's changed her shifts at work and her meal times, so that we eat together at lunch and tea.

It comes as quite a shock to realise that this *together time* occurs between two people who are physically separated by 300 miles. Ken is visibly vulnerable, and what is keeping him going is his ability to live to a novel time-table, which harmonises his life inside with that of his wife on the outside. He has invested a life-time in his family, and the disruption to this family time has profoundly shaken him.

I've never been strong. Never. Never. I'm coping in here, only just. Only just. When you've been married 32 years, and you got a daughter 25, and two granddaughters, and you spend six years watching them grow up, and then it's taken away from you, it's a terrible thing. It's just something that you can't accept. I mean, I can't accept it. I can't. Not after all this time.

Alistair (coping, 'C' Wing) has, in complete contrast, the apparent capacity to adapt to whatever institution he is in:

I don't like to say it, but I'm an institutions person. You just go along with the flow. I just take each day as it comes, really. There's not a lot you can do about it. If they decide to bang us up early, you've just got to accept it.

So Alistair lives according to prison time, grumbling tolerantly if he is banged up early, but not feeling any unusual discomfort if his time is disrupted in this way. He sits passively enough in present time, but mentally orientates himself in rather an automatic way toward future time, and looks forward in time to his release, but it is difficult even for him to understand why he does so:

What keeps me going is looking forward to the day I get out, and what I'm going to do when I get out. I look forward to getting out, and my problems start the day I get out. Once you walk out that door, you've gotta think where you're gonna get money from again, and that's the tragedy about prison. You can be in prison 10, 12, 14 years, easy. The trouble starts the day you walk out, because you've got to try and get somewhere again.

How do I cope in prison? Well, it's more a case of having to, really. I mean, there's no alternative. You go out there, you do what you do, you know full well at the end of the day that you're gonna get caught, and you're gonna end up back in prison.

The offending, the conviction and the sentence are not just possibilities, for he expresses them as definite events in his future. Alistair's fatalism means that he can see no other future for himself..

What can I say...my life has been H.M.P. from day one to the end, you might near enough say, because that's how much time I've spent in prison custody.

So Alistair has allowed his life-*time* to be appropriated by Her Majesty's Prison Service. A victim of early institutionalisation, he never learnt to own and direct his own time. His socialisation in one institution after another from the age of nine was a long training in passivity, and the perfect preparation for prison.

Mike (now 'coping', 'C' Wing), with a life sentence behind him, gives a succinct summary of prison:

Everything in prison works through time. It's like a time machine. At a quarter past eight, you do this. At half past eight, you do that. Time controls your life.

But this adjustment was a long process for him, and a painful road to self-knowledge. In the first four years of his life sentence, he said that he was simultaneously in a trance, but also belligerent and violent. Eventually he was stabbed by a fellow inmate and nearly lost his life. He took a long look at himself and began the process of adjustment to prison time. He followed every course that was on offer, and he began to read voraciously, taking a special interest in the history of slavery.

Over the years, he learnt to exercise autonomy over his time:

I didn't choose to come to prison, but I can choose how to spend that time. I choose to watch a film - that's a positive choice for me, and so I'm passing those couple of hours positively. Mondays, I'm always down. I hate Mondays, and that's when I need to keep myself to myself. So on Mondays, I'll choose to stay in my cell, in bed, and not do association. It's better I don't see no-one Mondays, I'd only bite their heads off.

Bill (now 'coping', 'C' Wing) is only five months into a life sentence, and is perhaps still in the 'trance period' referred to by Mike. In his case, it has not made him belligerent.

I just keep my head down, and try to do what is asked of me. I don't look forward to anything, I just keep busy, with my cleaning job.

In the long bang-up, he reads, plays games, chats to his cell-mate and plays music. If he thinks about the future, it is in terms of his next prison. He thinks it is important to make friends:

They can advise you and help you. My cellmate, he's just finishing off a life sentence, so he's told me quite a bit about the past and how he copes with it, how he's dealt with it. It does help to help other people: you can always get help in return. I don't ever sit there thinking how I'm going to pass the next couple of days or couple of hours. As soon as I've done one thing, I do another, without thinking about it.

Bill is probably still in the 'dream' or 'trance' time, which prisoners doing life so often refer to. Just because he is apparently so well adjusted, it is reasonable to expect that an acutely painful realisation time lies in his future. In his favour, however, is his early conviction that he must make for himself a community - a place where he helps others, and others help him. This conviction helps to structure his overall approach to his predicament, just as an overriding desire to seek the positive structures George's approach:

There's enough negativity about, so you try and fill your time with a focus on good things. You might get out at exercise, and see someone from another wing, so you focus on talking to him. Sometimes I'll be able to go to the gym and meet some lifers who have done a lot of time already, so I like to talk to them, and they try to point out how things are, and how things were, and how things will go.

I find that useful...you think to yourself if you can get onto the right plane...even when you do talk to the ones that have made the mistakes and caused uproar, they will admit it, and be straight with you, and say, well that's not the way you want to go.

So it's helping you through it as well: if you can get into it, and keep in a predominantly positive frame of mind, then the time will take care of itself.

George is an interesting contrast from the non-copers: he does not over-invest the dimension of time, as they do, with painful meaning. For him, it naturally inter-relates with the efforts he makes to turn the prison into a place where he interacts with others and lives in a positive way. Other lifers have valuable and special time-knowledge: they can say *how things are, how things were*, and *how things will go*. He is eager to learn from them, and enlarge his time-place perspective.

Conclusion

Foucault (1979) points to the historically grounded capacity of the prison to make bodies docile in particular places at particular times. But because his analysis is structural and methodologically screens out any consideration of human agency or experience (Medlicott 1994), he fails to convey the forceful capacity of the prison not only to order time in seemingly highly organised ways, but also, in terms of personal experience, to render time itself as a source of terrible pain and suffering. For paradoxically, time-discipline in prison is combined with the ruthless emptying of time: meaningful activity which allows for personal development and the expression of autonomy is largely absent. The provision of meaningful activity has frequently been asserted as an imperative responsibility for the Prison Service (HM Chief Inspector 1991). In this particular local prison, there was an enormous variation in this aspect of the regime. Some prisoners had jobs which proved a source of satisfaction and personal development: very many others had endless tracts of empty time to cope with.

The non-copers exemplify the way in which time can be the most potent instrument of punishment. It is empty, slow, relentless, and it has been appropriated by a powerful agency. This agency has the power to fill the time, but, for those defined as needing the special 'care' of the medical centre, it chooses not to do so. So the time-markers are trivial matters, such as the television going on. Even this is precarious, since it lies within the power of the staff to deny it, a power which they exercise as a weapon in the maintenance of conformity. The care is of the body, as the object which must be sustained in order to serve the sentence of the court, or in order to be produced for trial.

In addition to suffering placelessness, the non-coping inmates feel both in the grip of an obsession with time and yet a peculiar *timelessness*, in that they have failed to evolve a workable relationship with their internal sense of time. They feel watched, but are not aware of any source of help or comfort which might slacken the grip of the obsession, or enable them to develop a *personal timeness*.

Hal is the only teller in the Medical Centre who purposively filled his time, mostly by making his greeting cards or by laborious self-injury. It will be remembered that although he was classified as 'at risk of suicide', none of the staff considered him suicidal, and I have characterised him as 'coping' ambivalently through constant cutting. Hal had a brisk and no-nonsense relationship with time, but he was of course very near the end of his sentence when I interviewed him. This produced euphoria in him, alongside the knowledge that he faces the same problems on the outside which caused him pain inside prison - his addiction to cutting, his mood swings, and his propensity to cause trouble, plus the added one of his inability to resist alcohol.

For the copers, there are a variety of strategies which have been employed in order to reach a reasonable co-existence with the enemy of time. Alistair (now 'coping', 'C' Wing) illustrates the passive acceptance of prison time, so common amongst many prisoners who have been shuffled from one institution to another all their lives. His years of training in one institution after another have taught him how to wait, and he waits for time to pass. For those who have adapted to prison time, such as George (now 'coping' 'B' Wing) and Mike (now 'coping', 'B' Wing), this lesson in 'learning to wait' has been quickly learned in prison, and is combined with their innovative capacity to make best use of personal time, whilst acknowledging the inevitable constraints.

Temporality is organised in different ways by each teller: time-consciousness is represented on different levels of complexity and integration. Most simply, there are the ordinary representations of present time. In the peculiar circumstances of the prison, the sense of being held in constraint in present time is magnified, and, for non-copers, time *now* becomes an obsession: they are taken over by an exaggerated awareness of time. They feel immured in now-time. They are unable to engage with representations which emphasise historicality, and when asked to attempt the task of recovering the past, they do so with difficulty. All their energy is spent on denying an enemy which still persists in filling most of their thoughts. They are, therefore, completely unable to engage with the most complex representations of time consciousness, which attempt to grasp at the unity of future, past and present. It is this deep temporal awareness which they must acquire if they are to accept the fact of the penal appropriation of their time, adapt to it and learn to talk to themselves about how best to move through the present and into the future.

In this chapter, I have used data from the narratives to explore the relationship of prisoners with prison time. But separating the time relationship from the place relationship is only justifiable analytically: in terms of the prison experience, the temporal and spatial aspects of existence, so important for the focus of this study, are experienced synthetically. As Lynch (1972) points out, we live in time-places. Inmates' experience attests to the fact that the prison is a sophisticated time-place, where the temporal and spatial characteristics are structurally productive of prison life and culture. The integrated prisoners, such as George and Mike (both now 'coping', 'B' Wing) exemplify a time-place integration. Acceptance of the *place* was acquired painfully, and with it came acceptance and adjustment to the dominant characteristic of the place, its subtle management of repetitive *time*. It is not possible to generalise about the manner and order of acceptance: it is an individual journey of integration, the originating threads of which are elusive for prisoners to identify.

Non-copers keep returning to the issue of time: *they are saturated in now-time awareness:* they cannot move through time but must endure the feeling of its slow passing as a kind of personal torture. Unfortunately, in the medical centre, they are in a location where time is especially empty and the markers which break it up are tenuous and unreliable. During the period of my research, staff shortages meant that no-one in the medical centre was able to visit the library on a regular basis. No-one I spoke to in the medical centre during the year of my research had had the benefit of anything approaching the six hours of daily purposeful activity, which is the standard of the Health Care Directorate. Stretches of empty time can produce the breakthrough into consciousness of much material which the prisoner would rather not re-visit, or a retreat into fantasy (such as Marty described), or an obsession with activities to kill time (Toch 1992:28). On the wings, many inmates laboriously built miniaturised worlds from matchsticks, but in the Medical Centre, apart from Hal (ambivalently 'coping') making his greeting cards, I saw no-one who engaged in such activities.

The difficulty of time management is in no way related to the longevity of sentence, and the length of time spent in prison does not have a direct relationship with the pain suffered, *because the ability of inmates to handle time varies so markedly from person to person* (Porporino in Toch 1992). Thus, Bud is suicidal because he just cannot face 19 months, whereas George is sure he can face his life sentence. Unless this qualitative aspect of suffering in prison is appreciated, policies to prevent suicide will always suffer from a major awareness deficit. Only the prisoner himself can estimate whether a sentence is bearable or not: this is not a judgement others can make on his behalf.

References

Cohen, S. and Taylor, L. (1972), *Psychological Survival - The Experience of Long-term Imprisonment*, Penguin, Harmondsworth.

Foucault, M. (1979), *Discipline and Punish*, Penguin, Harmondsworth.

HM Chief Inspector of Prisons (1991), *The Woolf Report: Prison Disturbances*, HMSO, London.

Leach, E.R. (1961), *Rethinking Anthropology*, Athlone, London.

Lynch, K. (1972), *What Time is this Place?*, M.I.T. Press, Massachusetts.

Mann, D.W. (1991), 'Ownership: A Pathography of the Self', *British Journal of Medical Psychology*, vol. 64, pp. 211-223.

Medlicott, D. (1994), 'History of the Modern Soul: Foucault's Genealogy and the Problem of the Subject' *Occasional Paper March, School of Sociology & Social Policy*, Middlesex University.

Medlicott, D. (1995) 'In Our Own Time: The Uneasiness of Modernity' *Occasional Paper March 1995, School of Sociology & Social Policy*, Middlesex University.

Sapsford, R. (1983), *Life Sentence Prisoners*, Open University Press, Milton Keynes.

Scraton, P., Sim, J. and Skidmore, P. (1991), *Prisons under Protest*, Open University Press, Milton Keynes.

Serge, V. (1970), *Men in Prison*, Gollancz, London.

Thompson, E.P. (1967), 'Time, Work-Discipline and Industrial Capitalism', *Past & Present*, no. 38, December 1967, pp. 56-97.

Toch, H. (1992), *Living in Prison: The Ecology of Survival*, American Psychological Association, Washington.

6 Self

Introduction

The prison experience, with its special manipulation of time and space, is, as has been shown, a peculiar time-place, productive of much discomfort. In confining persons against their will, it produces a special and acute rendition of Dilthey's (1976) foundational categories of willing, feeling, and imagining. It puts individuals into a situation designed to induce experiential extremes, and it is these aspects of human response that cause inmates their rare pleasure and their severest pains. Indeed 'imagining' is often construed as something that must be self-controlled, for it causes too much pain.

It is no exaggeration, therefore, to describe the prison experience as an existential crisis, the form of which is that control over one's time and space has been removed, and the content of which is the way in which the prisoner copes with this. The two previous chapters have examined material provoked by questions about time and place. In this chapter, that somewhat artificial analytic is abandoned, and material is presented which expresses the nature of the crisis for the self, and how it is dealt with.

Dealing with the crisis is an ongoing task, so that when inmates spoke to me, they were communicating not only with me, but with themselves. They were clarifying out loud how they were managing. As a listener, as well as a researcher, my task was, openly and with good faith, to receive the communication as only part of that ongoing process of clarification. They would return to their cells, brood upon which they had said and what they had - sometimes to their surprise - heard themselves say. And this reflection would feed into the ongoing process of the self trying to reach an accommodation with the prison place.

These narratives go behind what is today taken for granted as the official agenda of the problem of suicidal prisoners. In elucidating prisoner accounts, and going to the heart of subjective experience, it attempts to investigate a sorely neglected area in previous research (Liebling 1992). Additionally it is communicatively useful. The extent and reach of this usefulness, and its relationship to current and future practice, are issues which will be returned to in a later chapter.

Some fundamental assumptions relating to the *social* self, drawn from the symbolic interactionism of George Herbert Mead (1863-1931), underpin this chapter. The phrase *the self in society* is often referred to as a kind of shorthand for the subject matter of the *social* sciences. But the phrase is of course a tautology. For the social dimension of the self is not an optional extra when it comes to empirical research. It is not conceivable to posit a self that is *not* in society, except in a purely abstract and analytical sense, and it is not conceivable to conduct empirical research into such a self. The self is best conceived as developmental and interactionist, as Mead (1934a:135) pointed out:

> The self is something which has a development; it is not initially there, at birth, but arises in the process of social experience and activity, that is, develops in the given individual as result of his relations to that process as a whole and to other individuals within that process.

So research into the psychology of prisoner suicide is not adequate unless it recognises the validity and significance of the *social* context. The extraordinary nature of the prison setting is sometimes a taken-for-granted aspect of such research, and a failure to cope can be misleadingly translated as an individualistic failing.

But just because the extraordinary nature of the social setting is emphasised in this research, that does not negate recognition of the individual and all the ways in which he acts upon that setting (Mead 1934a:201):

> The fact that all selves are constituted by or in terms of the social process, and are individual reflections of it...is not in the least incompatible with, or destructive of, the fact that every individual self has its own peculiar individuality, its own unique pattern (Mead 1934a:201).

Some of the complex aspects of this interactionist self are made explicit, as each individual considers himself reflexively both as an object in the prison place and as a dynamic subject, responding in innovative and varying ways to social processes and projecting himself from the past, through the present and into the future.

Although my tellers share a common placement in prison, they experience this challenge in individual ways. For 'each slices the world from the standpoint of a different time system' (Mead 1934b:341). So the uniquely individual reference frame of pasts and futures is fundamental to the experience and activity of the present, and it is experienced and recounted in wholly individualistic ways.

Shared Responses

What is shared by those overwhelmed by suicidal feelings is a feeling of collapse into nothingness. Almost all of these tellers described feeling an utterly blank, absent or annihilated self. But if this is a state of collapse, where there is no awareness left of a special and unique self, we are obliged to ask 'Collapse from what?'. As an abstraction, can we conceptualise the private self prior to prison and the present crisis?

It would be unhelpful and misleading to assume that individuals enter prison with flawless self-identity, which the prison then proceeds to break down. The twentieth century, after all, has seen a preoccupation with crises in identity and ways in which individuals can achieve self-actualisation. This is not the place to explore that debate, and yet the historical context is not irrelevant, for 'even quite intimate features of man's inner life are best formulated as problems within specific historical contexts' (Wright Mills 1959:163).

The most relevant context for this study is the way in which powers in the twentieth century 'have come to bear upon the subjective existence of people and their relations one with another' Rose (1989:ix). Prisoners will have experienced some aspects of this extreme governmentality at the hands of experts whose job is the management of subjectivity, such as clinical, educational and occupational psychologists, social workers, personnel managers, probation officers, psychiatrists and others (Rose 1989).

Rose (1989) is not, however, indulging in a nostalgic lament for some lost private self. He points out that it would be profoundly misleading to describe the autonomy and security of the self as destroyed, as if some golden age once existed where the self could be comfortable with itself in private and with the world in public. He is pointing out the importance of recognising the self as the object of expert knowledge and systems of moral orthopaedics, so that a genealogical excavation can be done of those techniques that fabricate the self and help the self to fabricate itself.

As Foucault (1979) pointed out, Western man is an confessing animal, inescapably an ethical one because he is forever monitoring, testing out and giving feedback to the self, which fuels the motor of change. In asking prisoners to engage in these practices of the self, I was not asking them to do something they had not done before. They were familiar with the moral codes, ethical scenarios and techniques of the self to which Rose (1989) refers, and, although it was painful, they seemed to find answering questions about their self-image a rewarding process. 'So what do you see when you look in the mirror?' was an odd question, particularly as mirrors are scarce and inefficient commodities in prison. But all the tellers understood the level at which this question was pitched, and that they were being asked to perform this action in their heads. Given time, they all responded thoughtfully. Perhaps this is because, as Rose (1989) claims, modern selves have become attached to the idea of freedom and they want to try to live it in terms of their identity. The experience of prison concentrates the mind upon thoughts of freedom, and therefore upon thoughts of self.

All the tellers were aware that the experience of incarceration was productive of responses toward their fellow human beings of which they were afraid. Sorrowfully, some of them would speak of the erosion of their social selves, and how self-managing and self-limited they were becoming. Despite their best efforts, their private selves were decaying also. They related to me some of their awareness of the constituting effects of prison life upon their sense of self, and these included a range of complex effects which figured repetitively in narratives of interaction with the prison place. They spoke of the compulsion to act out tough *macho* roles, of living in roles until the roles took over, of acquiring false masks, of stress, fear, grief and suspicion of others, of the loss of integrity through forced relationships and/or forced involvement in illegal activities. They spoke feelingly of the lack of privacy, the despair, the degradation.

But they also talked of the opportunity to reflect upon the deep issues of life and self, and to decide upon change, shape a future and improve self esteem. They spoke of the opportunity to observe peers at extremely close quarters, and to use this observation to further their understanding of their own situated uniqueness. They spoke of the opportunities to speak with significant strangers such as the chaplain, Samaritans, Listeners and senior officers, and of the opportunity to do courses such as Thinking Skills which offer the possibility of change.

It can be seen from the range of these responses that prison has the capacity to be powerfully productive in both positive and negative aspects and practices of self. It is an extreme form of governmentality, and yet in often creative ways, some inmates grasp at every opportunity to live freedom and express self-identity. This is a dynamic of risk, for such grasping may prove enhancing and help adaptation, or it may prove intolerably painful. But in recognising the prison as a place steeped in the practices of power, it is necessary also to acknowledge that power is not necessarily merely repressive in terms of what it can offer the self.

No account of the prison is complete, then, without recognition of the fact that it is productive of an enormous variety of complex, ambiguous and contradictory responses. For instance, inmates will describe it as a lonely place, and in the next breath describe how difficult it is to get any privacy. It is said to be a place where nothing ever happens, but which is paradoxically crowded and frenetic.

The list above demonstrates that it is misleading for the prison to be described, as it often is, as a form of *human warehousing*. According to inmates, it does not merely hold people in suspended animation, in some sort of penal vacuum, and then release them unchanged. It is a place which is richly productive of effects in people, constitutive of change of one kind or another. This change may, ironically, include 'freezing' people in an uncharacteristically static story, from which they cannot escape, even in their deepest and most private self. But this effect is created through the dialectical interaction of the prisoner and the prison society, and is a process in which inmates participate, just as they do when the constitution is more dramatic and extreme.

The prison is a particularly interesting context in which to study this dialectical interactism, because of the peculiar intensity of governmentality combined with high expectations of personal responsibility. In terms of governmentality, the extent and reach of power exercised over everyday lives is self evident in a prison, whether one considers inmates or staff. In terms of the personal responsibility of inmates, there is a powerful ideology at work, concerning overt expectations about the need for prisoners to take responsibility, learn their lesson and *go straight*. This ideology puts an enormous pressure upon the resources of the individual self, for in many cases, offenders are only too well aware that they lack the capacity to change and learn, and they sit helpless before the enormity of the task of renouncing their former offending behaviour.

From the interview data as a whole, the tellings of different selves emerge through these accounting practices, and I have identified three categories which are significant in terms of suicidal behaviour. These categories are not exhaustive or definitive ways in which the self accounts for its situation, but my fieldwork came to a natural end when I stopped hearing new kinds of telling. Of course each telling is unique, and maps onto an individual biography, subjectivity and personality, but each falls explicitly, at any one moment, toward one kind of telling much more than to another. However, everything that an inmate says will not map neatly onto one kind of telling, without any echoes of another. Some inmates, for instance, present in exemplary form all the characteristics of one kind or another. Some have taken a faltering step toward change, and stand on the threshhold of another stage. In what follows, we meet inmates who are exemplary examples of particular stages, and one who stands on the cusp of change.

Stages of Telling: Waiting, Presentational and Dialogic

Waiting and Telling

Alistair Inmates who have experienced many years of institutionalised living not unsurprisingly evince a great lack of autonomy. Such inmates form a substantial part of the prison population. Yet they do not, on the whole, attract great attention, accustomed as they are to the demands one institution or another. I did not encounter any such prisoners who were the subject of F2052SH documentation, but I was often pointed in the direction of such prisoners as examples of 'good copers'. Alistair, on C Wing, was one such inmate, and he is a perfect example of the passive institutionalised prisoner waiting for his sentence to end.

Alistair has conformed obediently to the expectations of institutions all his life. He found the children's home 'quite easy', the approved school 'pretty much the same', and prison 'a holiday camp, really'. He finds any decision-making very difficult, and even when the cells are opened up, finds himself unable to make the decision to wander out onto the landing to mingle with others. The most reiterated phrase in his narrative is 'I don't know, to be honest', and this passivity is his habitual response to any suggestion of change:

> My wife said that I should go and see a psychiatrist. I don't know, to be honest. This is the first time in my life that I've ever spoken to someone like you, like this, about myself, to be truthful. I've never really had low times in prison, no, at the end of the day, it's just something that has to be done.

Alistair's conformity ensures that he never attracts the attention of the authorities. As someone institutionalised since childhood, he has been the object of many official assessments, and conformed to the expectations of them all. In all that time, he has never had a conversation in which he spoke to someone 'like you, like this, about myself'.

Alistair has a realistic view of who he is and how he copes. This is what he sees when he looks in the mirror:

I'm an institutions person. You just go along with the flow.

For Alistair, time and place are just impersonal forces which happen to him. He just waits for the scenery to be changed, and for time to move on. He does not exercise any care over the self, or look for ways in which to grant it autonomy. He has never developed any reflexive dialogical capacity. He looks at himself and sees someone who has always been looked after by institutions: in the face of this unending governmentality, and with the acquisition of a passive self, it is not surprising if he finds the notion of a private self quite puzzling.

Alistair is on 'C' Wing, where the prisoners are free to come out onto the landings for most of the day, but this privilege is wasted on him as he never emerges:

I come to prison, I don't do nothing except stay in me cell all the time. I don't really associate with people, to be honest. I get on with my cell-mate, I get on with anyone who's banged up with me, but that's as far as it goes. I talk to me cell-mate, I'd class him as a nice person. I'll talk to other people that come in my cell. But whether it'd go any further when I got out...I suppose no, really. I've met some famous people in prison, they've given me their phone numbers to get in touch when I get out. But it seems to be that once you walk out of prison, you're too busy trying to keep up with what you missed out on that you don't really want to...I suppose I should have done really, because if I did, I would have been financially secure I think by now, the connections that I've known.

When I had heard a few narratives of this type from prisoners who had been in one institution after another, I realised that this group of Waiting Tellers have needs which demand urgent address. They were all regarded as good copers, which is not surprising, for they have been trained for prison all of their lives. But deep down there was a despair waiting to engulf them, and they did not have the tools to deal with it. Their needs would never be identified through official assessments hurriedly undertaken. For the Waiting Teller would cope with these through habit, endlessly producing the schooled responses so often repeated before. But it is not surprising, either, if, one day, the emptiness of this breaks through to the passive self, and the realisation dawns that Me, Here, Now is all that there will ever be, and so there really is no point in continuing to wait.

No-one ever talks to Alistair about himself, because he is a model prisoner and keeps himself to himself. He does not engage in relationships in prison, except of the most shallow kind. This failure to present a social self to the prison community means that he slides through prison life, almost unnoticed. But one day he may join the statistics of successful suicides with no previous psychiatric history, and no F2052SH documentation. He exemplifies the prisoner which no amount of risk assessment or management will identify, unless that process involves an empathetic encounter in which he inadvertently betrays his ultimate emptiness and desperation. Even if identified, such prisoners present establishments with an enormous problem. Despite their prevalence in prisons, these institutionalised inmates would need a different kind of 'care' from that presently offered, if they were to be helped to learn how to want to live outside of institutions.

In terms of suicide prevention, the Alistairs scattered through the prison system present a greater challenge than would first appear, and perhaps the greatest challenge of all to the system as it presently is. For all they do is wait, until they cannot bear the waiting any longer.

> There's one of two ways out, you can either walk out the door or you can try and kill yourself. (Pause) It has crossed my mind...

An unreadable expression flits across Alistair's blank face and is quickly gone. There is a long silence and then he adds:

> I'm looking at a 12 or a 14, now, you know, if I'm convicted.

> It has crossed my mind...yes it has...my wife turned round and said to me a little while ago, if it got bad we'd do it together. Because if you look at it, what has she got and what have I got left? I'm 43 and she's 48. If you look at it logically, by the time I come out, my life's finished really.

Presentational Telling

Hal (ambivalently 'coping' now, on F2052SH documentation in the Medical Centre) is an example of an inmate who has a very firm view of who he is and what he is like, and is able to present this picture in an articulate way. But it is a shallow presentation which does not match his personal situation or problems, and he cannot see beyond it to anything deeper:

> Before I came in, I took every day as it came. People called me happy-go-lucky. But I've got a bad temper, a split personality, I'm a bit of a Jekyll and Hyde. I like my good side, the side I am today. But my bad side, I hate it, I really hate it. But it's the way I've been brought up, and not only that, what

I've been through, over the years. I've got a split personality disorder, me. One minute I'm o.k. and the next minute I can change like the weather.

If I've got the time, I'm prepared to sit down and help someone by talking, and if they want advice, or something like that, I give it to them. And that J... who came on the ward yesterday, he says to me today 'Hal, I ain't never going to forget you, you've really stuck by me.' And he's really in a very bad way, yet twice I've made him laugh since he's been on here. (Pause) That's the type of person I am, very caring and very helpful.

I value myself very highly. I like myself a lot. I do. I like the good side. But I hate the bad side. Prison's made me do a lot of thinking. It's made me understand that prison ain't a place for me. The first time, that was only a 12 month sentence and it didn't give me a lot of time to do any real thinking. I was always working in the laundry. But this time, I've been banged up constantly for the last 17 months. It's given me a lot of time to a lot of thinking and come to terms with being in prison. That way, I know I'm not coming back. Sort out the Ifs and Buts.

It's made me better in myself. I mean, as I say, I may have a split personality, but I'm going to do something about that as well, and if I still carry on with this obsession of cutting myself, then I'm going to seek some proper psychiatric help when I get out. I don't want to go on the rest of my life scarring myself like this. My arms are in a bad way now, I don't want to be no worse.

Me cutting has gone from a habit to an addiction, and from an addiction to an obsession. But I'm a loner, I don't mix with anybody, I don't trust anybody. I've lost my trust in people, because a lot of certain people have let me down in the past, and I don't trust anybody any more. I mean, I might make friends with one or two on the ward, but there's no telling what they'll do behind your back, so I don't get involved.

I remind him of the 'very caring, very helpful' side he mentioned to me earlier, and he quickly says:

Oh yes, you're so right, I do care for people. I may not trust anybody, but I care for people. It doesn't stop me from caring for certain people.

So Hal holds firmly onto this picture of himself with a caring, helpful and insightful side, alongside the bad-tempered, suspicious, solitary and untrusting side. He has found a fixed story of the split personality which accounts for the way he is, and yet he has projected a good outcome, when he is released, of a person who has sorted out the Ifs and Buts and knows he will not return to prison.

Goffman (1959) points to a structural division between the performer who fabricates the impressions, and the character who is the impression that is fabricated by an ongoing performance which needs and entails both selves. The performance consists of both talk and enactment, and when it is performed, in talk, as Hal did, it brings to life, for the performer, the self 'who is sealed inside a story' (Young 1989). Hal is telling a story to the listener, in which he defines himself as an object to himself, and as the subject of the story. The next chapter in his personal accounting is the one in which he sees himself as returning to the outside world, coping well and never returning to prison.

But Hal's own accounting practices also reveal his propensity to self-injure, his pride in provoking fights on the wing as well as a high level of tension in other inmates and staff, and his desire for constant and heavy medication. Although he is due for release in 37 days, this has not prevented him from further self-injury, and he is heavily swathed in bandages as we speak. He came into prison equipped with a record of self injury, from cutting as well as overdoses combined with alcohol, of which he speaks with pride. He will be kept in the Medical Centre until release. The self that he presents is not a self which has yet acquired the means with which to manage the next chapter he has so cheerfully written.

This inability to follow through the story he has written for himself is not a realisation that he is able to confront. For he needs, like everyone, to present a self, in order to sustain a reality (Goffman 1959). The reality at stake is that most significant of realities for human beings - the reality of self - which, through the peculiar temporal and spatial constraints of prison, has become fixed and static for Hal.

Some of the performative content can be identified in the brief extract above. When Hal speaks of the 'caring' nature of his identity, and his 'lack of trust' in others, these two somewhat contradictory aspects do not well up implicitly out of his words. He speaks of each aspect separately, repeating his claim to each, three times in quick succession. But these aspects are not sustained in the rest of our two hour talk, and he is not able to explain the coexistence of many somewhat contradictory aspects to his identity except by reference to his 'bad side' and his 'good side'. It is a brave attempt to present a self, in order to sustain a reality, and yet it remains merely performative and presentational.

Looking back to Hal's personal timeness, it will be remembered that he had a childlike approach to the issue of passing time. He kept himself busy, by making cards, and he counted the days of his sentence already done, and the days that yet remained, as if he were a child who was shortly to go home for the holidays. He never spoke of time passing in terms of internal change, as some of the other 'copers' did.

Hal was proud of his inability to settle on a wing. The many occasions on which he produced violent responses in other prisoners, extremes of frustration and irritability in staff and a general atmosphere of turmoil and unease are produced as anecdotes, which show him as 'amusing', a real 'character' and 'well-known' throughout the prison. But he also likes the attention he receives in the Medical Centre following self-harm, and, once there, he achieves a limited sense of place, by being possessive about his locker and personal effects. He exercises autonomy over some meaningful areas of life, but these areas are neatly circumscribed and do not relate to personal development:

> It's funny you should ask me about choices and decisions, 'cos I do do that. I'm fussy about what they do give me to eat. I always make sure that I save a boiled egg, or some jam, or something like that, so I've got something to eat at night, so my stomach doesn't talk to me in seven different languages!

Paulo is 43, and fighting extradition to serve a 24 year sentence for a murder committed 20 years ago. He was in the medical unit for some time when he first came into this prison, and I interviewed him then, when he had been in prison for only two months. He wept a lot then, and expressed guilt and remorse. He was desirous of paying for his mistake, but he just could not reconcile himself to the length of the sentence. His troubled relationship with time and place can be summarised in this quotation from that first interview:

> You think, you have 24 years to do in this little space...you are in it for 23 hours a day...well, you can imagine for yourself...(weeps). Trying to survive is a problem...it's not possible.

Paulo is the only prisoner that I follow up and interview for a second time some months later. The second interview, some of which is presented below, is conducted on 'B' Wing where he is managing to cope. His out-of-cell time is about 12 hours, and he has a cleaning job in the mornings. He is going to English classes from time to time: each day he collects up all the newspapers he finds on the wing, and in the long bang-up from 8 p.m. to 8 a.m., he reads carefully through them, and he has a dictionary. He says his

English has improved a great deal, and this is evident in our interview. He reads the bible in his own language and in English.

In this interview, Paulo repeatedly asserts that there is no evidence against him, and he is not a murderer. Much of this talk is peppered with quasi-legal jargon, and he begins many sentences with the phrase To be honest... He remembers me and our first interview, so he is aware that he is now telling me a very different story. I resist the temptation to refer to the obvious discrepancy in the two interviews, for, methodologically, it is extremely important that Paulo presents the self that he now considers himself to be, without challenge from me. We pick up the interview at a point when I am asking him about his time in the hospital, and the occasion when I first interviewed him. This is, for me, an oblique way of checking that everything he says to me, he says with full awareness of our first encounter. He confirms that he remembers our talk, and adds:

> To be honest, is a different atmosphere on the hospital, psychologically, because you are in a big room and it is not like to be in prison. It is more like to be in hospital. Even if you know you can't go out. But what is hard is to be closed in a small room like this one (gestures), is like a claustrophobia.

(But you seem to be coping a lot better with this than in the hospital?)

> Well to be honest, I was feel better in the hospital, I don't know, maybe it was the medication they used to give me, or maybe because to be in a big room doesn't make you feel to be in prison. I used to coping better. This is why I was scared, I was terrified, because I knew that once you were out of hospital, I knew you had to be in Induction or on A Wing - I was terrified. Even now, I would do anything to stay on this wing, because I know we are open during the day. I don't know if I would cope...I don't classify myself as a criminal because I didn't commit any crime, I am in prison for nothing. Maybe that's the reason I feel like that, I don't know.

(So you don't feel like the others in here?)

> No, not at all. I've been in London for 20 years: in the beginning I was drinking and smoking. I gave up the smoking, I gave up the drinking, because I couldn't afford it.

Paulo then gives a long account of his time here, preceded by some remarks about the 'mistakes' he made in Italy as a teenager, stealing cars etc. But he reiterates that the robbery with murder, for which he faces extradition was nothing to do with him. I refer at this point to our previous interview, and remind him gently that he admitted his 'mistake' and he slides around that rather by saying 'Well, everyone makes mistakes.' I leave it at that: this is as close as I wish to come to confronting him with the reality of his double narrative. He moves on from that remark to a reiterated account of his life in England, which consists of a penniless immigrant washing dishes, working his way up to owning his own business, and remaining absolutely honest. After some time, I am able to turn the talk back to the issue of place:

(Tell me about your cell, Paulo: does it feel like your space?)

Well in prison, really, you got no privacy. Like, yesterday morning I was working and I finished working and went back into my cell to wash my hands, and there was the officer, the security, so they stretched me, they strip searched me.

(Do you find this upsetting?)

Well not really, well, I think it depend how.... if you got nothing to hide. I got nothing to hide: if they tell me to check it, they can check it. It doesn't upset me at all: actually I think it is a good idea, because in prison there are lots of dodgy people, and I think for security it's better that they do. Prison is full of criminals (laughs).

((Laughs) So...have you made any friends then?)

To be honest, few, very few. I'm not socialised with many, because I know this...the way they think, most of the people, not everyone, the way they think, that's the way I was when I was a teenager. Like, going to do things dodgy, and commit crimes, and I've learned better.

He then goes on to say that he feels quite safe on B wing, confident that if there is any trouble, he can go to Mr. B...and things will be sorted out. I ask him if he ever befriends other prisoners who may be having a tough time.

Well I'm friendly with another guy who is awaiting deportation: he is a 60 years old man. And I'm quite friendly with him, actually. And poor guy, I feel quite sorry for him, because he has finished his sentence five or six months ago, and he is still waiting. Well, he said 'I can buy my own ticket and go, but they don't let me'. He put in an Appeal, and so now they have to wait for the Appeal before he can go. He is American, been involved in some credit card fraud or something like that, and he's not really criminal, to be honest, not dangerous, a 63 years old man. And I'm quite friendly with him. To be honest it's not my mentality to socialise with many of the people here. Is like, I see these people, they jump and have a good time playing table tennis or pool table, and laughing, a good time...to be honest I feel to cry all the time. (His demeanour cracks very suddenly and he begins to weep).

(And so how do you cope?)

(Weeps) I just pray God all the time.

There is a long silence while Paulo struggles for self-control. In the distance, keys rattle and doors clang. Someone starts whistling. I wish that Paulo still smoked so that I could offer him a cigarette. Although I am a non-smoker and only carry them to share with prisoners, I long to smoke. I wish that I could give him a hug. I note that my discomfort is greater because this is a second encounter, and that follow-up interviews present, methodologically, a challenge to the maintenance of disciplined empathy. The long pause is useful, therefore, in enabling me to pull back from an unbalanced empathy.

After a time, I ask him if he has changed as a person in any positive way, whilst in prison:

Not really, no. I can't say that. I improve my language, slowly, slowly. Because I read a lot, and I never had time to read before.

(Is that a pleasure?)

It's not a pleasure, because I just read anything to pass the time, because after all, this is the cell (gestures), and the way they are, and there's nothing to do, and if you put your mind in something, and try to pass the time until you fell asleep. In the meantime I try to learn to read English, because before I don't read English at all. I have two bibles and I read them all the time. One I brought in with me, and Father S..., he gave me another. From time to time I do go in the library and read some Italian book. But most of the time I'm reading and not concentrating. I find that to read English I concentrate the more. Sometimes I am reading Italian for maybe one hour or two and I have understood nothing at all, because my mind is somewhere else.

(So you are still suffering anxiety a lot?)

Yes. 24 hours a day. But nothing I can do. My hand is tidied. And there is nothing I can do. It is like - no it is not *like*, it *is* that I am in prison for nothing and there is nothing I can do. Is very bad thing to feel like. You only be in my place to know how I am feeling. If only 6 months or one year, you can go over. But 24 years is a long sentence. Coming to this stage, there is nothing you can do.

The only way you can put yourself out of this thing is if you are not going to live in this world. That is the only way you can take out from your mind. Otherwise you can't, and you have to live with it 24 hours, and nothing you can do.

I have thought of suicide, many times. Many times. (weeps).

(Have you ever talked to anyone about that?)

No. I don't like to. (struggles for control) I don't believe it's the right things to do. It doesn't help. They (Samaritans) tried to talk to me. But it doesn't help, because I find that most of these people are no help at all. Because they only want to know your problem...it is something you can't share. You can't...it is like when you are a little boy or girl, I don't know if you never felt, and your father and your mother beat you up and said you done this, and you didn't done it. I don't know if I can make an idea, but it is not only the thing that they beat you up, but to punish you mentally for the rest of your life. They make you pay for the rest of your life for something you didn't do. You cannot explain the way you are feeling. You have to be in that position, to feel.

(Does praying help?)

Yes, a lot. I can say that, yes.

(And your daily visit, does that help?)

Yes I look forward to that. But my girlfriend, she is in same state as I am. I try sometimes to forget my pain, and help her.

(And how would you describe prison as a place, to someone with no experience of it?)

Well to be honest I think prison is a nice place for criminals. Because if you do anything wrong you need to be punished. I believe in that. And some people, in this prison, they deserve to be locked up and have the key throw away. But it's not for everybody the same. But unfortunately that is the system and the way it works, and everyone picked up by the system is treated the same things.

(And have you learned a lot more about yourself in this year in prison?)

To be honest I knew myself already. I knew exactly what sort of a person I was. I stopped drinking, I stopped smoking, they are not easy things to do. I never used to go out.

(So when you look in the mirror, what do you see?)

I see they spoiled my life, they really spoiled my life. Because I am a man, by this time I like to be married, have children, and I've been run from my own country, from my own family for 20 years. And nothing I can do. Only because when I am young, I do silly things. Lots of people make mistakes when they are young. But I don't think it's fair, I am supposed to pay for the rest of my life. And nothing I can do. Nothing I can do. There's nothing I can do.

Paulo has the troubled relationship with time that many of the non-copers exemplify. He reiterates the 24 hour a day suffering, and constantly mentions the length of the sentence that he faces if he is extradited. The only way to dodge the pain from the enemy of time is through not going on living.

Paulo has a clear picture of himself, and this picture is reiterated without being expanded upon throughout the interview, in both quoted and unquoted extracts, as non-criminal, hard-working, different from the other inmates, and a conventional citizen in his views on prison and punishment The sort of person he is now is described, not in terms of personal qualities, but in terms of the control of personal habits. When he looks at himself in the mirror, it is 'they' that he sees. *They* spoiled his life and stopped him from further conformity in terms of citizenship.

Paulo does not find himself able to associate with the other inmates, because, in their criminality, he perceives them as utterly different from himself. He makes an exception for another inmate who, like himself, is of a different nationality, of a mature age and not really criminal. In singling out this inmate, Paulo has chosen someone who can give him positive cues with regard to his own position.

Ken (now 'coping' on 'B' Wing) is visibly shaky and often tearful. He has days where he refuses to come out of his cell. A senior officer, whom he greatly trusts, has on occasions had to pull him out in order to help him integrate on the wing. Here he is talking about the requirement to attend anger-management classes:

> They say you've got to talk about your violence. What violence? How can you talk to someone about violence if you've never been violent? I mean I couldn't talk to you about violence 'cos I've never been violent. I'll be honest with you: I've always been put on. Even when I've been on the wing: I've never argued with anyone, I've took abuse. When I first came on the wing, I went down to use the phone, and because of who I was, there was things like 'You're not using this phone, get back to your cell or you'll get it.' So I'd just go back to me cell, and sit in me cell.
>
> I mean, you lose such a lot in prison. Dignity. Some of the officers, not all of them, because you've been convicted, they tend to say, well it's got to be true. Wrongful conviction never exists, they'd like to believe that it couldn't exist. But it does exist. If they were in the same circumstances, it'd be a different matter. Mind you, there's two that says they believe I'm innocent - Mr. D..., he knows I didn't do it.
>
> I've never been strong, you know. Never. Never. I've always been put upon.

Ken's repetitions emphasise his view of himself as weak and persecuted by others. This picture is static and serves to explain to himself and to others why he should have been singled out for wrongful conviction for murder.

(But you're coping, Ken, are you?)

> Well I've coped outside just because I've had me family.

(But you're coping in here, aren't you?)

> Well, only just. (voice trembles) I'm just. Only just.

Later, I ask:

(So what do you see, Ken, when you look in the mirror at yourself? What do you think about what you see?)

> (Sighs)   I just look at meself and know, that I've...that I've been con...con...convicted of a crime I didn't commit, and the person who

convicted...who comm...comm...committed that crime is out there gallivanting about and enjoying himself.

The stories that Ken and Paulo are sealed inside are stories of innocence and of being wronged. The question of what each sees, looking in the mirror, is answered in terms of this static story. It is not answered in terms of the perceived ownership of personal qualities of one kind or another, which was the response of other tellers. So, in a strange way, when they looked in the mirror, they only saw the story and did not see themselves. For a story sealed in stasis is a story without change, movement or personal timeness. It is also a story that voluntarily or involuntarily entirely neglects the reality of place. The tellers have not confronted the reality of prison and their placeness as protagonists there. In other words, their sense of self is divorced from an awareness of place and of personal timeness and change.

Nevertheless, Ken had a remarkable and innovative way of expressing personal timeness to himself. He lived by a different timetable, and he and his wife had a personal synchonicity which meant that they wrote letters to each other, ate together and thought about each other at the same time each day.

When these tellers look forward, they do not see themselves as engaging in events in a reciprocally changeful way. When, for instance, I asked Hal what sort of person he would like to be when he gets out, this is his reply:

I'd like to be a person who...I'm going to change my name when I get out, cos I want to start a new life and I want to find a nice lady, someone who I can really care for. Cos I tried that last year, but then I got done for this robbery and blackmail. I lost contact with her. That really upsets me to know that I lost contact with her.

I'm hoping I've a roof over me head when I do go. They wanted to put me in a hostel, but I won't go in a hostel, because it'll be a place full of ex-prisoners and so on, and it's going to be just like being back in prison, because you've got to watch your property because of people nicking it.

Hal begins to answer the question I have asked, but he is unable to sustain this, and instead presents a story which figures him a static protagonist in the midst of a set of interesting events. Despite a ready admission of guilt and a long account of his crime, in this extract his crime is referred to as an inconvenient event that happened to him and interrupted the pleasant flow of his life. In terms of his place identity and sense of personal timeness, he is able to picture himself living somewhere upon release, but not in a place where he has to watch his property, and his own status as convicted robber and blackmailer is not seen by him as incongruous with this desire. He can see himself in future time, and future place, but these aspects of identity are compartmentalised and only link up with self-identity in a purely presentational, shallow and unrealised way.

When these tellers look back, they are often unable to do so in a way that acknowledges a thread of connection between past time and present situatedness. Regardless of issues of guilt or innocence, Paulo overlooks the fact that the reasons he is now facing extradition is because he went on the run 20 years ago. Although he is happy to admit to offences committed when he was younger, these were 'mistakes', not crimes, and so he sees himself as an innocent forcibly incarcerated with what he terms dodgy people and criminals.

The reiteration in these narratives, particularly in the case of Hal and Paulo, requires a lot of emotional energy, something of the energy which is needed in a dramaturgical performance. The maintenance of an inauthentic image, for others to look at and for the self to rest within, can be hard work and use up energy which might otherwise be directed at the process of necessary change. These inmates present in exemplary form the characteristics of what I term the Presentational Teller, with all of the following characteristics:

- a static story which is not flexible or responsive in relation to passing time and the exigencies of particular places, but which overrides inconsistencies.
- a sense of personal timeness which is limited to the stasis of the story, and does not relate to a dynamic awareness of Me, Here, Now.
- a limited place identity, confined to highly selective and/or chosen aspects of the environment. Other aspects are avoided or denied, in thought and/or in practice, by reactive or proactive behaviours.
- a view of self as involuntarily and/or blamelessly cast as the main character in this static story.
- a marked incompatibility between the past and what is seen as the next personal chapter.
- reiterative performance of the characteristics which explain to himself some of the baffling dimensions of Me, Here, Now. This repetition looks to the listener for cues that will indicate she, too, is convinced, for such cues comfort and reassure, by providing validation of the performance.

- retold anecdotes, where the cues of others are invoked in order to endorse the presented story.

The Presentational Teller is usually strong enough to cope with prison without resort to extremes of suicidal behaviour. The self that is sealed inside the story takes comfort from that story, and is cocooned unchangingly within it. Nevertheless prisoners who fell into this category were, significantly, extremely vulnerable. They tended to present involuntarily and/or voluntarily some characteristics which ensure that they get noticed by staff: Hal constantly self-injures, and Ken is visibly shaky, weepy and, at times, refuses to come out of his cell. Paulo grieves and weeps, and only finds solace in prayer. Each is receiving attention, sufficient to maintain in stasis the protagonist sealed inside the story. This helps each of them to cope from the prison's point of view, and desist from suicide. In terms of suicide prevention policy, each must so far be reckoned to be a success.

But without much more attention of a particular kind, it can be theorised that the Presentational Teller will not change. Nor will he transcend the time-place exigencies and move on self-developmentally. The Presentational Teller looks for ways in which to exercise choice, as Hal does in relation to food, and as Paulo does in the classes he attends, but these tend to be decisions which are sealed within stasis, and are not (yet) part of movement toward change. Presentational tellers cling to their stories, in order to cope, but their stories may be too shallow to sustain them if they are subject to extra stresses, such as bad news from home, or a move to another prison.

Telling about Possible Change

Brendan (not now 'coping', Medical Centre) is an example of a teller who is apparently stuck inside a particular story, but desirous of breaking out of it. He is considered highly dangerous, and is on the ward after a spell in the ACU. He is serving life sentences for rape, and has been in prison for 14 months, about 5 or 6 since conviction. He is in the Medical Centre at the time of our meeting, as a result of cutting up. He says he has been cutting up since he was 16. The doctors have told him he is a psychopath, and the officers were anxious for me to be aware of this before we met. As I mentioned in an earlier chapter, we have to meet in a glass booth in the open-plan administration offices, visible on all sides. As a child, he was sexually abused and there is a case pending in connection with this.

Prior to this offence, he had just finished a five year sentence for armed robbery, and prior to that, a 15 month sentence. In all his sentences he has harmed himself or tried to commit suicide by hanging. The extracts below begin at a point in the interview when he has referred to these incidents, and so I ask Brendan if he regards himself as a suicidal person:

I regard myself someone who is not afraid to take his own life. And if I ever decide my life is going to end, I will be the person to end it. If that's suicidal, then maybe so. It's not like a pressure thing, not like the pressure gets too much and I want to kill myself. If I ever take my life, it will be a very conscious decision.

(These attempts - had you decided on something definite? Did they go wrong?)

I decided. Then they went wrong. The first time I decided, I was unfortunately spied...someone was walking through and spied on me and caught me. The second time was actually on the outside, and if it wasn't for my girlfriend, I wouldn't be here now. The third time was a heroin overdose, and if it wasn't for my friend,...well, the other times have been self-harm and not suicidal.

I'm the kind of person, ...when I was outside I didn't really have any...I'd give up on love and stuff. It was just sort of physical anyway. My days, I'd just do whatever I wanted to do. Oh I'll get up, I think I'll take some crack. I wasn't like I had to take crack, but anything I did after that was because of the crack.

There's absolutely nothing to look forward to in a life sentence at all. Apart from visits, letters, phone calls, canteen, that's about it. And music. I teach a guy on the ward, and I play keyboards, that's not exactly looking forward cos. it's on the wards, it's occupational therapy.

My first sentence, I used to look forward to going home and being with my girlfriend. That was that sentence. On my five (year sentence), I had nothing to look forward to at all. Just before I came in here, I had a wife, who's now had my child. And after my wife left, I had a girlfriend who had some children, and I looked forward to spending some time with them, but I also looked forward to having drugs, I used to be a drug taker. I was a crack addict, E's, speed.

(Do you think that part of your adjustment to this life sentence is constructing things to look forward to?)

No. I think that my adjustment is that I've been here in this situation before, so I'm not exactly a person who's like scared of the sentence. I'm actually not scared of this sentence, I'm quite, unfortunately, calm through it. It's just something that happened, I did my crime, I'll do my time.

(So how full or empty is your time here?)

Empty. There's not much you can do. Exercise, you get to watch TV, recreational really, it's either listening to my music or my tape or my C.D. Or organising discussion groups with the lads on the ward, ourselves. Apart from that, there's not much you can do while you're on the hospital wing, you're restricted in what you can do. I've been told I can't go anywhere except under secure conditions, i.e. the ACU or a segregation unit. At the moment I'm on the ward because I seem to have proved to the doctors that I'm no longer...that I'm curbing my temper problem. So they're giving me a chance. And if there's any complaints about me, I'll be back downstairs in the single cells (ACU).

Whilst talking about the sort of person Brendan is, I ask him if he has ever felt safe in his life, and his face lightens as he says that this has happened to him on only three occasions, which he remembers vividly:

The day my wife decided she was going to marry me. The first time I went out with my very first girlfriend, when my nan died, that was the girlfriend I had for four and a half years. And then when my wife left, and I started going out with Tracy. Basically I've had three females make me feel safe, cos. I've been loved, and that what I've basically needed most of my life. Apart from that I've never really felt safe. I've usually fought for things or caused problems that aren't really there, because I don't feel safe. I never really did as a child. And my childhood is something which is good, bad, very bad, and...if I can call it a childhood. I don't really think I had a childhood, but I grew up, from a baby to a man of course. But whether that was a childhood, or just a growing process, I'm not too sure.

We talk some more about the issue of safety, and he sums it up in this way:

That's what I mean, with each partner, it's felt warm and safe within the confines of a loving relationship, and I felt like they'd protect me from the bad things out there that I'd bring to myself and also that I do to others.

(How safe do you feel in here?)

I'm very good at looking after myself, physically. I don't feel threatened by any inmate or any member of staff. I don't want to be violent but if I need to be, I can be. I feel more...that makes me feel safe in a way, but because of the system as it is, that's what I don't feel safe with. Because I know, every time I think I know something, they've moved the goal post a bit wider, so that's where I don't feel safe. It's the fact that, I suppose I used to be heavily into power, so I feel powerless, and that makes me feel scared. But if I thought someone was going to hit me, then I wouldn't really be too scared about that. It's what they can do to me in the long term, not the short term, that's where I'm scared. People who have big power can create big problem...that's what I feel.

Emotionally I'm not safe. Mentally I don't think I'm safe. Physically I'm very safe. But I'm no good at protecting my mind or my feelings. I can protect my body, but the rest I can't protect.

When we discuss the issue of choices and decision-making, Brendon makes it clear that this is a deprivation which is related to his suicidal behaviour:

I try to do what I want to do within the realms of law and being here. Basically, the only decisions I can make is what time I go to sleep, and when I go to the loo, and what time I decide to eat my food. It's either, do I leave it, or I don't want to leave it. Apart from that, if I want something, I make an application. Anything else is out of my hands. I miss being able to make toast, or go for a walk. Because they're decisions that I miss. I want night-time exercise, because that's the time I like to walk around. But I can't make that decision. So in a way, yes, there is a little thing that I can say 'that's still mine', but the biggest decision I've got is the fact that I can take my life or I can keep living. That's my...that's the only bit of power I can hold onto...which is a fair assumption of power, really. You know, you might take my life, as it is out there, liberty-wise, but you won't take it the other way. My body will be here, you can take that, but my mind is still free. Until you start plugging it...my emotions the same way. But the beating heart is something I control.

Any decision I take is really special for me. Because they're still things that I do. You see, at the moment, I am...all prisoners are robots for the system. They're on programmes to conform to what they say is the norm. But they can't tell me when to sleep. That's where I've still got one over, so it's very important for me, to get through my sentence, to know that I haven't lost all control. If I lose all control, I cease to live, I just exist. And I don't want just to exist, I want to live.

The reason I'm in...all of it is a control thing, I think. When my self-esteem goes low, I blame certain people, and I think 'why don't I kill them?' I haven't killed anybody, that's what I think, but that's why I don't let my self-esteem get low. So I try to keep it on an even keel. Cos. when I feel low, I think 'they've made me feel low, it's their fault that I'm here'. I never blame it on myself, it's always someone else. And then when it does hit me that it's my fault, then I do go into wanting to harm myself, because I think to myself 'See, all you've ever done is brought pain. It's time to punish yourself.' Because I don't think this will punish me. The punishment thing is something I've had to live with all my life, basically. It's just the thing…Bad, you've done that, punish yourself! I don't believe that anybody outside of this body has got a right to punish me, even my parents. It's something that I will do. So I'll let them give me life sentences, retribution and rehabilitation. But I get my own form of retribution. This'll do. Whenever I look at my arms, recently, more so, these two here (points to recent mutilations), I will always remember I did these the day I got life. So I will always have memories of what I've done wrong. To punish me, basically.

(Do you feel yourself changing as a person?)

The staff say I've changed a lot recently. I think it's a route I'm taking subconsciously to be able to adapt and cope with such a long time. You know, I've realised that all the arguing and fighting, jumping up and screaming will get me nowhere, will get me no quicker out. Whereas retaining calmness and everything else is probably going to get me out someday. In other words, I've decided to play by the rules. Not that I haven't already, I mean I have. But obviously not enough.

(If you were writing to someone who didn't know you, how would you describe yourself?)

A bad person you want to stay away from.

(So when you look in the mirror, what do you see?)

I see an evil person looking back at me, 'cos I see everything I've done, which…I see things that I know, that no-one knows about. So, you know, I've got the darker side of my past, as well as the side that everybody else knows about, looking at me. And it scares me that I can be that bad, or even worse.

(Even worse?)

Yes. My charge sheet was quite tame. I think the victims, basically, didn't say everything in court. For their own reasons. Their embarrassment. And I didn't say anything. So they made it a little bit weaker than it actually was. Which I actually...in some way, I'm not grateful for. I wish they both had said...'this is basically what happened'. Instead of putting in what really happened, they put in what happened, plus some bad stuff to make it sound worse. But I'd rather they told the whole truth. I mean I understand that it was a terrifying ordeal, I understand that people feared for their safety, their lives, their everything else, including their family's lives. And...they just sort of used half-truth, and part collaboration. I'd rather they'd used whole truth and no collaboration.

(Do you think you cope well with change?)

I hope so. I think I've coped well with the change of environment on this one. Umm...change is something I'm frightened of, though. Because I don't know what's going to happen when I change. I know me now. I want to change, don't get me wrong, I don't want to be this bad person on me life, I want to change, but I've got this 'Right. What happens when I do change? What actually is left? Nothing: it's a new person'.

So it's fear of the unknown. But it's also in a way...change is, at the moment, it has been for the last couple of weeks, pulling me...saying 'You need to change.' You know, it's not something the system says, it's something that my heart says, it's time you left all that behind and changed. And because I don't really know how to change, I'm looking for ways to help myself, improve myself.

(Are you frightened that you might not be able to?)

Possibility. I'll lose a lot when I change. I'll lose a lot of the confidence, I'll lose the power basically, to tell the truth, I got to admit I'll lose the power. And that's the problem. I'm scared of what happens when I'm completely powerless. I won't need to show people how nasty I can be, I'll be a nice guy. And I'm thinking, when I was a nice guy, I was walked over. That's what I went nasty because of. Do I really want to get hurt again like that?

(When you were a kid, I guess you were a nice kid, and (he interrupts):

I suffered a few things. But the thing is, a lot of my mind is going back to racism. As a mixed race...you know I didn't ask to be the colour I am. I didn't ask people not to like me. I certainly didn't make a racist law or rule which says you can't like somebody. And in a way, it's like, when I change I think I'm going to be vulnerable like I was when kids picked on me about my colour. Because now I can say, get out and don't come back.

But when I change, when I learn to accept, respect, admire, and them things that go with the human race, then I get hurt. I don't know how I'll get hurt, or who'll hurt me. I feel sometimes I'll end up being the scared child I always have been. Which is why I build so much on being the aggressor, more than the victim.

But there is a tender caring side of me, which only comes out of me when someone brings it out of me. There's people who can bring out the best in me, and there's people who can bring out the worst in me. But I never seem to know which side to bring out, I can never repeat the good side. So usually...I'm very quick tempered, I don't take 'no' for an answer. I have the last word. What I say goes. Them kind of things! That's because I feel if I carry on arguing with somebody, they'll hurt me. They'll say something hurtful, like my wife for instance. She'll say something, throw something back in my face, from my past that I've said in confidence. So I've stopped the arguments, and if she carries on, sometimes I threaten her. And if that doesn't work, I either leave, tell her to leave, or show her that she's gone too far. Which is not something which I like to do. But it's something I feel I have to do. If someone says something to me that hurts me, I then re-live it. I then see it, and it's screaming in my head. And it won't go away, and I don't like that. 'Cos it makes me feel like I did then. And I don't want to feel that again. Nobody wants to feel terrified twice. Once is enough. Also I know how people who are terrified by me feel. That's all I can say on that one.

(When I asked you what you saw in the mirror, you replied that you saw your evil self. Why do you think you didn't tell me about your vulnerable self, or the self that wants to change?)

Well why pick your weaknesses? You don't go into a boxing ring and say to the boxer, oh don't hit me in the left eye because it's in the habit of bleeding. You never give someone that position when you know they can hurt you. So what I see is that bad person, 'cos if I see that good person, God it hurts. 'Cos to see the good person I got to see the times where I got hurt in the first place. Also, it doesn't give somebody enough door open to get in there and start breaking things up inside or something. I think everybody does that, and not just me. We all do it, it's part of life.

(You're hard on yourself, aren't you?)

Not hard enough, sometimes. I suppose I can cope with the bad things more than the good things, as well. I can understand the bad bits, I'm comfortable with them. The good bits, they make me look weak, they make me feel weak, they bring back too many memories.

(Can we return to something you said earlier about suicide? Apart from it being an opportunity for you to exercise ultimate control, is there any other way that you look at it?)

Yes, sometimes I do look at suicide as such a drastic, a desperate measure of where you can't take it no more, you have to stop. And if that gets to me, that's exactly what I'll do. For instance, I know that when I get to the dispersal system, there's plenty of heroin around. If needles are on offer for phone cards, I can overdose on heroin. Because if I know I'm never going to be released, I'll need to stop it. Because it will become too much. When I think of the fact that I could be 54, and going outside, I could be 60 and going outside, and taking my flask to bed at 8 o'clock, no more kids, no more sex or anything like that, it makes me want to end it. It does. But then there's another part of me that wants to give me a kick up the backside and says 'Oh come on, it won't be that bad. You're hard, you'll get through it.' And that's what I do.

(So what you're saying to me is, whether you do it, or you don't, it won't be because of external things will it?)

If I take my life, it will not be for these people. I will not let these people be the cause of my death. I won't give them the satisfaction. If I do it, it's because I can't take it, or I want to end it. It won't be because I never got a birthday card, or nobody wrote to me on Xmas Day. It'll be because I'm never getting out, or I'm too scared to come out. It'll be one of them reasons. Or if me mum dies. If my children are injured, if my wife dies. Anything like that. If my mum died tomorrow, I'd go tomorrow.

(She has to die sometime, I suppose...)

Yes. But she hasn't got to die at the age of 42, while I haven't any chance to be with her and say I'm sorry.

It will be noted that Brendan's narrative begins with a firm picture of himself. This is a self who is not afraid to take difficult decisions, who prides himself of being in charge of himself, and who is unafraid of situations that would scare most people. But it is hard for Brendan to sustain this self, in answer to some of the questions. Asked about life on the outside, his answer discloses a self who is not at all in control.

But it is the simple question 'Have you ever felt safe in your life?' that prompts a long eloquent sigh, a change of tone and the beginning of a telling of a different and more complex self.   This is the self who knows he has always fought for things and caused trouble, who needs love in order to grasp at a feeling of safety which has eluded him all his life, who does bad things to himself and to others because he is a bad and evil person, who has been so troubled by feeling unsafe all his life that he grasps greedily at every bit of power that comes his way.   This self has a tender and caring side, but not one that can be sustained. Threatened with pain, even if only in the form of hurtful remarks, this is a self that lashes out.

Profound feelings of non-safety do not allow the self to acquire a strong sense of rootedness in particular places, or a generalised strong place identity. Nor can the self acquire a sense of personal timeness. Brendan suffers terribly because of the disjunction between 'then' and 'now': it is the hurtful remarks in the 'now', which relate to 'then', which cause him to feel the unbearable pain of 'then'.

So Brendan has a dislocated and unresolved relationship with the personal chronology of his life. He is 'numb' when he considers how long he might be in prison. Like other prisoners in the grief stage, he struggles not to think about 'time' but of course it obsesses him. His time markers are still those of the life he has lost. He finds it hard to consider the concept of 'looking forward to things' in terms of his placement in prison. For him, 'looking forward to things' relates to sex, drugs and time with loved ones - all things he has 'lost' by being in this place. He has not yet acquired a coherent sense of Me, Here, Now.

Nevertheless, change is pulling at him: something tells him not only that he must change, but that he is changing. This terrifies him. If he loses the sense of power and control, he loses the presentational self, because the key supports of this story of the self are his exercise of power, if necessary by force, over others.

This presentational mask, however, is hard to relinquish. It is worn like a habit: admitting to the deeper, more complex and vulnerable self behind the face in the mirror is, in his view, giving the listener the opportunity of hurting him. He understands the bad bits, and they fit neatly into the hard man image he has constructed. But the other bits make him feel weak.

At the beginning of the above extract, Brendan stressed that if he committed suicide, it would be a very conscious decision. It would not be out of desperation. This fits in with his presentational story: here is a self, he says, who is not afraid to take his own life as the ultimate act of control and power.   But by the end of the extract, he admits to his natural desperation.   The interview has gone full circle: in the end, the performative utterances of the presentational self will not meet the reality of suffering in this time-place. He cannot deny the latter in any sustained way, and he knows that he needs a less shallow self picture to deal with what is confronting him in the present.

If Brendan is to move out from behind the presentational self, and evolve into a person with a less rigid and more fluid set of responses to his time/place situatedness, he will need much support and attention. Already suicidal, he presents a complex challenge to the suicide prevention policy. One of his problems is that he has been pinned like a butterfly within the discourse of psychopathology. He was not regarded as someone who was capable of change, and several officers helpfully pointed this out to me before our encounter.

Dialogic Telling

Gerry, George, Mike and Bill Some coping inmates disclosed a self engaged in dialogue with itself. This dialogue involves the gaining of a sense of personal time, integrated with a sense of place. In previous chapters, I have already quoted Gerry and George, showing their personal timeness and/or sense of place, analytically separated for the purposes of this study. In this section I can show the synthesis of these aspects of the self, integrated in expressive self-accounting. Here is Gerry, talking about aspects of himself that he works to maintain, because they form an important part of his self-picture:

> I make sure I read a paper every day, and I try to get hold of business journals. Keeping in touch is important to me. I make jottings about business ideas for the future all the time, and I keep press cuttings. People go inward here, rather than outward. But it's a time thing, isn't it? This is after all temporary, time will pass and they've got to let me out eventually.

Gerry has a thread of narrative in this short extract, which links Gerry-in-the-present with Gerry-in-the-future. This is a story in which he can grasp at the processes of change, and where time and place are reflected on as they inter-connect in this changing self:

> I think I've become more aggressive in prison. It hardened me up a lot last time. I wouldn't say boo to a goose last time. I mean, I started work at a very young age, when I was fifteen or sixteen, and although I would say that I was an aggressive business person, I wouldn't ever confront people. But now, if someone confronts me, I will confront them. That's a change that has arisen out of being in this place.

My companies are so squeaky clean now that it's not true! The SFO (Serious Fraud Office) are still out there, still sweeping the streets. Everything that I run now, it's legit. So that's a big change too!

I suppose, this sentence, I look upon prison not as a punishment but as something that's pulled me back from the brink. It's made me re-think, in a positive way. There's a lot of positive sides to it. I think that the last three years before I came in, I was in a self-destructive mood, not giving a shite because I didn't know if I would live through the next year.

Part of the process of recognising and monitoring change in the self is registering dissonance, and approaching that dissonance in a dialogic way. Like Paulo, Gerry is aware of the criminality of other inmates, but, unlike Paulo, he does not use this as an excuse to avoid their company. He registers the dissonance caused by the enforced socialising with people he would not associate with on the outside, and, through internal dialogue, produces something positive for his own self-development:

I think the negative aspects of prison are to do with the fact of becoming institutionalised. You tend to live in an unreal world - what people would hang around with rapists, murderers and child molesters for choice! And I say this to their face!

I mean, you can be talking to someone, and you suddenly think 'Hang on, he's got five life sentences for rape!' And you ask yourself, would I do this on the out? So you tend to pull back on the odd occasion - I can't say it's an unreal world, because it's really happening. But it doesn't feel like reality. It's a false reality, I suppose.

I think everybody tells themselves that they are different and that they don't really belong here. But they can't do that to any big extent. One of the biggest problems everybody's got in prison is that everybody is innocent. And until you've got over that stage of thinking you're innocent, at the end of the day you're doing your bird the hard way. Because as time goes on, and you carry on with that line, when it comes to making parole reports and things like that, and you're showing no signs of remorse - well, it's not good.

So it's back to reality thinking. As a fraudster, or an ex-fraudster as I am, reality thinking is a very difficult thing to do, because your mind is running at very fast paces, seeing all the angles.

Gerry is aware that, because of the nature of prison, inmates are tempted to 'act' a part. He himself does this, as a coping strategy. Like Brad (not now 'coping', Medical Centre), he protects himself by maintaining himself in a state of constant alert. But these characteristics do not supplant Gerry's constant internal dialogue, as the following extract shows:

> Life in prison is like taking part in a long-running play, where you're on stage all the time. You've got to play your part, have a front. It's a guard, and you never drop it. Yes, I even continue it in my cell, you tend to keep yourself switched on 24 hours a day.

> If you show any sign of weakness, you've had it. Cheerfulness is the most important defence of all. It's nothing to do with personality or temperament - my cheerfulness is learned. Learning guards and learning parts - that's what it's about.

> When I look at my actual sentence, I can recognise that some of the awful stages are already over. Parts of my torment are gone, and in past time now. The arrest, the police handling, the trial, those parts of my torment are over, and I have to face the future. I am bereft of certain things, but, nevertheless, I still must turn to the future without the comfort of those things.

Gerry's achievement is not kept to himself, because, in quite natural ways, he lives on the wing as in a community:

> I think I'm quite lucky. I have plenty in common with both inmates and staff. I can communicate with both levels. I think there's a fine line there: I can sometimes relate better to staff than inmates, because of the age level, and because many of them have done jobs that I have done in the past.

So Gerry's internal dialogue is rounded out by non-trivial, authentic dialogue with others:

> We have lots of conversations in here about coping: people sometimes come up to me and ask me how to do it. I think the expression that covers it is 'finding the mark'. We each of us have to find our mark. You know, that's a time thing, too. The past is gone and I must face the future. That's the reality principle again. You do your time. In your head. I've had a cell mate who sat and cut away at his wrists in front of me. I said - 'well, get on with it, it's your choice, but please do it quietly'. And I waited until he'd had a cry, and then we sat and talked for maybe three hours. I said 'You've got to get yourself out of this, but I am here, and I can understand. Don't use the past as an excuse, deal with here and now'. It's the time thing again, dealing with here and now, and then you can face the future.

In another part of the interview, Gerry returns to the subject of his cell mate, and speaks quite unselfconsciously about the 'us community' on the landing:

> He's been with us down on the ones for four or five months, and he's got a job and he's a different person. And that was really because people like me turned round and talked to him in reality terms instead of fantasy terms. You know - 'Don't be a silly sod: you can't do that!' Because he still tends to do it, you know (the self-cutting). He's got to go out on licence soon to a hostel, and he's saying 'But I want to go to my mum's' and all the rest of it. And I'm saying, 'Well you can't. You're still on licence for a period of time, and you have to be where they say you have to be.' And a lot of people seem liable to drift into that fantasy world, which is a protection I suppose. I mean we all do it, I mean I used to.

Gerry was very intrigued by the questions in my research which hinted at the significant status of the concept of time. He had thought about it himself, and he focused on it in a way which neatly encapsulated the time problematic of prison experience. He was able to draw on past experience, transferring its lesson to the very different context of prison and using the insights gained to aid his own adaptation, and to reflect upon the coping of others:

> Being a funeral director was the most excellent training for me, for this, because it was all about the problem of temporal reality. When you're planning a funeral, everyone gets the tense wrong, you know. Everybody's planning the funeral, and they are operating in the past tense. They say things like 'Mum used to like this, Mum said that.' But the reality is, Mum's still there! She's with me, physically, and she's still with them because they are planning something for her. She's not gone until the coffin slides into the cremation machinery. That is when you are finally bereaved, and you enter bereavement time, and you have to turn to the future without that person.

Through his own experience and through observation of others, Gerry has formulated a stage theory about the process of coping with prison:

> I think there's a cycle of stages to coping - everyone goes through the same stages but at different speeds and in different ways. There's the loss stage - 'I'm bereft, because I've lost so much, so many lost times and lost places, and all of that is outside'.

> If you can move on from that, there is the enquiry stage -' I've got to find out how the system works, and try to understand it'.

Then there follows the knowledge stage - 'now I know how the system works, I can try to manipulate it, and make it work for me. And I have to work with it'.

That phrase of Gerry's 'You have to be where they say you have to be' is a succinct statement of the temporal/spatial constraints of prison, which even follow the licensed prisoner into the outside world. Reality, in terms of Gerry's stage theory of adaptation, means a state of mind where there is first of all an acceptance of the special time/place characteristics of the prison, so that the changing self is grounded in this acceptance, and able therefore to move on to the process of learning how to adapt successfully in ways that maintain autonomy and enhance one's situation.

It is significant that Gerry's telling of this knowledge is related as a dialogue with himself, just as Mike's telling (below) of a similarly special insight is also re-enacted as a reflexive dialogue. George is another inmate who engages in reflexive dialogue. His, however, is conducted through writing as well as through reflection:

> When certain things happen I write in a journal, I write a little piece about it. If I've got to thinking about something one day, or something particular happened on the legal side, and how it's made me feel...so I do, yes. I don't keep it religiously, sort of Dear Diary, but I think sometimes if you can write down what you're feeling, and what may have caused you to feel that way and stuff, you can kind of analyse it a bit later on. And maybe you think, when I reaction that way I could have reacted another way. So you can go back to it, and add that to your experience, I suppose.

So George is engaged in a dynamic personal timeness, in which he moves through time, engaging in a process of checking and balancing. Despite being a lifer, he is not obsessed with the passing of time in the sense of it as an outside entity which is ticking inexorably away. He is not, like Hal, counting time. He is not, like Ken, living to a dramatically different clock. He is in a relatively comfortable relationship with the enemy, in that his personal timeness is integrated into his sense of who he is now and who he might be in the future.

Similarly, he has a different and more highly developed spatial awareness than those at the presentational stage of telling. He has made his cell his own little sanctuary, and yet it is not his only source of spatial comfort. He talks about the exercise period, and being able to enjoy 'being in the air and feeling the sun in the sky'. Similarly, he can take advantage of what other places in the prison have to offer:

Sometimes I'll be able to go to the gym and meet some lifers who have done a lot of time already, so I like to talk to them and they try to point out how things are, and how things were, and how things will go.   I find that useful...you think to yourself if you can get onto the right plane...even when you do talk to the ones that have made the mistakes and caused uproar, they will admit it, and be straight with you, and say well, that's not the way you want to go.   So it's helping you through it as well: if you can get into it, and keep in a predominantly positive frame of mind, then the time will take care of itself.

George's personal timeness is demonstrated in the above remarks: he is considering how things are, how things were, and how things will go, and he is keen to take advice from men who have mastered the enemy of time through reflection and experience, and the acquisition of personal timeness. He is expressing a synthesis of Me/Then, Me/Here/Now, Me/Here/In Future, in which his sense of place, his personal timeness and his sense of self are all bound up in each other. This is not a fixed picture, it is ongoing and is affected by others in the community. He speaks about adding to his experience and knowledge, and his picture of himself is not fixed and static. At one point, I observe that he seems to be a strong person, and he picks up on this, not in a dogmatic way, but in a reflective way that shows a dynamic time sense:

Well...I think I am. I try hard to be. Umm...it's alright to fail, but as long as you fail trying, then it's not a real failure. And if you keep trying, then you can turn a failure inside out, into a success. The trick is, never to give up. You can always make some changes.

For others, like Mike, the dialogue is engaged in through reflection, and the process of actually talking to oneself, as if to an other:

Yeah, of course at times over the sixteen years, thoughts of suicide come into yer mind. And sometimes they just won't go away, you know? I'd talk to meself, 'Come on now Mike, this won't do. Make yourself busy, man, read a book, and don't think this stuff.'

As he recounts this and similar crises, Mike puts his head in both hands, and then slaps his forehead, and vividly conveys the image of a man trying to talk himself out of a course of action.   Later, he says his worst suicidal thoughts came when he was remanded on a rape charge whilst out on license following his life sentence. He says that the thoughts were provoked by the nature of the alleged charge (for which he was acquitted), and would not have occurred had he been pulled in for something less nasty, such as alleged theft. The thoughts lasted for four days, and he held a razor to his wrist and stared at it for a very long time. Again, he reports a dialogue in which he talked himself round, reminding himself of his partner, his daughters, and his self-development during his life sentence. Again, the dialogue is re-enacted with the same body language, so that although he is recounting it cheerfully and informatively, the full flavour of the self in struggle with itself is conveyed.

Bill, five months into a life sentence, is another inmate who engages in dialogue with himself, and he describes it as occurring in the long bang-up when he reads, plays games and music and chats to his cellmate. Underlying all this is a process of reflection about personal change:

> I think I'm thinking during all of this time, thinking about what's to come, and what me next prison will be like. It's not about when I come out, that's too far off. I think I'm changing, I was reckless and full of fun before all this, now I'd say I'm becoming more patient and more reliant on meself. I think it's change for the good, it depends on how you do it. It's up to you, how you want to change. I've just chosen that way. I knew I was going to be sentenced, never any doubt, so I thought I'd make the best of it.

Making the best of it means, for Bill, acceptance of place. With this vital stage under his belt, he is open dialogically to negotiation and change, and the changes can assume a momentum of their own:

> It does surprise me that I'm coping a bit better than I thought I would. It's just something I'm going to have to do.

Being presented with choices can prove more difficult than if there were none, and yet it is the coping with choices which provokes more change and development:

> Having the 23 hour bang-up (on 'A' Wing) in some ways was better, for getting on with the thinking. Sometimes you want to be banged up, and get on with it. Then there's other times you don't want to be banged up. But you just have to take it how it comes. Here (on 'C' Wing) you got the choice - you can either bang yourself up or be out. It can be harder, having the choice.

This issue of choice, referred to by Bill, is an important dimension in the tellings of 'coping' prisoners. It was evident that when coping tellers were engaging in the processes of adjustment, they looked for ways in which they could exercise autonomy, and these went further than the small yet meaningful acts such as saving a boiled egg for later consumption (Hal, ambivalently 'coping', Medical Centre). For the dialogic self, such as Gerry, a less static and richer process of adjustment has evolved, in which the arenas of autonomy are significantly to do with aspects of the self integrating itself in something ongoing:

> It's just a case of trying to get through. My mind's always active. I'm always picking up things from the paper, cutting them out, you know, and stuff like that. It's just a case of trying to get through: you set goals. Will I get a shower today? - the little things of life. You set a goal, and that keeps you going until the next day. So I try to read a newspaper everyday, and I listen to the radio every night as well.

> But I learned from my last sentence that you had to do these sorts of thing to survive. And the whole reality is, that you've got to do your sentence. It's not something you can run away from: it's not like life outside where you can run away. You're stuck, you're in it.

Like the presentational tellers, Gerry uses repetition a lot in his narrative. But, in the extract above, Gerry's repetitions disclose (i) acceptance of the here and now of prison ('you've got to do your sentence') and (ii) orientation toward movement and future time (e.g. as in the setting of goals). Gerry speaks from inside a story, but he is not sealed inside it in a static way. Movement and contingency are implicit, and his story of himself is subtle and non-rigid. He is, for instance, aware that 'coping' is an ongoing and fluid process:

> Some people have stronger minds than others. Just as some people are physically stronger than others. And it's how you cope with it in your mind that determines how you get through your sentence. But, you know, it's actually *learning* (his emphasis) to cope with it in your mind, it's not automatic that you do or you don't and there's an end of it.

The narratives of Gerry, George, Mike and Bill tell of the dialogic self, a self that suffers, but is fluid enough to be open to learning and change. The stages of coping which Gerry describes are crucial ones: the acceptance stage is the stage at which many inmates get stuck, and from that position they proceed to express a purely presentational self story. But the dialogic self grapples with the reality of a place that seizes time, makes sense of this predicament, and, settling down into present time, is able to turn expectantly toward the future. It is worth stressing that one of these inmates, George, is serving a life sentence. In terms of Gerry's stages, George has moved through the first and second stages, learning to accept the time/place characteristics of prison, and looking around him to see what resources there are to help him, including the valuable help of others in the community of lifers. Making his cell into a kind of home is an example of Gerry's third stage of knowledge. When I ask George if he has any plans for the future, aware that this could be considered a savagely ironic question for a lifer, his face lights up and he replies in an open and frank way:

> Yes, I've got a few plans. A lot of it depends on availability, I suppose. I've got some ideas and intentions but I can't do anything in the short-term. I'll have to see how things develop. I'd like to get involved in music - I was a sound recordist till I came here.

Individual narratives do exemplify the stages of individual coping of which Gerry speaks, but when the body of narrative from dialogic selves is considered, it can be seen that these narratives additionally exhibit different levels of time consciousness (Ricoeur 1984), ranging from the narrowness of 'within-time' to 'deep temporality'.

The body of data echoes Ricoeur's view that narrative is not some dry, coded vehicle on which explanation rides. On the contrary, it is a symbolic discursive form which symbolises events, making judgements about their status for the narrator, and telling the narrator what sort of a person he is. The presentational self can manage the ordinary representations of 'within time', and even achieve a told story of self which has a shallow or limited sense of place and personal timeness. As such, this self can, for the present, cope with varying degrees of unease.

The waiting teller can also handle 'within time' but with a sense of place and personal timeness that are essentially passive and non-innovative. Neither the presentational nor the waiting teller can achieve any authentic synthesis with representations of past and future, which would permit of the change and development that is so necessary in all lives, and so hard to achieve in lives disrupted by the prison experience. The presentational and waiting tellers do not achieve a stable or easily sustained form of coping, and with the absence of the necessary stakes of a properly integrated sense of place and personal timeness, there is always the risk that some event, or the painful absence of any significant event, may precipitate them into suicidal behaviour.

The dialogic self, however, can turn to the past and recover it in terms of personal historicality in a way that achieves a connecting thread with what is going on in the present. Despite the prison experience being productive of a grim view of future time, the dialogic teller is able to consider the future, and make representations of it to himself. In a highly demanding environment, at an extraordinarily difficult time in the life cycle, the dialogic self can manage the most complex representations of time consciousness, which attempt to grasp at the unity of past, present and future in a lived and sustaining unity of deep and complex temporality.

Presentational tellers, such as Hal, would sometimes boast about their suicidal behaviour, as if it were a behavioural item to be admired or envied. It is perhaps partly because of this practice that it is commonly believed amongst staff, and often reiterated, that the inmate who constantly talks about it will never do it. On the back of this assumption rides another: that the really 'serious' suicide will not speak about it. Such assumptions can act as straitjackets and are notoriously unhelpful. Nevertheless, it is true that some prisoners with deep-rooted suicidal feelings find it very difficult to speak of their suicidal feelings, which often appear to form part of a secret self.

The word 'secret', first used in the fifteenth century, comes from the Latin word meaning to separate or to divide, and Levy (1976) points out that its original usage dealt with the sifting and separating of grain, the edible from the non-edible. This suggests a parallel: the edible, which is expressive or bearable, is separated from the inedible, which is inexpressible or unbearable. What prisoners divulge in relation to their secret selves is the bearable and expressible: what they still hang onto and do not as yet divulge is inexpressible, unbearable, non-edible. The listener who is open to what is divulged cannot help but be aware that many secrets remain unexpressed, awaiting a listener who may never come along. The secrets that are expressed remain provisional. What is said may go some way toward constructing another layer of selfness for the teller, or another level of knowledge about selfness.

In this research, I heard a lot of secrets, in that inmates told me repeatedly that they had told me things they had never previously told anybody. Many of these things were often imbued with humiliation, shame and fear. But, importantly, in many cases, because they had not spoken these things out loud previously, they had never heard them spoken. Such things had been known, and carried within the self, but, because never heard, kept 'secret' even sometimes from themselves. Once spoken, such things would be added to other self-knowledge, but there would still remain further aspects of the secret self, as yet unspoken and carried around as a weight.

So, perhaps one of the most enduring characteristics of self is uncertainty and unknowability, because however much one comes to know oneself, and conveys oneself to others, one is never sure about how much more there is, and what of it could be capable of expression. Much of the self lies beyond words. It is only of the self in place, and the self in time, that the tellers can speak. In prison, the uncertainty and unknowability are experienced paradoxically in a situation where there are infinite vistas of time spent only with self. If the dialogue cannot begin, in such a place and at such a time, then the outlook, in terms of change and development, looks bleak.

Conclusion

These tellers exemplify different moments in their relationship with the prison time-place. They are not fixed types: nor are these kinds of interaction exhaustive or exclusive. For, within whatever limits are chosen, rising out of human potentialities, a panorama of types confront us (Wright Mills 1959). The danger of 'typing' human responses is sufficiently well-known to justify confining my analysis to what are, after all, not human types as reified categories, but stages of telling.

In a sense, we all spend our lives developing successive selves, and our coherence and identity as a person involve time in at least three ways (Elster 1986). On one level, we cease to be coherent people if our time sense lacks integration or is disintegrated by profound change. On a second level, however, we sometimes have to change our attitude toward everyday time. On a third level, we can experience the forcible violation of our internally nested system of memories and anticipation. The anticipation of future time that used to be present is destroyed, and therefore the bearer of memories must enter into a different relationship with those memories (Elster 1986).

In prison, these ways of involvement with time are put under severe stress and are productive of deeply felt responses. They are interwoven with the crisis in place identity induced by the prison, and the combination is productive of changes in the way in which the tellers experience their inner selves.

Nevertheless, these changes are not fixed or inevitable. What tellers experience is contingent. The potential exists for each and every prisoner to remain fixed at a particular stage of telling, or to move to another. Nevertheless, it is likely that tellers of the Waiting type will remain fundamentally fixed, for their lifelong institutionalisation may not have provided them with the inner resources ever to move on. It is impossible to specify in detail the particular spurs to contingent movement for individual prisoners, for much of this remains hidden in the dark recesses of the unconscious, where, for many, much dark material from early trauma casts its long shadow. In the next chapter, two prisoners who have accomplished dramatic inner change try to identify what the spurs to change were for them.

References

Dilthey, W. (1976), *Selected Writings*, translated by H. P. Rickmann, Cambridge University Press, Cambridge.
Elster, J. (1986), *The Multiple Self*, Cambridge University Press, Cambridge.
Foucault, M. (1979), *The History of Sexuality: An Introduction*, Allen Lane, London.
Goffman, E. (1959), *The Presentation of Self in Everyday Life*, Doubleday, New York.
Levy, A. (1976), 'Evaluation Etymologique et Semantique du Mot Secret', *Nouvelle Revue de Psychanalyse*, vol. 14, pp. 117-130.
Liebling, H. (1992), *Suicides in Prison*, Routledge, London.
Mead, G.H. (1934a), *Mind, Self and Society*, Chicago University Press, Chicago.
Mead, G.H. (1934b), *On Social Psychology*, Chicago University Press, Chicago.
Ricoeur, P. (1984), *Time and Narrative*, Vol. 1, translated by K. McLaughlin and D. Pellaner, Chicago University Press, Chicago.
Rose, N. (1989), *Governing the Soul: The Shaping of the Private Self*, Routledge, London.
Wright Mills, C. (1959), *The Sociological Imagination*, Oxford University Press, New York.
Young, K. (1989), 'Narrative Embodiments: Enclaves of the Self in the Realm of Medicine' in J. Shotter and K.J. Gergen (eds), *Texts of Identity*, Sage, London.

7 Same Time, Same Place, Changing Self

Les

> I wanted to die: that's all I wanted to do, just die. What happened was, I came in and for about 4 days I was on the induction unit, and then I got moved to A wing for about a couple of hours, and I just...for the first 4 days I was numb, I didn't really feel anything, and all of a sudden it just come on that I didn't want to do this no more, I couldn't cope with it no more. I couldn't handle the fact that I was away from the family, and I didn't want to go through it no more.

(How did you cope generally in the hospital here?)

> There's always someone in the hospital, always someone in the box there, and if you get low you can always go and talk. They'll always talk to you, and sit and listen. So I did find that helped. The fact that I could always talk to someone when I was feeling down. Plus the fact that I could get on the phone: it seemed that the only thing that could calm me down was to talk to me wife, and there's the phone in the ward so I could talk to her and she could calm me down.

(Did you talk to the other inmates on the ward?)

> Well I did, but I didn't really want nothing to do with them, because they all had their problems and every time you started talking to them they all started reeling off their problems, and it was adding to mine. It was adding to the situation I was in, so all I wanted to do really was to be left on my own.

> I felt suicidal. I felt that I wanted to kill myself, and yet I didn't want to. Basically every time that I was saying to someone that I wanted to kill myself, to stop myself I could talk and get it out of my system. And no, I

185

didn't find it difficult at all (to approach the staff in the box); it helped me. It's what I needed to do.

The feeling of numbness and not feeling anything at all lasted about four days. And then the feeling that I wanted to die, I wanted to kill myself, and all this, I'd say it must all in all have been about three and a half months that I felt like that. I just couldn't get my bearings, it was like I was falling off a cliff. It's only recently, the last month and a half that I've actually not wanted to. I still get depression, I still get down days, but I phone up my wife, I've got friends here, they all help out. It's still hard, I still don't want to do the time, but I've got no choice.

Education's helped a lot: I mean, I'm so busy now, I'm doing a computer course, City and Guilds, an Accountancy course, which I get so much homework for to do in my cell that it kills the time in the cell. So I'm making good use of the time, but I'm not doing it, because, like, it's hard to explain like, I'm not doing it just for the fact that I'm furthering my education. I'm doing it for the fact that I'm killing my time. Although it's helping me in the long run, it's also me getting a hold of my time, so I don't get time to think, I don't get time to sit there and mope around and think. But it does sweep over me from time to time and will do right until the time I get out, I should imagine. But I've just got to learn to control it. If I'm out on association and I feel like that, I just go and talk to someone. Not talk about the problem but just go and have a laugh, and try and get over it.

There's always someone here (on B. Wing) if I wanted to, but I feel I don't need to, now, you know what I mean? I mean, I feel that I'm on top of it now and I can cope with it and I can deal with it on my own the way I feel best to.

(Have you ever spoken to a Listener?)

Yes I spoke to one for a while.

(Did you cut yourself at all when you felt suicidal?)

I did try to, once, over on the hospital. Because I couldn't get a razor nor nothing, I punched one of the walls in the bathroom and toilet, and broke one of the tiles and tried to cut myself with the tiles, but it wouldn't cut. It's like what I say, I didn't want to kill myself, I didn't want to die, but I felt that I had no control over the situation, and the feelings were that I had to, I must do it. It's hard to explain, cos. I've never felt like it before, and I never want to feel like it again. The feeling was that I wasn't good enough for my wife anymore, I'd let her down, I'd let my daughter down, basically that I was no good for anybody, that I was no good for...that I was no good. And what's the point of going on if you're no good for anybody?

I was always in control of my life, and then all of a sudden I had no control over it. Everything was taken away from me: I couldn't do nothing unless I asked, basically. It was things like that, you know what I mean? I felt totally useless.

(What sort of person were you before you came in?)

Very strong-minded, very independent. Just that.

(What sort of things did you look forward to on an everyday basis?)

Coming home. Coming home to my wife. I used to look forward to coming home from work. I used to look forward to the weekend, when we could go out, and like take Emma out and have a good time. And then when this happened I had nothing else to look forward to anymore. Two years is a long time.

(When you look in the mirror now, do you see a very different person?)

Now, yes. I've just done a thinking skills course. So it's changed the way I think and that, the way I feel. And yeah, I'd say yeah I have changed. When I was on the out before, I'd say I was very selfish. If I wanted it, I'd get it, no matter what, you know what I mean? If there was anything I wanted, no matter what it took, I'd get it. And it didn't matter who I trod on or who I hurt to get it. Now, I'd say that was wrong and I'm a much better person. I don't get angry anymore, I like...I look at a situation before I think about it and start acting on it. After I've thought all the options through, then I do something. And it just seems to be better that way, no-one seems to get hurt or nothing.

(Will you take anything with you when you leave, from the thinking skills course?)

If you'd of asked me that two weeks ago, I'd of said no. But I had a few problems with me Nan and me wife and that, on the phone, yeah? And normally I would just of blown up and gone into one, and I've thought about it and handled it properly. I would say it does work, and I'd say to anyone going on it, stick with it.

(So you're finding things out about yourself?)

Yeah I am. But I'd rather of found out about them in another way. Yeah, you find things out about yourself: you actually spend more time with yourself than you do anyone else, so you learn things.

(In fact you're realising that you're a deeper person than you thought you were?)

Yeah, I'd say that. But it's took me a long time to realise it. And if it wasn't for the fact that, like I say, if it wasn't for my wife, I wouldn't realise it, cos. I wouldn't be here now. It was only through her. If I'd of stayed in the hospital, I'd never of got better. I'd of never got over it. And I know that. It was only through Sue phoned the prison up and spoke to the B. Wing Governor, and he come and got me and brought me over here. Now at the time, I must admit I was nervous about coming over here, I didn't want to leave the hospital, I had all the help I needed at the hospital, and I thought I ain't going to be able to cope with coming over here, you know what I mean. Single bang-up and all that, on me own. All the time on me own. And it was only a few weeks after I got over here that I realised that, yeah, I can get on with it here, I can get over it here.

In the hospital, how can I put it, there was always somebody there. And I was getting used to the idea of that person's always going to be here. That person...that person can now think for me. I didn't think for myself, I didn't think about nothing. I was just like...in limbo. Like part of the machinery, and somebody else was controlling the machinery, and they were controlling me. And I was going down and down, and worse and worse. And you were seeing people come in there, and trying to kill theirself all the time and it looked so easy. And Sue realised this and phoned up the prison and said, Look something's wrong, and it's not right and all this. And Mr. M... come over, and brought me over here.

I weren't ready for over here, I don't think, or at the time I didn't. I wasn't afraid: it was worse than fear in a way, cos. it was like I'm going to have to start doing for myself again, I'm going to have to start thinking for myself again, I'm going to have to live. And it was like trying to reverse my whole system. D'you understand? It's really hard to explain how I was feeling, but I knew...well I think I know that if I'd stayed on the hospital much longer then I would have killed myself.

On the hospital I surrendered all control over to somebody else. Perhaps you don't have to but I did. That's what I done. I surrendered everything over to someone else, because they were doing all my thinking for me, they were telling me what I've got to eat, when I've got to sleep, when I've got to get up, what to do all day, you know what I mean? It was...there was no thinking at all, it was just like the brain stopped. My brain was dead, and my body wanted to follow it.

(And how did you cope with that first 8 to 8 bang-up on B Wing?)

Well when I was first brought over I was in the ins-and-outs, so I was banged up from 5 in the evening till 8 the next morning, and to be honest with you, it gave me time to sit and think. And I tried to pull myself out of it then. I was on my own. I had no choice. If I wanted a drink, I had to get up and get a drink. I had to decide whether I wanted it or not. The only think I didn't like was that I couldn't get on the phone. That was the thing that I couldn't get on with, not being on the phone. In a way I think it did me good to be on my own for a few days and few nights. Then they moved someone in with me for a few weeks, then I got a job in the kitchen, then I went up on me own to a single cell. Everything's just been getting better and better since then.

The other thing that's helped me is that I started going to church. I've started finding religion and that, yeah. I used to be an atheist, I never used to believe. And the person I was banged up with used to go to church every Sunday. And there was a few Irish people in here I was talking to, and they're right religious. And I got talking to them, like, and then I asked to see Brother Philip. And I said to him, if you want me to believe, then you've got to prove to me, or convince me. So he said to me, come to Church, and I went to classes as well on a Thursday, and, yeah, you know what I mean, like, now I'm ...if I get bored or lonely, I just read the Bible.

(Will that carry on when you leave?)

Yes, most definitely. When I get out, because we just got married in a registry office, we're going to get our marriage blessed in church. And I've never been baptised, so I'll get baptised. Get all that sorted.

(Going back to this loss of control that you experienced in the hospital, do you think anything can be done about it?)

No, short of giving everyone a bunch of keys. I mean you're still in prison, whether you're in the hospital, in a dorm or in a cell. You've just got to learn to accept it really, and get on with it. A lot of the people I met when I was on the hospital were only there to ride their bird, cos. it was easier. That's what I found. And it seemed to be them, like the people that was just riding their bird that was being given medication, all the help they asked for. And there was me - this is the way I saw it when I was on there - I was really in need of help. I really wanted help and I didn't want to feel the way I was feeling. I just wanted help. And I was getting nothing. And it just seemed totally unfair to me, to be honest with you. But now, I'm glad that I didn't get any medication, because now I'd probably be dependent on medication and I don't want that. On the outside, I won't even take a headache tablet.

This teller is 27 and is serving a two year sentence. He has completed five months since conviction, the majority of it on 'B' Wing, where I interviewed him, after a short spell in the hospital and some time at another prison. He did not serve any remand time in prison, has never been in prison before, and has never had any mental health problems. He has been married for seven years and has one daughter. His account has many echoes and similarities with other accounts from non-coping tellers, but unlike them Les has turned some kind of corner and is on the way back up. He has put his suicidal behaviour behind him and made what he feels are real and lasting internal changes. The story is of a dialogic self, who was in utter despair, but, using what resources there were on offer, has engaged in reflexive care and moved to a qualitatively different experience of self.

His account demonstrates the validity of Gerry's stage theory about the process of coping with prison, and the necessity of moving through the loss stage into the enquiry stage, and finally through to the knowledge stage. Les's loss stage was typical of many prisoners, in that it consisted of two significant parts. The first part consisted of a numbness and total absence of feeling. There quickly followed a period of about three and a half months when he was seriously suicidal. He felt that he was falling, and over a period of time going down, and down, and down.

His place setting in the medical centre was significant in a number of respects. It exaggerated the loss of control over his own life which he experienced upon coming into prison, and produced profound feelings of dependency. He stopped thinking and acting for himself, and got into a situation where he was afraid to leave the hospital, although he experienced himself as deteriorating there. It was only through the combined intervention of his wife and the 'B' Wing staff that he was rescued from the hospital, and, once on 'B' Wing, he was able to embark more actively on adjustment to prison, with the support provided there. He describes himself as 'me getting a hold of my time'.

Nevertheless, Les was able to use one particular resource in the medical centre to his advantage. Whenever he felt suicidal, he approached the staff behind the window, and found them always willing to talk and listen. This contrasts strongly with Marty's experience of a precious confidence being broadcast to the whole ward as ribald humour.

This unevenness in response may be related to staff perceptions about deservedness. Even swamped by grief, Les would strike prison staff as 'one of them' - a young, white, talkative and articulate Londoner presenting a mixture of deference and spirit. Marty, on the other hand, was of mixed race, very diffident, inarticulate and self-effacing. Such presentations of self (Goffman 1959) are often a crucial factor in informal contact where participants can respond with reference to consciously or unconsciously held beliefs. The problem of differential responses to 'vulnerable' prisoners has largely been recognised as one of prisoner interaction. 'Vulnerable' prisoners are most likely to be threatened or abused by other prisoners because of their offence or behaviour (McGurk 1996). But the place characteristics of prison encourage staff also to adopt differential responses on the basis of deservedness.

The initiative that got him moved to 'B' Wing was out of the ordinary: it involved a wife who, like Les, was young, determined, bright and articulate. The Prison Service theoretically welcomes such initiatives, and has a commitment to shared care. In practice, however, it is difficult to make such initiatives happen. Many inmates have no significant others on the outside who are in a position to stimulate or participate in such ideals of shared care.

Les made a significant remark in relation to his suicidal feelings. 'It's still hard, I still don't want to do the time, but I've got no choice'. Here, he is endorsing Gerry's view, that much of the pain and grief at the loss stage arises from a non-acceptance of the time and place of prison. Until this acceptance is grasped, inmates cannot move forward and begin dialogically to engage with the process of coping. Significantly, Les was not able to do this acceptance work in the hospital: it was only on the wing that he achieved this:

> And it was only a few weeks after I got over here that I realised that, yeah, I can get on with it here, I can get over it here. I can survive this.

Tel

I went as far as thinking through how to do it, to hang meself. That seemed to me something that I was quite capable of doing. I didn't make the rope: I was contemplating ripping the sheet up and twisting several strands so that it would be strong enough. And I found out a place where I could climb up, and stuff like that. That was one night, where I was up very late, and I really did come close to it. I'd like to say to you that, when you are in that mode of thinking of just topping yourself, it's a very hazy kind of thing. I'd liken it possibly...the other experience near to that is perhaps when you are out of your mind on drugs. You know, things are just hazy, and it's not quite what we normally perceive as reality, anyway.

I came real close to it one night, and I think it was the thought of me family that finally stopped me doing it. There was a lot of emotion the early hours of the morning: I was in tears, and eventually fell asleep.

The next morning I actually got a razor to shave with, and that was my intention. I didn't think of it. The night before was kind of hazy, I hadn't been awake that long, it was maybe fading in and out of my memory, but then there was the routine of breakfast being served, and that was probably taking me concentration away from it, and after breakfast I asked for a razor to shave, and actually used it to shave.

I...I've talked about this a few times before, and the best thing is it's like that unreal sort of thing again, it's like your automatic pilot. You didn't really think about it, it's like one minute I was shaving and the next minute I was sat on the bed and I found out that I'd broken the razor open and cut me wrists. And I think...you know, that wasn't a suicide attempt, it was just a cry for help. Because I'd been bottling a lot of things up at that time, thinking that there wasn't anybody that could understand and that I could speak to about this. I think that when you are talking about your feelings and sensitive things, I've mentioned to you that in prison, you know, it's a little bit like the macho thing, boys don't cry and things like that, and you have to put this kind of tough exterior on all the time, and that is how it is in prison. Prisons are the kinds of places where showing feelings can be seen as weakness and can cause trouble and friction: it's not something that's done in prison: that's the general consensus.

Anyway, I realise that there are people you can talk to about this, now, but even so, I think that you have to have a certain amount of trust in somebody to share this, because, for example, you know, I'm a Listener. I think that is a good scheme. The confidentiality - that's tricky, I mean, it just could be that you pour your heart out to somebody on the Wing and it's the wrong person and it's all around the Wing, and you're ridiculed, which obviously would make the situation ten times worse, if not more. So I just was dealing with a lot of remorse, depression, missing my family, all the usual things, and I was bottling things up, and it came out that way, you know.

(Were you conscious of having low self-esteem then?)

Yes definitely. I don't know how to...yes I was conscious of it. There was self-hatred, because I'd been looking at what my life amounted to. Over the past ten years, I've served four prison sentences and two lots of remand. And it's sort of progressed from taking cannabis and then that progressed to taking the heroin habit, and theft progressed to burglary, and I was seeing a lot of the other side of it then, with drugs putting a veil up against the side of it, where I would see burglary and breaking into people's houses, whereas at the time you have your set of excuses which you use to justify this to yourself, whether it's that you're out of it on drugs, or that they are probably insured. But you take all this away, and you start feeling the things that you've done. Even though you've never seen it physically, you imagine about when that person arrives home and finds their house burgled, and they find out that their things, which they worked hard for, are missing. Obviously this causes them a lot of misery. So I was looking at this... although this was my life, it's not been all crime and drugs, over the past ten years. I have made attempts to straighten meself out, but I would say that they were half-hearted, although it isn't an easy thing sometimes. I was looking, just this need to look at meself, and that's what caused the low self-esteem.

The only thing I don't agree with is that a lot of people, although I can understand how this job could make people cynical and stuff like that... But I think some people adopt the attitude that, especially if you've been in once or twice before, that you'll never change, you'll never make anything of your life, you'll never amount to anything, you're a criminal and that's all you'll ever be. And I don't think that that is strictly true. As I do say, they do see a lot of people coming in and out time and time again, and it must be disheartening, especially if perhaps on a previous occasion they really tried to turn them around. And maybe the officer tries to help them and spends some time talking to them, and then hears...one of the commonest statements you hear is ' I'll never be back in', and then invariably they are back in.

And as I say that must be disheartening for the staff, but just to give up hope on somebody is...I really don't think that that is the way forward.

This sentence is a significant turning point for me. It's down to a lot of things. The only other time I was suicidal was on a sentence which was a wrongful conviction and I went three weeks without eating. It was a different motivation, from self-pity if you like, and this one is out of real remorse, self-disgust if you like and self-hatred. I've seen a lot more things a lot more clearly now, you know, mainly that there are no short-cuts and that there are some sort of universal laws in life. It's been said a lot of different ways, like 'what you sow you reap'. 'What goes around comes around' is how it's said in prison. And it's basically that if you do good actions, you get good reactions, but if you do bad action, you get bad reactions.

The thinking skills course helped me a lot. I did it last July. It taught me a lot of things about problem solving, and also about impulsive behaviour, about not thinking things through, and not thinking of the long-term consequences. I use it in more or less everyday ways, there's always an opportunity comes along where you can, say, take short-term benefits for immediate gratification. It's going to bring you a certain amount of pleasure in the short-term, but it's going to be more costly possibly in the long-term.

(Are you making plans now for your future?)

Yes. I'm aiming to go to a drug rehabilitation centre after release, and I see that as some sort of support, a chance to meet some people who have maybe had similar experiences, but want to do something about that and change their lives. I've now found that, you know, just as I said, doing something worthy and worthwhile, that may not be particularly well paid, is better than doing something well-paid that you don't get any satisfaction from. After the rehab., I'm thinking of doing voluntary work. But obviously I have to let time take its course, because different opportunities may arise on the rehab. There are things I want to work towards, I'm pencilling in some aims and goals.

From my work in prison, I am getting a sense of when people just want to talk. Sometimes...each situation is different, and you have to try and assess what's happening, and interact with people to show that you are really listening. But there are some things that are common to everybody, and we all want to feel a little bit better, a little bit more loved, a little bit more complete, a little bit more sense of meaning and purpose into our lives. So, I just feel that from the people I talk to in this, I'm getting a good idea, a kind of sixth sense, when to let people talk on and when to sit with people in silence for a while and just make them feel comfortable by telling them that they don't have to say anything, if they just want to sit and think things through. I say 'Take your time, we can just sit here in silence together'.

We then discuss how Listeners work on this Wing: approaches are informal, maybe through other inmates, or officers. They are considering having formal application forms. Tel agrees that this work has raised his self-esteem.

It took me a few months of going up and down, wanting that and then not wanting that. You make the decision for yourself, either to get on with it and top yourself or start building your life back up. You know I can remember times when I just never envisaged me getting out of prison, certainly not alive anyway. But now, as I say, I'm making plans. I do a little bit of writing, and I've had a few articles published. Pottery... I think the Listeners' involvement has been the most rewarding and maybe the most challenging, which is usually the case isn't it? What you get out of something is what you put into it. That's not a new feeling, more a forgotten feeling.

(Do you think about time passing, or just get on with tasks?)

Both, I think. You have to think about time passing, in that certain things are happening, different events in the near future, and you think about your release date. I find that that's inevitable, but you've got to keep it in perspective, that you're in prison, and, - I think this is a big thing - that you just accept it. This is where you are, you want to get out. If anybody had the chance they would rather not be here. But this is where you are, so what can you do about where you are right now to make the most of this situation?

I remember how it really is outside the gate. A lot of people, after quite some time, people remember all the good times outside and they fantasise about when I get out, it's all going to be great. I'm going to walk through them gates, into freedom and we're going to have a big party, and all my friends and family are going to be glad for me, and it's all going to be great. But then, you know, you forget about the bills there are to pay, and there's living to make, and family problems, and all the rest of things that everybody has to deal with. So I remind myself about that, rather than tending to forget about all the things that aren't easy.

I hadn't done much work before I came in. I was earning any money I got from crime. I was spending mostly on drugs.

(Do you do your time in weeks or months, or do you not think about it in units?)

Think you're always glad to see a new month. I think it depends on...I seem to...I've talked to a number of people and they seem to go through the same phases...they might be a bit restless for a couple of weeks, or just less energy, not quite as content as normally, and that period might drag a bit more. But I would say that generally you say that's another week and that's a little marker or milestone, but generally I probably mark it by the month. Towards the end of the month you think, there's another one nearly out of the way.

(And when you go, will you be a different person to the one that came in?)

Yes, certainly. Yes. Yes. Very different. But, you know, I think there are certain parts of your character that don't change as well. But it's channelling them towards fulfilling things, things that help people and help yourself. If you're honest with yourself, I think you'll be honest with other people.

(Do you think you will always have to struggle to keep yourself on the straight and narrow?)

Not so much now, to keep on the straight and narrow. I just think that I've not got the same outlook and the same attitude to life. I've got a different attitude and outlook to life in a lot of ways that I've never had before. I mean, saying that, I don't envisage that things are going to be easy out there and a criminal record is a disadvantage that is going to follow you through life. But it's not something that can allow you to defeat you. That would just be surrendering to that attitude I talked about before, and you'll never make anything of your life. If you tell yourself something enough times, that's what will happen. Whereas if you tell yourself, OK it's a disadvantage, it's a kind of handicap if you like, but I can still do something useful and make a contribution. And the longer the time goes by when you are living a decent, constructive and useful life, the criminal record just fades more into the background. As I say, it will always be there but it will be less significant.

I've done quite a lot of study of religions while I've been here. And that's another universal law. I think that promoting one religion over another can be quite divisive and you can see the effects all around, but I see that actions in this life may well have a bearing on what happens after you die. And that's not a central theme of me life, you know, that's just something...but I have my beliefs and I think I've built on them. And the other thing I've found, that while money and material things are relevant to our lives, the more fulfilling things are different, to do with contentment and happiness. And what adds to contentment is doing something useful and constructive with your time.

I've also...through opening up, through realising that it's not only possible but important to speak about your feelings, and as I say, you don't pour your heart out to someone you've just met. But you meet someone, you build up a bit of trust, and it's usually a two-way thing anyway. And you talk maybe about things you're finding difficult, about anything you may feel apprehensive about, not sure about, things that you are not sure about whether you are supposed to know, just being able to speak about your feelings and be a little bit more open. And trusting people. And sometimes we make bad choices, and sometimes we have good intentions that don't come to pass, but I know that the contentment comes from doing something worthwhile and it doesn't necessarily have to involve money or drugs, which were the things I've used in the past mainly as blinkers to hide things that I don't like about my life or the way it's going. If you get stoned, you forget about your problems temporarily, but they don't go away, you just forget about them for a while, and when you come down, the problems are still there plus the effects of the drugs wearing off.

(What about the negative aspects of prison? Do they leave a lasting mark?)

I think you've got to let a lot of things go. I think that some things in life, even when we're right about something, and it might be clear to everyone so it's not just you thinking that, unless you are trying to point out things to that person, and if you are doing so in order to help that person make a change, that's in order. But if you're only pointing them out to be self-righteous, even if everyone agrees things are wrong, it doesn't always serve a useful purpose. There are things that happen in prison, and nobody could justify them, certain things. I could give examples...things that are quite obviously wrong. And they happen. But they happen also in life, you know. And you have to let them go, use patience and forgiveness: sometimes people just get caught in their anger.

I think that a lot of people do get released from prison feeling bitter and angry about the way that they were treated, and that may have served some purpose, in the sense of retribution and in the case of keeping the public safe from harm for that amount of time. But what about when you are out again? If you are worse than when you went in, you know, that to me, is an injustice but not one that has an easy answer. And, as with everything, there are thin dividing lines between where you draw the line between giving someone adequate kind of therapy, and should that therapy be able to be enjoyed? I just think that a lot of people, not just young people but mostly young people, if they are starting to fall into the cycle of recidivist behaviour, if you can catch them early, by helping them to help themselves to become better people and people with a goal and an aim of making something of their lives, if you catch them then, in the long run it will be a lot cheaper. All the court cases, all the sentences that are probably going to happen to them in the coming years would be saved. It would have to be done in Centres, and of course you get an outcry in the press if it appears too lavish, but you have to try these things out and ask - is a year of that less costly than a lifetime of offending? And what about the cost in misery, you can't put a price on that, you know. And that, in some ways, is more important. And, I speak as someone who is as guilty as anyone, sometimes the material issue is put before the feeling or the person.

(Has there been a specially significant person, in this change of yours?)

I wouldn't put it down to one particular person. I would say that some people are more significant than others in helping me change. But the other thing is that I always had an interest in mind-quietening, and I found that gave me more of an insight into myself, and this is when ...so long as your mind is full of excuses and this is what you are backing up and propping up your actions with, well, people can tell you your life isn't worth a row of beans all day long, and you are not listening, so it's water off a duck's back. But once you see that for yourself, it's different. Even if you have always known it deep down, you have got yourself so well trained to cover it up, and something may keep touching on it, but you instantly bury it. I went on a long time like that, and maybe some people go on a lot longer, maybe all their life. So I would say it was a combination of things, some people just come to a certain time in life when they need to take stock. I've heard a few people say, officers and other people, a Chaplain and a probation officer, that when people offend from a fairly young age, they seem to take stock in their thirties. A combination of a few things.

(What changes would you make in the prison regime if you could?

(Laughs for the first time). I'd have everybody walk round with one of these on (taps his Listener badge). There's always room for progress and improvement. Especially in big institutions of all kinds. We're never going to have a perfect system, and people are fallible by nature, and we all make mistakes. I think the type of person that becomes a prison officer seems to be changing, from not quite so much ex-Forces. And in the time that I've been coming to prisoner over the past ten years, I have seen a lot of changes in prisons. Yes. In attitudes. The hostility and the negativity still exists, in the Us and Them thing between prisoners and officers, but it has lessened, which is a good thing. I still think that it needs a lot of work doing on it, and it's a lot worse in some institutions than in others. In some prisons, the prison staff and prisoners speak minimum. And to an extent, some people are like that in here. They speak when it's necessary to ask for an Application, and there's no general conversation. I'm not putting it on anybody, I think it's up to them both to find common ground. There are different roles in life and people can be seen as the kind of people that don't usually mix. But if people are willing to sit down and talk, they can find common ground. It might be the same football team, that can be quite a good thing to bring some people together. And you just feel that tension ease. OK, they still have a job to do, but it's not personal.

At the time of this interview, Tel is 36 and serving four years for drugs offences. He spent some time on remand at another prison. He comes from a loving home, with parents who always worked. He lived in a respectable working class area and never truanted from school. He never took drugs as a youngster. After leaving school, he became a despatch rider, buying his own bike through hire purchase. Later he trained as a typesetter and led a steady and relatively prosperous life. It was following redundancy, during a period of casual work, that he experimented with drugs and mixed with the wrong crowd. This life-style eventually led to a series of convictions for drugs offences.

He describes himself at the time of his trial as pretty mixed-up, and was examined by doctors and psychiatrists. They did not consider him to be suffering from a classifiable mental condition. He says at this time there was an outside influence of whom he took notice for a while, suggesting that it would be in his interests to feign mental illness. After a while he decided against that, and after conviction he was feeling a lot of remorse for what he had done, and was seeing a Samaritan.

There are a number of significant points in Tel's narrative. Throughout, he endorses the value of talk, but stresses that the bestowal of trust on others is a precarious action. He reiterates what so many prisoners stated, that the dominant culture encourages a tough and 'macho' exterior, and this militates against the display of feelings and sensitivity toward others. He illustrates how the nature of the prison place, combined with feelings of guilt and remorse, contributes to lowered self-esteem. He shows a remarkable tolerance toward the injustices of prison life, emphasising that such things happen in civil life also, and sometimes the mature thing is just to let these things go, rather than hold on to bitterness and resentment.

These points illustrate Tel's growing awareness of the nature of the prison place, its limitations and its possibilities. This awareness is part of the achievement of a sense of place, just as much as the inmate who makes his cell into an imitation of home. He has passed into the third stage of which Gerry spoke - trying to make the system work for him and his developing sense of self. He is taking all the opportunities on offer that can help him gain new skills, and revive forgotten skills and feelings. He emphasises the value of talk and interaction to arrest the process of pain and confusion which results from confinement in the prison place.

Tel's narrative crystallises what so many other prisoners disclosed, in terms of the difficulties of prison, but in his case it does so in the context of personal development and the over-coming of suicidal behaviour. For Tel, it is as if he merely existed on the outside: in the prison place, through a long dialectical process of interaction with the environment, he comes to decide who he is and who he will become. Driven to extremity by finding himself in this place, he has engaged in subjective reflection, which he terms mind quietening. It is surely not too fanciful to liken this reflective work as a passion of inwardness (Kierkegaard 1962) through which he has become aware, in relation to his own life, of the essential significance of existence. He has turned away from suicide toward the future, and is resolved to make some congruence between his thinking and his existence. He has turned to tend his self-identity, and, in giving it some care, he finds new potential and capacities within himself.

Conclusion

These two tellers demonstrate the sheer hard work of overcoming suicidal frames of mind. In Les's case, it was a change of place setting that he feels saved him. On the wing, he is able to fill his time with work, classes, and association with others. He has defeated the enemy of time, and in the process he is educating himself, expressing his social self, discovering a spiritual self, and changing certain key personal characteristics. His remark, 'you actually spend more time with yourself than you do anyone else, so you learn things', shows that he is nurturing himself, as he would nurture a best friend, and this care of the self is resulting in change which he feels will be lastingly beneficial. Such change is only enabled by the place setting in which he fortunately finds himself, a setting where staff offer him opportunities at the same time as providing support. He has moved on from limbo, and the experience of falling without any bearings to anchor him. Through talk and the intervention of significant others, he has arrested this process of descent. Not only has he put his suicidal behaviour behind him, but he has moved into a qualitatively different experience of selfness.

For Tel, it is harder to pinpoint the catalyst for his change. He bottled things up inside himself until there was a crisis, and then he slowly realised the value of talking to others about his feelings. He dug deep into himself, and interacted with certain aspects of the prison place in a determinedly positive way. The long overnight bang-up, for instance, gave him the opportunity to meditate. He found ways to drag his low self-esteem up, and mobilise his self-respect.

It would be wrong to draw the message from Tel's narrative that, given the requisite personal strength and resourcefulness, any prisoner can overcome suicidal behaviour and learn how to adapt to prison as a time-place. What these two triumphant narratives show, however, is that there is a relationship between personal identity and context (Kroger 1993), and in a variety of sometimes obvious, sometimes innovative and subtle ways, individuals can create their own personal development even in highly constrained settings. Les and Tel have resolved crises: each narrative expresses experience of crises overcome, of continuity and development of identity, and in each case, the setting has been used in the service of this trajectory. The act of telling means further confirmation to themselves of their success: in telling it to me, each heard it told aloud, thus aiding the next stage of the journey.

The psychiatric/pathology model (see Chapter One) as it is presently utilised in prison is too blunt to recognise the sophisticated dynamics of interaction between prisoner and place, and the contingent nature of adaptation to prison, exemplified by Les and Tel. The official categories of 'coping' and 'at risk' are not subtle enough to access the complex and broken trajectory of Les and Tel's journey from acute suffering and into a state of acceptance and self-development. The models of interactive change which prisoners themselves articulate should be utilised as a resource in suicide awareness and prevention, so that what Les and Tel learnt can be communicated to others in dire need.

References

Goffman, E. (1959), *Presentation of Self in Everyday Life*, Doubleday, New York.

Kierkegaard, S. (1962), *Philosophical Fragments or A Fragment of Philosophy*, Princeton University Press, Princeton.

Kroger, J. (1993), 'Identity and Context: How the Identity Statuses Choose Their Match' in R. Josselson and A. Lieblich, *The Narrative Study of Lives*, Sage, London.

McGurk, B. (1996), 'Experience and Perceptions of Integrated Regimes for Vulnerable and Non-Vulnerable Prisoners', *Home Office Research Bulletin no. 38*, HMSO, London.

8 Attention, Care and Talk

Introduction

Critiques of the prison as causative of recidivism, of splitting families and pushing them into poverty, and of stigmatising and disqualifying individuals from participation in society, have been cogently voiced for 170 years. There is a substantial literature on the prison which, using a historical perspective, shows that the institution can better be understood with reference to the analysis of political economy, social class, ideology and power, rather than to benevolent ideas of progress (Ignatieff 1978, Foucault 1979, Melossi and Pavarini 1981, Cohen 1985).

This perspective is entirely compatible with one that acknowledges the efforts made every day on the part of some staff working in the prison system to operate a system which is humane within its overall parameters of purpose. But it is these parameters of purpose, rather than the day-to-day ameliorating efforts of the best prison officers, which give the prison so much of its intensity of place identity.

The prison is a 'total institution' and a 'forcing house for changing persons' (Goffman 1961:22) which may indeed share some characteristics with the asylum, whilst remaining quite unlike it in important ways. Then, too, the prison has some resonance with the camp: in particular, its extreme place characteristics produce some of the psychological defences and the craving for autonomy of which Bettelheim spoke (1960:183). Many tellers, for instance, spoke of the emotional detachment they experience, from all that is left behind, and Sean (not now 'coping', medical centre) exemplified Bettelheim's (1960) findings in relation to ambiguous attitudes to power, whereby looking down upon other prisoners was an important psychological defence against his own fears.

And yet the prison is very definitely not a concentration camp, and the threat of disintegration of the self is not of the same order. Concepts which derive from the study of other institutions cannot be lifted from the historically specific place to which they are attached, and applied like an analytic blanket to the prison. The prison is not like any other place: it is itself, and that is enough. It has its own special identity, and that identity is largely obscured not only from public knowledge but also from the sensibilities of policy makers. Those who have experienced the prison, either as staff or as inmates, are especially well equipped to communicate the nature of the place, and analytic identifications of it through their eyes help those of us without such experience to understand it better.

Although we are now equipped, through historical studies and studies of comparative institutions, to understand the prison better than we used to be, this understanding does not enable us to re-design the institution with a reformulated blueprint. Despite the variety of types of prison, the prison as institution exists as a punitive monolith, heavily encumbered with the weight of its overall purposes, past policy and practice. It is only open to intervention and change through negotiation, and the remarks of this final chapter are made in the full awareness of how slow, limited and careful such change must be.

In the context of rising prison numbers and reducing budgets, staff morale has deteriorated in the last few years, and has resulted in sometimes elementary security lapses (Woodcock 1994, Learmont 1995). In this climate, staff find it difficult to resist protecting themselves through the adoption of cynical attitudes toward the value and goals of innovations in prisoner management. Nevertheless, because of the seriousness of the problem of suicidal behaviour in prison, innovation and sustained development are urgently required, and attention to the narratives of tellers must inform that process.

The special place identity of each individual prison, to which every teller attests, is first of all structured by the purposes of the institution of prison, and comes about because, through a historical scientifico-legal complex (Foucault 1979) it has been granted the power to punish. To punish is to establish a state of artificial danger, for punishment is organised hurt (Hentig 1937). It is in and through the law that punishment finds its harshest form and most energetic expression; its application enters into every human relationship (Hentig 1937:1). The punishment principle imparts a sense of implicit shame over every human relationship in prison, and when men are condemned all their life to false relations with other men, they become false themselves (Kropotkin 1971:332).

Kropotkin was writing from personal experience in 19th century Russian and French prisons, at a time when the prison was coming of age in terms of the understanding that it was economic, efficient and rational to incarcerate and invigilate, rather than subject bodies to physical punishments (Foucault 1979). Such knowledge is integrally bound up with the exercise of power

(Foucault 1979), and the prison is one institution through which this power/knowledge relationship is expressed in exemplary form. Within the prison place, therefore, every human relationship is overshadowed by the institutionalised expression of this relationship and by the weight of historical practice, and the principle of punishment through incarceration and suffering is an implicit ingredient, whether manifest or latent, operating dialectically in every relationship and every encounter.

Relationships within prison do not operate passively: they require maintenance and attention. Attention must be paid to inmates, for they must be contained in security without disorder. The act of paying attention to someone or something is an act of intentionality. It involves setting aside the distraction of competing pre-occupations, in order to attend to the phenomenon in hand. The prime goal of security and order means that the care principle is secondary: to ignore an inmate sitting weeping could be considered justifiable: to ignore him attacking the bars on his cell with a file is not.

The overarching type of attention which is paid to inmates within prison is, because of the nature of the place, a punitive attention, for it must intend and will the continuing secure incarceration of inmates. The legitimacy for this punitive attention is afforded by the decisions of the court, whose legitimacy, in turn, derives from principles of retribution, deterrence, incapacitation and reparation, which are often invoked either singly or in various combinations to justify imprisonment, despite their sometimes uneasy fit.

Because it is a place to which individuals are sent as punishment, the principle of less eligibility or 'non-superiority', (that conditions inside prison should not be better than those prevailing outside) is an actuality, even if unvoiced, in every relationship and every encounter, and a significant marker in the act of punitive attention. In my research, staff were not my primary source of data, but it was impossible to ignore the fact that staff often voiced this principle, in a variety of ways, in relation to discrete aspects of prison life, such as the quality of meals. They would comment on the inappropriateness of giving people such as prisoners healthy and well-balanced meals, when others could not afford these. Such aspects would be discussed in isolation from the total experience of being in prison, and, if prisoners were perceived as having access to an isolated good, to which access on the outside might be more problematic, resentment was expressed. The principle of 'austerity in prisons' voiced so vehemently by Michael Howard as Home Secretary during the Thatcher administration of the 1990s provided ideological and populist affirmation of the 'less eligibility' principle.

The principle of less eligibility has historically always been significant in the development of penal institutions and issues of reform and change within them (Mannheim 1939). It is a measure of the nature of the punitive monolith that the weight of this principle acts as a drag on all attempts to make prisons more humane and more productive of change and development in inmates.

The highly regulated nature of the prison place exacerbates the capacity of punitive attention to produce real consequences in the innermost selves of inmates, and punitive attention provides the conditions of possibility for a wide variety of responses. The effects of punishment upon individual lives can never be absolutely categorised as 'positive' or 'negative', for many of the effects are so politically complex, so shifting and so unfixed within the lifetime of an individual, that any such categorisation would always be historically, socially, politically and individually specific. Such is the complexity of human responses to attention of any kind that such claims would always be built on the essential unpredictability and unknowability of the deepest wells of human behaviour, as well as on essentially contestable value judgements. The 'coping' prisoners themselves exemplify such contradiction, from the case of Len, who 'likes' prison because it is no worse than any other known setting, and Gerry, who does not like prison because he has experienced better places. For 'non-coping' prisoners such as Bud, the punitive attention is a massive case of overkill, which degrades him and fills him with terror, for 'if I'd got a non-custodial, those seven weeks on remand I'd have kept in my head for the rest of my life, so that I didn't do anything wrong, ever ever again' (Bud, not now 'coping', Medical Centre).

But it is precisely because the prison is a place of punitive attention, that it can be claimed, structurally and systematically, to be a machine for elimination (Foucault in Simon 1974). These effects of elimination of which Foucault speaks are not routinely and consciously practised by staff: they arise as an inevitable by-product of the nature of the prison place. Thus it is that inmates like Ramon (Induction, 'coping' now) say, in tones of wonder and surprise, that 'the staff are just doing their job, they just seem normal people'. Thus it is that Tim, (Induction, 'coping' now) having prepared himself for the worst, enumerates the shock of being admitted at the age of 50 for the very first time, the degradation at the loss of privacy, the claustrophobia of his cell, the lack of access to clean clothing or regular washing facilities, the emptiness of time, the worry of being confined with a stranger, and the nerve-wracking uncertainty about what is to come.

Nevertheless he can say openly 'the prison officials are fairly good, you know. If you ask them, they give you an answer'.

That the place has special characteristics is evidenced by the stresses suffered by the staff. In a study by Liebling and Krarup (1994), 90% of staff claimed that the experience of depression, anxiety or unreasonable levels of stress were common. 58% knew (an) officer(s) who had attempted or committed suicide.

The tellers in this study have related how prison crushes their deepest selves, producing anger, loneliness, boredom, guilt, apathy, and self-loathing. It is not the conscious actions of individuals that produce these responses, although on occasions they may contribute. It is the nature of the place, and of the punitive attention that is its *modus operandi* which effects this crushing of inner self.

How, then, can this punitive attention coexist with principles of care? How can the Woolf principles of security with care and justice be combined? For it is only if this synthesis is possible that a policy of suicide awareness and prevention can be actively pursued.

That such a synthesis is possible is due to the extraordinary ambiguities of prison. Structurally and systematically it is harsh and punitive, and yet within that framework, some staff strive to do their jobs with honour. As a place, many other ambiguities exist. It is 'closed' in the sense that full information about the prison population is hidden, and yet 'open' in that there is a constant traffic in, out and in again. Individuals 'disappear' in many senses from the community when they enter prison: for instance, they are almost universally absent from national health statistics (Levy 1997), and yet many of the same individuals repeatedly leave prison, re-enter the 'visible' community, only to return again. It is a place of both extraordinary drama and extreme immobility: keys clang, doors open and slam, people whistle, feet tramp, but when the prison locks down for an hour in the middle of the day, it is impossible for the outsider to move around, and, obliged to remain confined for that hour, she experiences some of the helpless immobility that prisoners feel 24 hours a day. Ambiguities over time are infinite: inmates complain of endless stretches of time, in which there is nothing to do, whilst the staff on wards in the medical centre are visibly stressed because there are insufficient staff to allow staff-inmate interaction and their time is almost wholly preoccupied by attending to the security and invigilation aspects of their jobs.

But the most striking ambiguity for the outsider is that there is so little deep talk, in a population of individuals who are, by their own admission, desperate for someone to talk to. Large quantities of human beings are confined together, and yet the culture and routines of the place militate against them engaging in talk, either with each other or with staff. From the way in which prisoners flooded me with talk, and staff either studiously ignored me and avoided even necessary talk about access and arrangements, or surreptitiously approached me with an urgent need to talk at length and in confidence, it was apparent that talk was both longed for and yet feared, as a subversive activity.

Talk in prison exists in the historical shadow of the silent prisons of the nineteenth century. In the huge prisons of the United States, the silence of up to a thousand men impressed observers in chilling ways. Everything passed in the most profound silence and the silence within those vast walls, which confined so many, was like that of death (Beaumont and Tocqueville 1833/1964). In our own culture, both the separate system and the silent system were devoted to the prevention of association between prisoners (Preface by Walker in Emery 1970). Even when, in 1900, as part of the Gladstone Committee's reforms, prisons had to allow conversation between prisoners at exercise, conversation was viewed as subversive and grounds for suspicion. When the chairman of the Prison Commission declared in 1952 that the rule of silence no longer prevailed in English prisons, he went on to describe the conditions of restriction, and a culture of discouragement of talk. The change in attitudes on communication only began to reach the local prisons in the mid 1950's with the so-called Norwich experiment, in which, in a small provincial prison, 'helpful conversations' between prisoners and between officers and prisoners were encouraged. The Norwich experiment became the Norwich System, as other local prisons began cautiously to follow suit. McConville (1994:271) has noted that, historically, even when educational policy embraced instruction in classes, the curbing of communications between prisoners was entailed by the priority of maintaining penal discipline.

Informal talk is, traditionally, a powerful element in human affairs. One of the most powerful slogans in the Second World War claimed that careless talk costs lives. In the prison, staff often seem to feel there is an unwritten rule that talk with prisoners is dangerous. So, in a sense it is, for more talk might lead to empathetic engagement, and the twin principles of care and talk might begin to challenge the principle of punishment.

Talk is an expensive commodity in an institution like the prison. In some sense, it is added value, provided by voluntary agencies such as the Samaritans, as if it were some kind of luxurious but unnecessary extra. Place is not made for it. Inmates like Ramon would rather do without this 'luxury' than cope with the humiliation of having to talk and weep with a

Samaritan in full view of the ward. Listener schemes, whereby prisoners volunteer and are trained by Samaritans from local branches, have been established at more than 80 prisons since 1991. Their value is inestimable, but in local prisons, where the need is often greatest, it is hard to keep Listener schemes up and running because of the rapid turnover of prisoners. In this particular local prison, a Full Inspection Report by the Prisons Inspectorate during the period of my research disclosed that there were six active listeners in the whole of the prison, but they could not meet as a group, and they were only permitted to attend part of the proceedings of the wing-based suicide awareness groups.

Care

In relation to suicidal feelings and behaviour, I turn now to the issue of care, commencing with an analytic of what it is that is to be cared for. Prisoners may lose much when they enter prison, but it is often forgotten that they also acquire rights. In summary, they are entitled to protection from harm, and access to services (Tomasevski 1992), which includes the specific right to health care equivalent to that available to those outside in the community (Council of Europe 1991).

This research has shown that talk between prisoners, and between staff and prisoners, is an invaluable aspect of care. Because I adopted a philosophy of empathetic listening, my tellers even experienced my interest in them as 'care', and, in conversation after the interview, they would express their gratitude for what they perceived as attention and care through talk. Prisoners consider the availability of talk to be the most valuable tool not only in relation to suicide awareness and prevention but also in reducing the pain of imprisonment and helping them to come to terms with their situation.

But the principle of harm is so explicit in prison. To be sent to the prison place is the punishment: it involves the suspension of all social roles and of temporal and spatial choice, and submission to the routines and timetables of the place. Whilst in prison, the harm of this punishment is continuous and inevitable: additional punishment or harm is not supposed to be administered unless regulations are infringed. However, because of the nature of the place, the social individual inevitably experiences some changes to self image, conscience and internal states of mind. Faced with a crushing edifice, inmates' reactions to institutional life are indeed expressions of self, of harm to that self and of their care needs.

This research has afforded glimpses of these expressions of self. Tellers have spoken about the pain of having to follow daily routinised practices and participate in events which are not, in the main, autonomously willed, and over which they have no control. This package of enforced routines is accompanied by a lack of reliability, for it is never certain that time-tabled events will happen at the time they are scheduled, or even at all. However this is enriched by the innovative practices of individuals, this combination of constraint and uncertainty produces special experience, which, at the level of social being, may be characterised as deep unease or ontological insecurity. This special experience of unease consists of a constrained absence of an autonomy of bodily control within predictable routines and encounters (Giddens 1984:64), and of confidence or trust that the natural and social worlds are as they appear to be, including the basic existential parameters of self and social identity Giddens (1984:375).

This deep unease can usefully be conceptualised at the ontological level, but there is also a need here for a concept that expresses the here/now/me actuality of experience, drawn from both the manifest and latent content of what my tellers disclosed. My research has recognised the importance of, and attempted to follow Wright Mills' (1959) demands for social research. Thus the project was formulated and the data collected with an abstract space left available for a concept that would bridge the structural properties of the prison, and the psychological depths of experience, but without soaring above the level of analysis enabled by the interviews, or plunging below it into assumptions about the unconscious. Nevertheless, any concept that purports to describe the experience of individuals must recognise both structure and experience, for the life of an individual cannot be adequately understood without references to the institutions within which his biography is enacted (Wright Mills 1959:161).

When I began the research, I did not know what that concept would be. Nor did I know exactly how it would relate to the two dimensions of the prison experience that I had decided to focus upon - the experience of time and space constraint. However, as prisoner after prisoner, whether apparently 'coping' or 'at risk', in terms of official definitions, related their experience of entering prison and suffering numbness, loss of feeling, time disjunction, loss of place identity and, as time passed, the overwhelming experience of grief and loss, their common state, albeit experienced in uniquely individual ways, presented itself as 'falling'.

In its literal and physical sense, 'falling' means involuntarily descending, and persons in this state lose their habitual contact with, control over, and awareness of, time and the objects in space for the duration of the fall.   For my tellers, it is not their bodies which are falling, but their sense of self.   Such are the exigencies of time and place that they lose their habitual contact with the self that managed a daily round of experience (Goffman 1961) in the outside world.

The event which precipitates the experience of falling may, in some cases, be the offence itself, or the trial, or a number of markers along the way.   Such is the theatrical nature of a court, that it can easily be the trigger for the realisation that one has been singled out for special attention by the criminal justice system, and in connection with this event, tellers often described themselves as reeling.

But the event which is of the most significance is the realisation of entry into, and presence in, the time-place that is prison.   Those convicted are the focus of penal attention, and, for those sentenced to imprisonment, this attention is provided in a place which is largely closed to societal observation.   Tellers feel this closure acutely: they speak of the entry into prison as they would speak of a bad dream, where something extraordinary is happening and yet no-one takes any notice of it whatsoever.   The routines of admission are so very banal, and yet the self is aware that an extraordinary threshold is being crossed.   Often inmates steel themselves to be strong, expecting the suffering and barbarism to begin suddenly and immediately: when nothing dreadful happens to them in the first 24 hours, like Ramon and Tim, they feel some relief, not yet realising that falling is not always an explicit experience, but one that may gather momentum as time passes.   For the punitive attention which is bent upon inmates as they enter prison is paradoxically both all-seeing and blind.   In its generalised form, it is attentive to detail, to routines, to rules and to security in so very many ways that recipients feel its weight and power.   Yet, at the same time, they are made aware that it is blind to them, as individuals, and to their particularised vulnerabilities, needs and responses.

For suicidal prisoners, such as Pradeep, falling is so acute, painful, disorientating or long lasting that it cannot be endured, and the sufferer resorts to extreme behaviour in order to avoid its continuation.   For some prisoners, falling is initially painful, but after a time, they manage to orientate themselves, in acceptance of the place they are in. They acquire a manageable sense of personal timeness.   From there, they move through the stages that Gerry described.   Les (Chapter Seven) is able to look back on his experience of prolonged suicidal feeling, and liken it to falling off a cliff, and, over time, going down and down.   This is sometimes a physically disorientating sensation, but it is never exclusively confined to the physical, for 'embodiment' involves the unity of experience, whereby the body in a particular place interacts dialectically with environment, in ways which are productive of suffering and change in self-identity.

In an earlier chapter, whilst referred to the suffering which the prison place can produce, I quoted Serge (1970: 96), who spoke of an element of authentic clarity. This can emerge from falling, as it does for Les, or alternate with it, as it does for Jimmie. Prison provides inmates with much time and opportunity for reflection: emergence from falling arises when inmates begin to use the subjective products of their reflections and engage in expressive self-accounting. They stop falling because they grasp at the sides of the time place they find themselves in, and begin to anchor themselves in ways that re-discover that tolerable sense of self (Goffman 1961) which was lost upon entry in to the prison place. I have shown (Chapter Six) how tellers make entry into dialogic states, through gaining a sense of personal timeness which can be characterised as 'deep temporality', and acquiring or fashioning a sense of place. This sense of place is always limited by consciousness of the punitive place, and is a source of anxiety and guilt. Nevertheless, inmates such as Les and Tel engage in an exploration of experience, and an examination of the possibilities of exercising free will within the given constraints. In this sense, they are exploring self-hood (Jaspers 1951) and moving toward a more authentic existence. They have ceased to fall.

Falling cannot be arrested without communication with self and others, for the magnitude of the place experience, with all its overtones of punishment and crushing elimination, can not be sorted and made sense of except through inter-subjectivity. Jaspers' (1951) principle that individuals only exist insofar as others reflect them, is, however, a dangerous principle to follow within the prison setting: disclosure to the 'wrong' person can result in further harm to the suffering self. Some inmates, such as Gerry, seem to have an extraordinary capacity to engage in self dialogue, which is enough to arrest falling. However, further probing always reveals some significant other, who has helped to provide the loving strife of communication (Jaspers 1951) which is the key to arresting the fall and stimulating the process of anchoring oneself in time and place once more.

If care can help to arrest falling, what is the nature of its coexistence with the punitive attention which necessarily prevails over other forms of attention in the prison place?

The most explicit form of care practised in prison is health care, and yet it is necessarily a secondary function to that of security (Home Office 1991). Rule 17 (Prison Rules) states that the medical officer has responsibility for the care of the health, mental and physical, of the prisoners in that prison. Health care in prison has been a cause for political, ethical and clinical concern for some time.   The quality varies considerably, with some prisons providing health care broadly equivalent to NHS care, but many are characterised by low quality care, inadequately trained and professionally unsupported doctors, and a failure to meet proper ethical standards (Reed and Lyne 1997).

There is an obvious conflict of roles for medical officers, in that they are involved in administering a system of punishment, and, at the same time, 'caring' for the health of those being punished (House of Commons 1985/86). This conflict is embedded deeply in the history of the prison, for the original introduction and expansion of medical knowledge were entwined with the disciplining of the inmates, and in making their bodies and minds acquiescent through discipline, regulation, and exclusion (Ignatieff 1978). So, although medical discourse places itself historically on the side of enlightenment and against ignorance (Sim 1999), in penal history it is steeped in the practices of institutionalised barbarism.

Although the worst excesses of physical punishment are no longer practised in prison, with corporal punishment ended as recently as 1967, it is still the case that medical officers in prison must sanction the use of punishment by cellular confinement. Given the nature and quality of the punitive relationship between carer and patient, how can it be possible to be responsible for the physical and mental health of a prisoner and also to sanction his punishment, on the grounds that he is fit to receive it, by methods which may be prejudicial to health? (Bowden 1978).

Clearly, for many medical officers, this conflict is managed, and the job is considered possible, presumably with the aid of painfully gained neutralisation techniques. But, despite the overall tendency to ignore or erase prisoner responses, the relationship cannot be defined solely by how medical officers rationalise it. It is only adequately defined if all parties to it share the definition. Patients who are prisoners are aware that medical officers are presenting as carers, and they wish that that role is definitive and exclusive, sometimes, like Sean, working extremely hard to maintain the fantasy that they are in hospital, with the full expectation of being cared for uncritically. But in their hearts they know that medical officers are enlisted agents of a system of punishment, and that this is not some optional extra but is integral to the human relationship, so integral that it must on occasions take precedence over the care principle.

Given the nature of institutions, it is not surprising if medical officers, within the isolated Health Care Service for Prisoners that is in turn enclosed within the Prison Service, cannot maintain the independence of mind necessary to formulate, develop and express criticism of that organisation (Prison Reform Trust 1985). But it is not surprising, either, if medical officers strive, consciously or unconsciously, to continue the isolation from mainstream health care which Bowden (1978) observed, for the conflict between principles of care and custodial punishment could be made even more painful for medical officers by closer proximity to the principles and ethos of healthcare in the current market culture.

Current moves toward a greater integration of the Health Care Service for Prisoners and the NHS are widely supported, but realistically this alone cannot solve the present problems in the current contexts of a rapidly rising prison population and a reducing budget. Additionally, this integration will not, of itself, overcome the paradox of care within punitive containment, for the issues of control and regulation through medical practice in prison are, after all, embedded deep within the institution of medicine (Sim 1990). A better ethical framework is essential (Reed and Lyne 1997). But a closer relationship with standards of health care in the community may, eventually, improve the currently patchy and deficient implementation of the current Health Care Standards of the Prison Service (Reed and Lyne 1997). It has been known for some time that there is a direct relationship between the ill health of inmates and the level of overcrowding (Home Office 1980), and that reduction of overcrowding is the single most important change which would improve both prisoners' health and prison healthcare (Smith 1984). Some (Coles and Shaw 1996) see the problem of suicide as inexorably linked with the rising population, and maintain that the rate will only decline if the prison population can be reduced, and regimes for the remaining made more humane, healthy and constructive. Unfortunately, current projections, using the usual regression model, anticipate a yearly average prison population of 82,800 by 2005, noting however that if the overall custody rate continues to rise, that figure may well be 92,600 (Home Office 1998). Realistically, then, efforts must be made to improve the existing culture of care, despite rising populations, and these efforts must take account of prisoners' experience of care. Where suicidal feelings are concerned, the culture in some prisons is clearly inadequate and unhealthy (HM Chief Inspector 1999).

The phenomenon of suicide is a special challenge in prison, because it presents such extreme requirements for care, in a context that is already crisis-ridden, and to a service which is struggling to cope. Just because a prisoner is suicidal does not excuse him from continuing to receive the special effects of a 'blame culture' (HM Chief Inspector 1999), yet at the same time he is considered to need special attention and medical care. This produces contradictory responses in staff, clearly evident in the use of one particular tool of special attention - the F2052SH documentation.

During the pilot study of my project, I was allowed access to F2052SH documents, but was unable to perceive any correspondence between the entries on them with the narrated histories, experiences, and feelings of the subjects of the documentation, and, rather than be side-tracked into this admittedly fascinating anomaly, I decided to carry out my main study without the benefit of sight of this documentation.

The F2052SH documentation, only a few years old, already carries with it a profound weight of cultural baggage. Officers described it to me as a discipline document, in the sense that there would be disciplinary consequences for them if the associated procedures and paperwork were not carried out properly. Prisoners regarded it as a device to absolve the Service of responsibility in the event of a death. 'It just covers the system if I do anything to meself' was how Thomas put it.

The F2052SH documentation, implemented in establishments from 1993 onward in a rolling programme, forms part of a policy move towards a more multi-disciplinary team approach to the problem of suicide. It is the responsibility of the Suicide Awareness Team within each establishment to co-ordinate and manage the F2052SH system. Support and help with implementation is always available from the Suicide Awareness Support Unit at Prison Service headquarters, which develops policy on suicide awareness and prevention, provides advice on establishment policy, practice and training, and support for prisons and individuals following a suicide inside prison.

Naturally, the identification and maintenance of a prisoner requiring F2052SH documentation and management must depend upon sound communications within the particular establishment. No risk management system can survive successfully unless an appropriate level of open and/or frequent communication is the norm.

The potential for communication failures in the F2052SH system is substantial. Firstly, this potential occurs at the level of inmate subjectivity. There are inmates whose intention to commit suicide is so fully formed that they will feign successful and cheerful adaptation to prison, in order to avoid attention and permit them the opportunity to carry out that intention. Additionally, the majority of inmates enter prison with acculturated norms of masculine behaviour which discourage the sharing of feelings. Many of them do not know how to communicate on the subject of their own feelings, and have not acquired the social skills that enable them to approach officials. The place effects of prison, in this sphere of self-expression, produce an exaggerated form of this behaviour, which is best summed up by Mike ('coping' now, 'B' Wing):

> Prison's all about acting. No matter what I feel in my cell, when I come out onto the landing, I'm hard. And everyone sees I am, and that's how I get respect. I'm not gonna get any respect if I'm shaking and crying, am I?

Secondly, there are significant place aspects to prison which interact with the norms mentioned above, and enhance the potential for communication breakdown. Reticent and limited communication between staff and prisoners is the norm in prison. Direct, frequent or friendly communication between an inmate and a member of staff may produce suspicious and/or aggressive responses from inmate peers or other staff. At the worst level of communication failure, members of staff react inappropriately to attempts to communicate on the part of suicidal prisoners. When a bad outcome follows, in the form of a suicidal incident, the guilt that staff feel can produce even higher levels of strategic distancing from the sufferings of prisoners. This strategic distancing from suffering, often done for self-protection, can make it hard for staff to talk to each other in empathetic ways about prisoners. So there is a lethal cycle of non-communication.

So the internal culture of prison militates against openness and the practice of listening with special attention. Nevertheless, the ease with which my tellers spoke to me indicates a tide of communicative material pressing against the floodgate, awaiting the appearance of the listener who is good enough to receive the flood. It can seem savagely ironic to inmates that relative care is taken of their bodies, and yet the turmoil of inner suffering is either ignored or expected. Punishment used to focus on the body as the object of punishment, and suffering was marked upon the body and visible to all: the historical transition with which Foucault deals (1979) is to a system in the modern age which keeps the body secure and unmarked, and where suffering is internal and often invisible. The body deceives, masking the suffering of inner disorder, and the problem for inmates is how to communicate their need.

To receive special physical care in prison, like patients everywhere, they demonstrate deservedness, by being visibly ill, and by co-operating with staff and with regulations. When prisoners evince suicidal behaviour, they too must demonstrate individual deservedness in order to receive care. Care, in prison, is always inhibited and always individualised: this is the strength of Foucault's (1979) critique of the modern age: power constitutes - it normalises but it also singles out and individualises. There is, however, an important corollary to this which Foucault neglected: that when power fails to individualise, it can seem even more punitive to the inmate who, though needy and desperate for attention, is ignored, because he is not deemed deserving of care.

The Medical Centre, as a place within a place, is where the principle of deservedness is practised in the most acute way, partly because of the resource limitations to which I have referred, and partly because punitive attention is allowed to dominate the principle of care. It is, then, both a place with extremes of suffering, and extremes of inhibition in the practice of care. The staff, who are overwhelmed by the former, practice the latter as a routinised way of doing the job, and as a psychological defence to prevent them from being swamped by the tide of need. They cannot afford empathy. The question they must always unconsciously ask is 'Does this person, who is after all here as punishment, really deserve my care?' Suicidal prisoners in the medical centre, undergoing prolonged mental anguish, were often unable to recall for me the last time that someone had made eye contact with them and taken time to talk and listen. They felt their undeservedness keenly: the knowledge that humane attention was a scarce resource, which they had not managed to earn, added to their suffering.

In my research, it was only the really deserving suicidal inmate - the apparently blameless, the articulate and the compliant, who could report having received concerned care and talk in the Medical Centre. Alan, the Falklands veteran, who killed whilst suffering Post Traumatic Stress Syndrome, was the only prisoner I encountered, suicidal or 'coping', who reported having had a proper conversation with a medical officer, in which the latter had really 'listened' to the former. His place on the deservedness spectrum was secure, since he had acquired his condition whilst fighting for Queen and Country.

It was clear that where deep conversations occur, which produce that significant sense of being cared for, they do so in this establishment generally outside of the arrangements currently in place in the medical centre. From the body of narrative of my tellers, it emerged that care in the form of deep talk was much more common on the wings than in the Medical Centre. There were officers on 'B' Wing, whose names came up over and over again in the narratives of prisoners. To prisoners, these officers provided attention, care and talk. It is clear that what was in place on 'B' Wing was a system of attention, care and talk which was responsible for arresting falling and stimulating the development of the dialogic self.

There is, then, a set of problematic issues surrounding the whole notion of what constitutes care of the suicidal. Many officers, as well as prisoners, still view suicidal behaviour as a problem that is largely owned by medical and psychiatric staff. There is an understandable reluctance to acknowledge the whole thrust of suicide awareness policy since 1992, that prisoner suicides are part of the whole social nexus of prison life, and that it is therefore the entirety of the prison experience which must fall under scrutiny in developing strategic policy. It is not surprising if other specialisms within the prison service are not clamouring to share ownership of the problem, not least because of that seemingly endless stream of definitional problems, and because, despite increased attention to the problem, the rate continues to rise.

But the failure on the part of prison authorities to recognise and own the problem as part of the whole social nexus of prison life derives from a failure to recognise the nature of the prison place. The prison as a place with special qualities and effects must be acknowledged: part of this acknowledgement must involve a recognition of the value of prisoner contributions, both to knowledge about the experience of prison and the phenomenon of self-inflicted harm. It is nearly 30 years since Cohen and Taylor (1972) drew on prisoner experience to point out the contexts of stress, despair, and the urge to self-destruction in prison, as well as the amazing strategies for self-preservation, autonomy and survival which prisoners demonstrate. Yet there is still a cultural failure in many prisons to recognise both the essential nature of the place, and the value of prisoner experiences in analysing its most powerful effects (HM Chief Inspector 1999).

Inmates have a special knowledge of the prison place, and of surviving and transcending place, and their voices can make valuable contributions to knowledge about the phenomenon. My key methodological principle has been disciplined empathy in both gathering and analysing the data: it is perhaps worth stressing that the force of this principle extends to the reader, for research which attempts to understand the situatedness of extreme suffering is not to be read with a cold eye.

Such inmates need attention, care and talk, and, in the eyes of inmates, the Medical Centre in this local prison is not the place where this is presently provided. Care and attention can only take place in the context of a moral relationship. It is in the nature of prison as a place of punitive attention that moral accountability is put into crisis. The medical centre is a place within a place where the moral relationship is most muddied and ambiguous, and the principle of health care fights with that of secure containment, exemplified most neatly by rule 53 of the Prison Rules which state that it is the Medical Officer's responsibility to certify a prisoner 'fit' to be punished. It is easier to see such action as complicity rather than care (Tomasevski

1992). Yet it is easy, also, to understand what inmates report as high levels of resentment in staff in the medical centre, over inmates who are not explicitly ill, yet who, through being placed on F2052SH documentation, appear 'undeservedly' to demand care.

Some inmates, such as Gerry, are quite unequivocal about the appropriate place for providing care:

> They're best off on the wing. There should be a suite of cells on the wing for those who are suicidal. Then there'll always be someone to talk to.

Since the Prison Service attained agency status, there has been an accompanying expansion of a managerialist culture. An implicit assumption of managerialism may well be that non-rational form of behaviour can be designed out of prisons through the use of actuarial techniques, risk assessment strategies, key performance indicators and a host of useful yet bloodless policy initiatives. Sometimes this official approach is merely rhetorical: many so-called policies, after all, exist more at the level of claim and representation on paper than in operational practice (Garland 1990).

For instance, the Service currently states that health needs assessments in each establishment are, for instance, an appropriate managerialist goal, but if the current context of rising numbers and budget cuts continue, such assessments could never be matched by implementation. The phrases 'Standard practice', 'Performance Indicators', and 'Risk Assessment' can seem bloodless and chilling to the prisoner who just wants someone to talk to, and to staff who want to be able to respond humanely to need. Tumin recognised this when he quoted this robust remark by a governor (HM Chief Inspector 1990:6):

> My own view is that the ethos of an establishment, how inmates are treated, will determine the amount of self-injury. While I understand the need for form-filling and insurance policy-type activity, it is not a substitution for investing in time spent with staff. Firstly, letting them know that it is part of the culture to demonstrate concern with inmates, and secondly, showing them ways of letting it show.

These narratives have shown that prisoners have special knowledge, which may equip some of them to play a part in awareness and prevention policies. Through suffering the extreme pain and misery of suicidal feelings, through extremes of placelessness and disorientation, brought upon them by the special characteristics of the time place of prison, and through moving positively through such extremes of experience, some prisoners have a special knowledge, which may equip some of them to play a part in awareness and prevention policies. Through suffering the extreme pain and misery of suicidal feelings, through extremes of placelessness and disorientation, brought upon them by the special characteristics of the time place of prison, and through moving positively through such extremes of experience, some prisoners have a special knowledge which non-prisoners can never have. More space must be made to utilise this valuable resource. Once released into the prison as a resource, it has the capacity to change culture in dynamic and life-saving ways. Such change will benefit staff as well as prisoners, and make the prison service more attractive to those potential recruits who are interested in the complexity of human behaviour in institutions and in building a secure and healthy culture.

Conclusion

A proper attention to the extraordinary nature of the prison place will recognise its capacity to put inmates into a state of falling. These narratives demonstrate the depth of need for attention. This attention should be expressed through care and talk as natural ingredients of the job of prison officer. The waiting teller, such as Alistair, wears a mask of institutional complicity. But behind the mask is a deep-seated desperation. He is not considered to be at risk, and yet the same judgement has been made in the past of many successful suicides. To be appropriate, attention to his needs must recognise his passivity and institutionalisation. This recognition could only occur if it were underpinned by an ethos of care and security, rather than one of suspicion and blame.

Because of the unpredictability of the phenomenon of suicide, it follows that attention, care and talk ought to be adopted as a strategic and yet a 'natural' way of working in a prison setting and interacting with all prisoners. Attention (without much talk) cannot be effective if it is instrumentally applied to selective prisoners, with an eye to their 'deservedness' status. All prisoners require attention which is other than punitive, care that recognises their social rather than strictly medical needs, and opportunities to talk unguardedly and empathetically.

Paying attention is an implicit value in the notion of the professional and each lawyer, doctor or other professional pays attention with special reference to her/his area of professional expertise. Listening hard is a difficult act of attention: it ought to form one of the professional value competences of prison officers. It does not entail the entire relinquishment of those vital reserves maintained by officers in order to protect themselves: it does, however, entail a disciplined empathy, which can be promoted on the job by appropriate training and by example from other experienced officers, and maintained by ongoing staff support. Those tellers who encountered this competence in wing officers attest to its value in this study, and it is probable that those staff who practice this competence feel a greater sense of satisfaction in their work than those who merely attend to the custodial aspects of the job.

Care, in the context of social relationships, is a vital ingredient in HMP' Mission Statement, and it can only be practiced effectively if it includes a proper recognition of the realities of the prison place. This recognition would acknowledge and respect the validity of inmate experience. These narratives provide evidence that, for prisoners, care entails talk. Initiating and maintaining dialogue amongst prisoners, and between staff and prisoners are shared social responsibilities on the part of all who live and work in prisons, and these responsibilities can be prioritised through strong leadership, training and example. There are points within the existing system where there has been proper recognition of the need for talk with trustworthy listeners, and recognition of the fact that the composition of the prison population is such that many inmates have never been properly 'heard' in their lives (Smithson and Harris 1998). Examples of good and creative practice are many, from the group sessions in Lancaster Farms (Smithson and Harris 1997) to the prisoners' committees being developed at HMP Doncaster in the private sector. But most therapeutic units within the Prison Service experience isolation and precariousness in terms of continuity (Lewis 1997), and some are not permitted to survive (MacKenzie 1997).

Those who fall into the category of Presentational Telling need dialogue to help them abandon their reiterated, rigid and inflexible stories of self, which bear no relationship to the plight they find themselves in, and merely serve as weak defences against their lack of personal timeness, their placelessness and their loss of control. The Waiting Teller waits resignedly, too passive to initiate a search for a listener, and yet deserving one in terms of need and the possibility of a fatal outcome. The Dialogic Self finds himself' through talk, both to himself and to others, accepting and orientating himself in the place he is in, and recovering some sense of personal timeness.

But attention, care and talk is not just another model which staff in prison must add to their weary load. It must be a shared cultural reality, shared by prisoners and staff. Prisoners, particularly those like Les and Tel, who were once seriously suicidal but who have moved on, have a great deal to contribute, if a healthy culture will allow.

The value of prisoner expertise has already been tangibly recognised in Listener schemes. The establishment and growth of so many Listener schemes across the prison system is a valuable initiative in encouraging communication.   In busy local prisons, however, such as the one where this research was carried out, the continuity of such schemes is constantly under threat by the large remand population and rapid turnover of prisoners both in specific locations and the prison as a whole. And it is significant in a symbolic sense that the organisation of Listeners is farmed out to a voluntary sector body (Samaritans) instead of being a structured and fully accountable part of the organisation.

But much prisoner expertise lies unused. Prisoners could routinely also be deployed to help newcomers through reception and induction procedures, as mentors on the wings, in appraisal schemes and a host of other   interactive roles. A seminar on 'The Responsible Prisoner' held at HMP High Down on 23rd November 1995 discussed these very possibilities.   Prisoners' committees on the wings can prove a valuable tool in promoting social and ethical bonds between prisoners, and in encouraging the development of responsible attitudes, amongst men who may never have been given such opportunities during familial or educational socialisation.   Many of my tellers exemplify extraordinary personal growth, despite the exigencies of place.   Others, too, could grow and become, in turn, a resource to other prisoners, if only the opportunities were more overt, and if only communication within prison, amongst prisoners, amongst staff, and between prisoners and staff, was valued and rewarded.

The expansion of Care and Talk within prisons is about changing the culture in the direction of the Healthy Prison extolled by HM Chief Inspector (1999). It would enhance the quality of life not just for suicidal prisoners, but for all prisoners and for staff as well.   Inmates need staff who recognise the reality of place, and who, in doing so, can act from that knowledge.   Being operationally efficient need not rule out disciplined empathy as a significant tool in dealing with prisoners. Individual prison establishments are now more at liberty than in the past to develop the expansion of talk, as governors are operating more direct management of their establishments. And yet often empathy is marginalised, and good initiatives are either not expanded or closed down (Prison Audit 1997). Disciplined empathy must be a valued part of the operational efficiency of everyone working in prisons. Recognising and rewarding it in specific locations will enable its dialectical spread throughout the system as a whole, to the ultimate benefit of all who live and work in prisons. The initiative of some staff in some locations are a dynamic testimony to the viability of care, attention and talk, even in situations with rapid turnover.

It is a huge task for the ideology of social care to stand up to either the ideology of punishment or the weight of past practice, in a context where prison budgets are reducing in relation to overall numbers. Nevertheless, the tellers from 'B' Wing are living proof that good communication is like a relay baton: each time it is handed on, it creates another participant. It needs energetic leadership, but once started, it creates its own field of energy. It needs investment in terms of committed practice and ongoing support.

Such cultures have, in the past, been shown to be both possible and effective in changing attitudes for specific inmate populations: the Wormwood Scrubs Annexe, housing up to 40 high risk inmates for periods of between four months and a year, lasted for twelve years, without any suicide attempts being recorded (Glatt 1984). Where a humane, constructive, hopeful and active atmosphere, characterised by supportive relationships, is set up, a positive social culture can be created, in which inmates learn to interact in mutually useful ways, and defuse suicidal feelings by ventilating and sharing feelings of aggression, self-harm, guilt and loneliness. Such a culture militates against the more usual psychological effects of institutionalisation, and can encourage autonomy, personal planning and the development of coping mechanisms (Glatt 1984).

Following the commissioning of the Relationships Foundation by the Scottish Prison Service in 1994 to carry out relationship audits, audit tools acceptable to the new managerialist culture are being developed to examine the quality of relationships in prisons in England and Wales. They offer opportunities for scrutinising existing practices, with a view to change and development, and for identifying and celebrating good practice (Brett, Schluter and Wright 1995). Relational audits are said to support the development of the responsible prisoner: it is to be hoped that this tool will be used to encourage, reward and support the responsible officer and the responsible community within prison. Audit tools tend by their very nature to consider either staff populations, or prisoner populations. An appreciation of the interactive attitude, however, is necessary whenever relationships and practices in prison are scrutinised and assessed with a view to change.

A model of Attention, Care and Talk is part of the natural progression of making the problem a shared social concern, in the way in which HM Chief Inspectors have consistently recommended for many years. The revised 1994 strategy emphasised the shared responsibility of all staff in caring for the suicidal, and developing multi-disciplinary responses.

It is time now to recognise the crucial role that prisoners can play in this. They have proved their worth in the context of prisoner befriending schemes, but there are very many other ways in which their knowledge and expertise can become part of future strategy. My research is part of an ongoing dialogue which asserts the necessity to recognise the value of prisoners' participation in what is, after all, an experiential crisis induced partly by the place characteristics of prison.

The narratives as a whole show that a model of attention, care and talk can be developed in specific locations, which builds on (i) prisoners' needs, (ii) prisoners' knowledge of the phenomenon of suicidal feelings in prison and (iii) on staff expertise, including that currently expressed in sometimes non-systematised, random and individualised ways. Such a model would, if developed and implemented with appropriate support for staff and prisoners, have the capacity to arrest 'falling' and seriously reduce the experience and fatal expression of suicidal feelings.

References

Beaumont, G.D. and Tocqueville, A.D. (1833/1964), *On the Penitentiary System in the United States and Its Application in France*, Southern Illinois University Press, Carbondale.

Bettelheim, B. (1960), *The Informed Heart*, Penguin, Harmondsworth.

Bowden, P.M.A. (1978), 'Ethical Aspects of the Role of the Medical Officers In Prison' in *Medical Services for Prisoners*, Kings Fund Centre, London.

Brett, C., Schluter, M. and Wright, M. (1995), *Relational Prison Audits*, Scottish Prison Service Occasional Paper no. 2.

Cohen, S. (1985), *Visions of Social Control*, Polity, Cambridge.

Cohen, S. and Taylor, I. (1972), *Psychological Survival - The Experience of Long-term Imprisonment*, Penguin, Harmondsworth.

Coles, D. and Shaw, H. (1996), *Deaths in Prison: Breaking the Wall of Silence*, Prison Report no. 37, Prison Service, London.

Council of Europe (1991), *Report to the UK Government on the Visit to the UK Carried out by the European Committee on the Prevention of Torture and Inhuman or Degrading Treatment or Punishment*, Council of Europe, Strasbourg.

Emery, E. (1970), *Freedom And Justice Within Walls: The Bristol Prison Experiment*, Tavistock, London.

Foucault, M. (1979), *Discipline and Punish*, Penguin. Harmondsworth.

Glatt, M.M. (1984), 'The Wormwood Scrubs Annexe: Reflections On The Working and Functioning of An Addicts' Therapeutic Community Within a

Prison' in *Prison Medicine: Ideas on Health Care in Penal Establishments*, Prison Reform Trust, London.

Giddens, A. (1984), *The Constitution of Society*, Polity, Cambridge.

Goffman, E. (1961), *Asylums*, Penguin, Harmondsworth.

Hentig, H. von (1937), *Punishment: Its Origin, Purpose & Psychology*, Hodge, London.

HM Chief Inspector of Prisons for England and Wales (1990), *Review of Suicide and Self-Harm in Prison*, HMSO, Cm.1383, London.

HM Chief Inspector of Prisons for England and Wales (1999), *Suicide is Everyone's Concern: A Thematic Review*, Home Office, London.

Ignatieff, M. (1978), *A Just Measure of Pain*, MacMillan, London.

Jaspers, K. (1951), *Man in the Modern Age*, Routledge, London.

Learrmont, Sir J. (1995), *Review of Prison Service Security in England and Wales and the Escape from Parkhurst Prison on Thursday 3rd January 1995*, Cmnd. 3020 HMSO, London.

Lewis, P.S. (1997), 'Sustaining Therapeutic Communities - The Grendon Experience', *Prison Service Journal*, May, no. 111.

Liebling, A. and Krarup, H. (1993), *Suicide Attempts in Male Prisons*, Home Office, London.

MacKenzie, J. (1997), 'Glen Parva Therapeutic Community: An Obituary', *Prison Service Journal* May 1997 no. 111.

Mannheim, K. (1939), *The Dilemma of Penal Reform*, Allen & Unwin, London.

McConville, S. (1994), *English Local Prisons 1860-1900: Next Only to Death*, Routledge, London.

Melossi, D. and Pavarini, M. (1981), *The Prison and the Factory*, MacMillan London.

Reed, J. and Lyne, M. (1997), 'The Quality of Health Care in Prison: Results of a Year's Programme of Semistructured Inspections', *British Medical Journal*, Vol. 315, pp. 1420-1424.

Sim, J. (1990), *Medical Power In Prisons: The Prison Medical Service in England 1774-1989*, Open University, Buckingham.

Simon, J. (1974), 'Michel Foucault on Attica: An Interview', *Telos* vol.19 Spring, pp. 155-156.

Smith, R. (1984), *Prison Health Care*, B.M.A., London.

Smithson, S. and Harris, P. (1998), 'Coping in Custody', *Prison Service Journal* no. 116.

Smithson, S. and Harris, P. (1997), 'Prison-Induced Stress', *Prison Service Journal*, no. 111.

Tomasevski, K. (1992), *Prison Health - International Standards and National Practices in Europe*, European Institute for Crime and Control, Helsinki.

Woodcock, J. (1994), '*Report of the Enquiry into the Escape of Six Prisoners from the Special Security Unit at Whitemoor Prison on Friday 9th September 1994*', Cm. 2741, HMSO, London.

Wright Mills, C. (1959), *The Sociological Imagination*, Oxford University Press, New York.

Subject Index

For Product Safety Concerns and Information please contact our EU
representative GPSR@taylorandfrancis.com
Taylor & Francis Verlag GmbH, Kaufingerstraße 24, 80331 München, Germany

www.ingramcontent.com/pod-product-compliance
Lightning Source LLC
Chambersburg PA
CBHW050426280326
41932CB00013BA/2012

9 781032 803098